To my mother,

and to Maureen Barden
and John Ricca,
for being there,
and to
Amanda Vaill,
for being here

SOMEWHERE
CHILD

PROLOGUE

Somewhere in the world I have a child who does not know me. She was taken many years ago by a man I hardly know. According to federal law he is not considered a kidnapper, because he is her father. But to me there is no distinction.

My daughter and I are strangers to each other against our will. We are among the many thousands of victims of the modern phenomenon called child snatching, an act whereby one parent takes and hides from the other parent the child or children of their marriage. This act has not been considered a criminal offense. We victims have been rendered helpless.

Since the time I last saw my then-five-year-old daughter, in August 1971, I have tried my best to find her. At times I have tried to forget her. But I have been unsuccessful at both. In searching for my missing child I have searched my own life to find, at least, myself. This is the story of that search.

1

April 20, 1979—It is a terrible thing for a mother to lose her child to Time. Death is an end; Time, a continuum. With death you grieve for days and months. With a live loss you grieve forever. The pain never ends because there is no resolution. The wound never heals because you can't forget your child is alive and missing. . . .

• • •

I wish I could forget. I wish I didn't have this hollowness inside where a child once was, a hollowness that surfaces to my face like a bubble in water and breaks on the blue of my eyes. Even strangers see it, when they get close.

I wish I could pretend it never happened, wash my memory with lye. But everything reminds me: other mothers with their children, teenage girls who might resemble her, even my own body. Blue-streaked breasts remind me they were once triple their usual size, filled with milk to feed the child I carried.

I wish I could live a normal life: remarry, have more children before it's too late. Eat meals at regular hours, have a reason to cook and to go to bed. Make a home as solid as an old tree, as peaceful as a green field. Raise a family, watch the garden grow. But who could marry someone with a hollow heart? And what if my future children should look like her? How could I say to them, "Darlings, you have a half sister somewhere . . . she is lost . . . I've had to forget her"?

I can't forget her. She is as much a part of my memory as my own childhood. I was the basket that carried her into life. She lived in me and filled my body.

After fourteen years I can still smell the baby-fragrance of her skin and hair. I can still hear her voice call me Mommy. In my mind I can see her plainly, as if through a kitchen window, playing outside in the sun. But that is only in my mind.

• • •

I live alone in a small room without a kitchen; in a city to which people from all over the country come to escape tradition's trappings, such as Home and Family; in a neighborhood where the word "mother" is half of an epithet. I am both a citizen and a foreigner here.

I live alone with memories I cannot forget, memories too painful to speak of, so I do not speak of them. Yet like demons they scream for release, threatening to drive me mad or kill me if I don't drive them out first.

I know I must do something. Perhaps it is this: Remember. Take the memories; spread them, as a painter might, on paper; then face them, as I would a separate life apart from mine. Every day, then, alone here at my desk overlooking the river flowing smoothly to the sea, I will try to lean over the paper and let it catch the memories as they fall.

When the minister asked whether anyone knew any reason why these two should not be joined together, she wanted to say, "I do." Instead, she stood there frozen, clutching her bridal bouquet and the small white Bible, freshly inscribed, "To My Beloved Wife, on this our Wedding Day, 12/19/64, Jim," wishing someone else would say it for her. But inside the old stone church decked with Christmas garlands, the handful of hastily invited wedding guests remained as silent as the snow outside.

It was a quiet wedding. Jim arranged it all and paid for everything. He even chose the white wool suit his young bride wore. She'd told him she'd never wanted a fancy wedding or a frilly wedding gown. Her father had told her and her two younger sisters, before they'd even reached puberty, not to expect any weddings from him. "Elope at seventeen," he told them, only half teasing. "I'll provide the ladder."

Jim and his bride had planned to be married in February—on Valentine's Day, she'd suggested—but Jim moved the date to December, "for income tax purposes," he told her. She suspected he was afraid she would back out.

He had reason. Several times before the wedding she had tried to break their engagement, but he wouldn't listen. During her last attempt, in the living room of his large home, Jim knelt in front of her and cried, "I've waited all my life for you. You're everything I've always wanted. You are the answer to my prayers." What could she, at nineteen, say to this man who was seventeen years older than she, a professional man with his own law practice, a man nearly twice her size, resting his head on her lap, wetting her lap with his tears? Jim was well educated and widely traveled, powerful and sure. He was everything she wasn't. And for reasons she was incapable of comprehending, he wanted to marry her.

He told her his law practice consisted primarily of matrimonial cases. "I know when couples don't have what it takes to make a marriage work," he said. "Our marriage will be extraordinary. We'll be like Kathryn and Bing Crosby, like Prince Rainier and Grace Kelly—"

Grace Kelly. How often her mother had said that name. "My girls all look like Grace Kelly," her mother would boast privately. "Let your hair grow long and swirl it on top of your head, like Grace Kelly," she told them. "Walk tall, like Grace Kelly. . . . Look rich—"

Her mother liked the fact that Jim drove a new black Cadillac and lived with his parents in a seventeen-room mansion in a nearby town, where he also had his law practice; that he bought her daughter expensive gifts—china and silver for her trousseau, a brand-new Chevrolet Malibu convertible—and took her to the best local restaurants, and treated her like a princess.

Her grandmother liked him because he supported his elderly parents, because he seemed charming and chivalrous in an old-fashioned way, and because, like her, he was of German descent.

• • •

A few days before the wedding, when she visited her mother, who was in the hospital recovering from major surgery, Jim's bride-to-be tried to tell her mother of her fears. "Mommy," she said, "it just doesn't seem right to me. I don't think I can go through with it."

"Don't worry, honey," her mother said, patting her daughter's hand. "Jim is a very successful attorney. He has a big house and can offer you a good life. You won't have to struggle. You'll be secure. You have no reason to be afraid."

There were, however, reasons for fear. But somehow she couldn't tell her mother, especially while her mother was in the hospital.

How could she tell her mother about the first time she met Jim's mother, the evening she and Jim became engaged? How the small, bent woman with dyed-red hair had stood on the bottom step of the hall stairway of Jim's home, leaning over the banister, glaring at her as she stood beside Jim, and screaming, "You're taking my son away! You're stealing my Jimmy from me!"

And how could she tell her mother about the night she spent at Jim's, because, he'd said, he was too tired to drive her home? How they'd slept in the same bed, without so much as touching, yet the next morning Jim's small, white-haired father had shuffled after her downstairs, shouting, "slut" and "piss pot" at her.

She couldn't tell her mother about the evening Jim took her to his own physician, who, without her prior knowledge or permission, gave her her first internal examination, to let Jim know whether she was "all right." Of course, Jim told her as they left the doctor's office together, he had believed her when she'd assured him she was a virgin. The examination was just to make sure she'd have no problems having children, he said. "All couples go through this procedure before marriage," he told her. And she, not knowing what to believe, believed him.

She didn't tell her mother, either, about the ominous phone call she'd received the night before, from an elder of her church, a man whom she called Uncle Mac, who'd been like a father to her for years. "My dear," he warned, "you don't know what you're getting yourself in for. Jim is not a good man. . . . He is not well liked in the business community. . . . He's been married several times. . . . He has a reputation for being a womanizer—"

She thought: *Uncle Mac must surely be wrong this time.* It was true Jim had been married, briefly, once before, but he certainly wasn't a womanizer. He actually seemed to disdain women—except, of course, his mother. And now her.

Her mother only knew about the happier aspects of their courtship. How they'd met at the bank where she worked as a secretary and Jim came in with clients for mortgage closings. How he embarrassed her with long-stemmed red roses hidden beneath his tan raincoat whenever he came to the bank on business. How he phoned her, flattered her, and fussed over her more than any man had done before. How determined he was to date her, not taking no for an answer.

Her mother knew about their first date. It was the first cocktail party the girl had ever been to, a party Jim told her he was giving in her honor, and at which he introduced her to his client-friends and their wives as if she were a pretty, talking toy he'd just bought. After the party, on the way back to her home, Jim parked his car on a side street and turned from the steering wheel to face her.

"I'm going to marry you," he said.

She thought he might have had too much to drink.

"You don't believe me?" he said. "You'll see."

"He says he's going to marry me," she told her mother when she got home.

"How wonderful!" her mother said.

Her mother knew the story of how they became engaged. It was the day she'd had an accident with Jim's car. Because her Volkswagen was being repaired, Jim had let her use his Cadillac to get to work. She'd never driven such a large car before. It was a dark and rainy evening in November, and as she pulled the long boat of a car out of its tight parking spot in the lot behind the bank, she turned too soon and scraped the whole back fender along the front bumper of an adjacent car.

Sobbing in fear, she drove through the heavy rain to meet Jim near his office. She was terrified he would shout at her the way her father used to: *"You fool! You stupid good-for-nothing—!"*

But when she showed Jim the damage, he didn't seem upset at all. Instead, he said, "Here, I have a surprise for you—"

The little black box he brought from his pocket contained an engagement ring. They hadn't discussed engagement. They hadn't looked at rings. She never had a chance to tell him she'd always dreamed of a small round solitaire set in yellow gold, like her grandmother's engagement ring. This ring, in its black velvet box, was of white platinum and held the largest diamond she'd ever seen so close. The huge rectangular stone was flat and colorless and had slivers of smaller diamonds on each side. The ring was unlike anything she would have chosen for herself.

Her emotions—relief that Jim hadn't been angry about the car; surprise at the unexpected ring; disappointment that she didn't like it and couldn't see herself wearing it; dismay that she was once again reminded she was unlike most other girls, who would have been thrilled with the ring; fear that everything was happening too fast—pulled her in so many different directions at once that she felt paralyzed, numb.

"That's more than two carats," Jim said. "Put it on."

She obeyed. "It's heavy," she said, laughing nervously and letting her left hand fall foolishly to her side. "I don't think I'll be able to type anymore—I can't lift up my hand—"

Jim stood stiffly beside his dented car. "A man in my position can't have his wife wearing small diamonds," he said as if his words were law.

When she got home that evening she showed her mother the ring. "I don't really like it," she confessed. "It just doesn't suit me—"

"Don't be silly," her mother said. "Any other girl would give her *eyeteeth* for that ring!"

She knew what her mother must have been thinking: *You* are *a peculiar girl.* Her mother never could understand why her eldest daughter read cookbooks instead of fashion magazines, why she did her homework every night in the basement instead of watching TV in the living room with the family, why she went alone to church socials instead of on dates to school dances, why she was so serious and shy.

9

"You're such a pretty girl, why don't you *do* something with it?" her mother urged her. But the girl could only respond with a look that said: *I don't know what you mean.*

. . .

How could she have told her mother about Jim's persistent questions regarding her family background? How he inquired about everything—her parents' divorce, her father's drinking, her mother's dating, her older brother's whereabouts, her younger sisters' social lives, her own religious beliefs—in intimate detail? He made her feel as if she were in court again, giving answers on the stand. *Perhaps,* she thought, *all lawyers are this way.*

"What was your father like when he became intoxicated?" Jim asked her.

"Sometimes he got violent," she said.

"Did he ever try anything with you?" he asked.

"Try anything?" She didn't understand at first. "Oh. Oh, no," she said. "Never."

"What about your brother? Did he ever try anything?"

"No," she said, "but he was always affectionate. Whenever I was upset as a child he would hug me and comfort me—" She wanted to stop and ask him, *What is the point of this?* But she didn't have the nerve to question him; rather, she chose to think he knew best.

When Jim asked her about her religious beliefs, she told him she believed in a personal, loving God; that she read the Bible and prayed; that she'd gone to church by herself since she was twelve; that the people in her church had been like a second family. She told him how much her faith meant to her, how it had given her strength and comfort, especially during the unhappiest years at home when her parents were at war with each other just before their divorce.

Jim appeared pleased by what he heard. "I am a Christian, too," he said. "I believe the same things you do."

—

How could she have told her mother about the nebulous fears for which she had no words? The way Jim's eyes refused to meet hers, the fact that they seldom kissed, he seldom touched her, and he never seemed to hear her when she spoke? How could she explain that she sensed there was a feeling missing but she wasn't sure what it was because she'd never felt it? *Perhaps those sorts of feelings are only for storybooks and novels,* she thought maturely.

That is how she saw herself then, at nineteen: sensible, responsible, mature. She felt as if she'd never been a teenager; she'd made one long leap from childhood to adulthood at about eleven and a half, when she'd asked her mother, "Why am I bleeding?" and her mother had answered, "Because you are a woman now." She'd always looked older than her age, and being the eldest daughter, she'd been given, and even welcomed, responsibility. She'd set goals for herself. She strove.

She'd even achieved a few distinctions: She'd been president of her church's youth group, a member of the National Honor Society. She'd won a scholarship to the best secretarial school, Katharine Gibbs, where she was elected president of her class and editor of the school's paper. She made her own clothes from simple patterns and plain, good-quality fabric. She wore sensible shoes.

She kept a scrapbook, not of mementos from places she'd been, because she'd never really been anywhere, but of decorating ideas for her "dream home"—a small, cozy, country-style house with rustic, Early American decor. She collected household hints and recipes. She was prepared.

That her husband would be so much older than she did not disturb her. There had been a seventeen-year difference between the ages of her mother's parents, too, and they had been happily married. *You are as old as you feel,* she told herself. And she felt as old as Jim.

But still, she was afraid. And as the wedding date drew nearer, her ineffable fears grew. She had difficulty eating. She couldn't sleep. Her mother assured her all brides-to-be felt this way. Her family physician prescribed tranquilizers to calm her, but they made her feel anesthetized, as if she were sleepwalking and dreaming.

The night before the wedding, her best friend, Kathy, who had been her roommate at Gibbs and who was to be her maid of honor, spent the night at her house, and they talked until dawn. They talked about their year at school, their first experience of living away from home on their own: going to the library at lunch hour to try to find books on sex because neither of them knew a thing; doing stripteases in front of their third-floor window to entertain the onlooking trees; roasting chestnuts in the broiler-oven and having them explode all over the room; sharing each other's food and clothing and innermost thoughts.

"Kath, I'm so scared. I've never been so scared," she said, as they lay together in the dark in the living room of her home.

"Marriage is a big step," Kathy said. "It probably scares everybody, but most people are too ashamed to admit it." Kathy was engaged to marry Carl in May.

"Remember how you used to type, 'I LOVE CARL I LOVE CARL,' single-spaced, margin to margin, and top to bottom on legal-size paper when you should have been doing your typing homework? What made you do that? What did you *feel?* I'm not even sure I know what love is. I don't know whether I love Jim. Sometimes I think I could marry anyone—"

"I don't know, Bon," Kathy said. "I just know that I love Carl and I always will."

• • •

Her mother was still in the hospital on the afternoon of the wedding. Her sisters were home, dressed and patiently waiting for one of Jim's friends, who'd misplaced the directions, to pick them up. Her brother was at his home in Florida with his family. She didn't know where her father was.

At last she found the strength to say, "I do." But by the time she did, it was too late.

I t was a good thing my father's car made noise. We called it the Teega-Teega Car because that's the sound it made. It was an old Hudson that rocked along the road like a boat in a bay. It needed repair, but he never bothered. So the cause of the noise was never found, and we were glad. The sound of the car was a warning signal—it gave us time to run for cover.

When we heard the TeegaTeegaTeegaTeegaTeegaTeega-Teega coming down the county road, one of us would shout, *"He's coming! Man your battle stations, girls!"* And like squirrels in an attic, we would scatter. We hid in closets or under our beds or behind the sofa—wherever we could squeeze—and we waited. Sometimes we giggled with fright.

The Hudson spun its wheels, digging deeply into the steep driveway, leaving open sores of earth in its wake. It stopped with a crash against the inside far wall of the garage attached to the house, shaking the house and us in it. But, like its driver, the large car remained unscathed.

We wondered how he could drive when he could hardly walk. *Perhaps the car knows its way home by itself,* we thought. *Perhaps it doesn't need him at all.*

13

From our hiding places we listened to the crashes and thuds. The voice—using all the words my mother pleaded with him not to use in front of the children—became louder, came closer. *What will he do this time,* I thought. *Who will he hit? What will he break?*

He can't break the banister again—ripping out the wooden spokes one by one and hurling them across the room at her, on his way up the stairs—*because the new banister is made of wrought iron, and even* he *can't break that. He could hit* her. He always tried to hit her, although she was half his weight and width. He hit us, too, when he could find us. Once he hit me in the mouth, and my tooth went through my lip.

He wasn't always like this. Sometimes he was a sweet man who smelled of Old Spice and helped us with our homework and put cool washcloths on our foreheads when we had fevers. Sometimes he brought surprises home from work, hidden behind his back. "Guess which hand!" he'd say, and we'd always laugh because there were more of us than he had hands and he always got the same surprise for all of us anyway. And he brought us each a heart-shaped box of chocolates every Valentine's Day because he said we were his sweethearts.

But something made him change, and little by little we began to understand. We developed a kind of sign language among ourselves, a sort of pantomime. The main sign that we used was an outstretched hand holding an imaginary glass, brought to the lips with a jerk of the elbow, a toss of the head, and a roll of the eyes.

Sometimes, as he sat at the dining room table listening to his favorite record play over and over—

> *Chanson d'amourrr,*
> *Rah-ta Ta-ta-ta—*

shouting abuse at people living and dead, we would creep into the kitchen and pour the clear liquid down the sink and then fill the bottle with tap water. By that time he didn't know the difference.

The next day he never seemed to know what he had done or said the day before. But he must have seen the damage. The

14

torn driveway, the ever-widening hole in the wall at the back of the garage, the stain of spaghetti sauce that couldn't be removed from the dining room wallpaper, the broken glass, the frightened little girls. He would simply take the checkbook and the Hudson and drive away.

Eventually he would return, sometimes sober and sorry.

"I'm so sorry, honey," he would say to my mother. "I'll never do it again. I promise. I'm really sorry. Please forgive me."

He became a gentle giant, filled with remorse. He helped in the kitchen and made his favorite recipes. He tried to joke and make friends with his family. He patted and petted his wife and danced her around the living room to the music of the radio. And, like a small animal on a short leash, she followed every step.

I watched the faces of the younger ones. Their eyes asked, *Who is this man?* and *How long will he stay?*

He never stayed long. It would all begin innocently enough. A Schaefer commercial at the top of the fifth when the Giants were winning, and then, "Hey, honey, how about a beer?" and then whole bottles of clear liquid would vanish in an afternoon, and then he would drive off, and then in the distance we would hear the Teega-Teega sound, and then we would run for cover.

Helen's hands were hummingbird's wings that fluttered above the typewriter and left no outlines in the air. All that remained of their flight was the steady sound of the keys beating against the bank's letterhead like a Gatling gun, and the finished letters that emerged from the machine like white doves from a magician's hat. I sat beside her quietly and watched in awe, the way I used to sit in the kitchen as a child, watching my mother deftly fluting pastry for pies. Helen's hands were like my mother's, feminine and quick, with slender fingers and well-shaped painted nails. I'd always wished my hands would someday be like that, but they were not and never would be, I knew.

My hands were like my father's, square and strong, with long, thick fingers that refused to grow nails. Good at hammering wood and kneading bread and smoothing sheets, or gripping a tennis racket or patting an animal's back, my hands worked well at any task that didn't require speed. At Katharine Gibbs I'd learned all twenty-six rules for commas, how to take dictation perfectly and center a letter exactly on the page, how to dress and comport myself like a lady in the business world. But try as I might, I couldn't make my fingers move faster than fifty-five words per minute, which seemed to be one-fifth of Helen's speed.

16

The bank hadn't hired me, however, for my typing speed. At my only interview, two days after graduating from Gibbs, the vice-president for personnel told me their new president was looking for a "young and pretty girl" to be his secretary. The new president, I was told, wanted to change the bank's old image to match his own: modern, aggressive, dynamic. Since the present secretary was "due to retire soon," the president wanted to replace her with someone "fresh from school."

I started work that Monday, to Helen's surprise. No one had warned her of my arrival, and as I later learned, she had no immediate plans to retire. She had been the bank's only secretary since it first opened its massive front doors thirty-five years before, and she seemed to know banking better than all five of the officers she worked for.

Helen had never married. She lived with her spinster sister in an apartment not far from the bank, to and from which she walked each day, wearing thick-soled shoes, a plain cotton dress, and her thin white hair pulled back in a bun. She walked with a limp.

It didn't take me long to sense that the bank had been Helen's whole life, and she looked on me, her replacement, as the harbinger of her death. Masking her resentment with forced politeness, she led me through her daily routine. Each morning we filed the letters of the previous day in the cavernous basement by the bank's main vault, where, in the ancient file cabinets that lined the walls, I noticed carbon copies of correspondence, with Helen's initials in the lower left, dated fifteen years before I was born.

She showed me where she kept the bank's forms and how to fill them in. There were new account forms, loan forms, financial statement forms, mortgage forms, estate forms, note forms—

"Is all this clear to you?" Helen snapped at me impatiently.

"Oh, yes," I assured her, although I wasn't at all sure.

And then there was the mail to open and distribute, the customers to assist, and the daily dictation from all five men . . .

———

By the end of July, Helen's limp had grown worse, and although she never spoke to me of it, I knew she was in pain. She rubbed her lower back when she thought no one was looking; she brought in a cushion for her chair; and whenever she sat down at her desk, she involuntarily moaned.

"Are you all right, Helen?" I asked her one day.

"My back's bothering me a bit," she said.

"Have you been to the doctor—?"

"No," she said firmly, ending the conversation. I could see she was afraid.

By the time Helen went to the doctor, it was too late.

I visited her in the hospital one Sunday afternoon and brought her some bakery cookies and a book entitled *Woman to Woman,* which I'd recently read. Helen was alone, looking out of the window, when I entered her room. When she turned and saw me come in, she began to weep.

"I'm sorry I was mean to you," she said.

"You weren't mean, Helen," I said. "Please get well and come back soon. I can't manage all that work without you. I'll never be the secretary you are. Perhaps I should have been a nurse—?"

That was the last time I saw Helen. The malignant tumor on her spine was inoperable. She died in the hospital soon after my visit. Her sister, who looked so much like her I thought for an instant it was Helen coming through the door, came to the bank one morning to settle Helen's accounts and pick up her things. When she left, carrying Helen's white cardigan over her arm, the sweater Helen hung behind her chair "in case of a chill," and holding Helen's cushion, I knew Helen was gone. Nobody mentioned her after that. Her work, her speed, her expertise, her devotion, were forgotten. And I, nineteen, fresh out of school, alone and frightened on my first real job, was left to do all the work that Helen had done so efficiently for thirty-five years.

I sat at Helen's desk in the lobby in full public view. All day from nine to three customers approached me with questions, few of which I could answer. Each of the bank's officers expected me to do his work first and became exasperated when he found it wasn't done. I tried to push my hands to type faster, but they only made more mistakes. I couldn't keep up with the filing. I couldn't keep track of the forms.

As the pressure at work increased, I began to get bad headaches; and the pressure inside my head caused my nose to bleed. On several occasions I stood bent over the toilet in the bank's ladies' room, letting the blood, which wouldn't stop, pour freely into the bowl. One day one of the vice-presidents I worked for came in, led by a teller who had seen me bleeding.

He pulled his fat cigar from his mouth at the sight of all the blood. "You all right?" he said.

"Yes," I lied. "It's nothing."

There was a strict rule at Gibbs—one of many—that graduates had to stay at their first job at least six months or they would lose all future placement privileges. Six months for me meant December. I would stay at the bank, I resolved, until December.

· · ·

From my desk I could look across the lobby to the hallway, where the elevator operators stood like sentries guarding the ancient elevators' accordion gates. Both were elderly Irish women with lovely, lilting brogues who called me their "little flower" and blew childlike kisses to me across the lobby whenever they caught my eye.

"How's our little flower today?" one or the other would say whenever I went to the sixth floor to use the building's only photocopying machine. "Been beatin' back those bloody slave drivers with a stick?" We'd put our hands to our mouths and giggle conspiratorially, as the elevator made its clanking ascent. But all the while I wondered how long it would be before the new president replaced these old, hand-operated elevators, too.

One afternoon as I looked up to meet the elevator operators' glances I recognized a handsome soldier standing in the hall. He was a boy I had dated for several months during the previous year when I was at Gibbs. We'd had a disagreement one evening before he joined the service, and I told him I didn't want to see him anymore.

"You're so old-fashioned," he'd said that night. "Why don't you realize you're living in the second half of the twentieth century. Sex isn't *bad,* give it a try—"

A force, fiery and strong, with a voice of its own, pleaded, *Yes! Please! Now! Try!* But my brain overruled, coolly. "I don't think it's bad," I said. "I just think it's wrong before marriage. I'd rather do things right and wait until we're married."

"*Us?* Married? I don't want to get married for a while. Who said anything about marriage? I want to become a pilot first. I want to fly, travel, live a little before I settle down. I've been thinking about joining the army and letting them train me to be a pilot. They need helicopter pilots in Vietnam."

"Vietnam? I said. "Why Vietnam?"

I left my desk and crossed the lobby to greet him. "Bob, what a nice surprise," I said, admiring how tan and trim he looked. "You look great in a uniform, as handsome as my brother looked when he joined the marines."

"Can you get away?" Bob said. "Can we be alone for a while?"

"I wish I could, Bob, but the president is waiting for this letter—"

"I'm leaving tomorrow," he said.

"Leaving?"

"For Vietnam. I've just come to say—well, what difference does it make, we—you—"

"Could you come back at five, Bob? We could go somewhere and talk then—"

"No, I've got to be going real soon. Lots of people to see—"

"I'm sorry I can't break away. I'd love to spend some time with you. I've missed—"

"Yeah. Me too. Well, nice seeing you." In the hallway by the elevators he kissed me good-bye.

"Who was the darlin' soldier-boy?" one of the elevator operators asked me.

"An old boyfriend," I said. "He's going to Vietnam tomorrow."

"Vietnam? Where's that?"

•   •   •

In early autumn a lawyer who, at first glance, looked as if he could have been my father's brother began coming into the bank regularly for mortgage closings. He had my father's broad face, light complexion, and pale blue eyes behind eyeglasses. Like my father, too, he was about six feet tall, sandy-haired, and heavy-set—over two hundred pounds. He wore a tan raincoat that always looked rumpled and dark shoes that needed a shine. He was not as handsome as my father had been; my father had a nicer smile, kinder eyes. But something about him intrigued me. Perhaps it was his power over people, his air of indisputable authority. Or the way he stared at me, unaware that I was watching from the corner of my eye. He made me feel visible, valuable. I felt as if I'd known him all my life.

Over time he became more bold toward me, more pressing. He phoned me daily, but I could never talk because I was too busy. He brought me red roses hidden beneath his raincoat and presented them dramatically, which he could see both embarrassed and flattered me. For weeks I refused his dinner offers; but when he proposed a cocktail party—in my honor—I weakened and gave in.

I couldn't understand why he was interested in me, why he should say repeatedly I was the answer to his prayers. I couldn't fathom why he wanted to marry me. *This man has everything,* I thought. *What does he want with me?*

When we became engaged, I gave him a print of a photo taken by a local portrait photographer who had asked me to sit for him. I inscribed it at the lower right, diagonally, "All that I can offer you is me—head, heart, hands—completely. Bonnie." I had nothing more to give.

Before I left my job at the bank, the elevator operators, with some ceremony, gave me a pretty box wrapped in wedding paper and a large white bow. Inside was a white peignoir that took my breath away.

21

"For your weddin' night, m'darlin'," one of them said.

"I've never owned such a beautiful nightgown," I said, blinking back tears. "I've always worn flannel pajamas or my brother's T-shirts to bed." The peignoir was the first thing I packed for my honeymoon.

I left the bank in mid-December. I had stayed there six months.

On the way to the airport, as Jim gave instructions to his friend Jerry about how he wanted the house prepared for our return, he didn't seem to notice me sitting beside him. I smoothed my white suit, adjusted my white fur pillbox hat, and took out my compact nervously. The hairdresser had teased my short hair and sprayed it heavily; she'd applied my makeup too—more than I had ever used before—so that I could hardly recognize myself in the compact mirror. *Who is this person with the darkened eyebrows and the stiff, lifeless hair?* I asked myself, and answered: *I don't know her.* I closed the compact, folded my hands in my lap, and stared out of the car window. As Jerry sped along the highway, driving us in Jim's black Cadillac to Kennedy, everything we passed became a blur.

"The kitchen's got to be painted yellow, Jerry," Jim ordered. "And make sure you're there when they install the wall-to-wall carpeting next week. . . . And don't forget to have the refrigerator and stove replaced with the new ones I ordered—"

Jim and I had agreed we would live in his smaller house, and his parents would remain in the large house on the other side of town. Jim owned several apartment buildings also, where we could have lived; but the small Cape Cod house, in a neighborhood of young married couples with young children, seemed ideal for us as newlyweds.

I had seen the small house and liked it. It had a sunny kitchen overlooking a small backyard, a nice-size living room and adjoining dining room, and two bedrooms and a bathroom upstairs. It was only slightly smaller than the house in which I'd grown up and was quite like the "dream home" of my secret scrapbook. I was pleased that Jim had agreed we could live there and proud of his generosity in leaving the Summit Avenue house to his parents. The small house would be *ours,* I thought, a place that I could decorate and make into a warm and cozy home.

Jerry listened to Jim's orders and nodded obediently. He seemed used to Jim's commands and anxious to carry them through. Jerry reminded me of a woodland animal: small, timid, darting. He seldom spoke, but when he did, his voice was soft. He lisped. I wondered how such dissimilar men as Jerry and Jim could have become close friends.

As Jim continued to instruct Jerry, I studied our honeymoon itinerary:

Sat. Dec. 19	6:45 p.m.	Leave Kennedy Airport via American Jet #15
	9:45 p.m.	Arrive San Francisco Airport
Sun. Dec. 20	8:30 p.m.	Leave San Francisco via Pan Am Jet #841
	11:35 p.m.	Arrive Honolulu Airport
Fri. Jan. 1	9:30 a.m.	Leave Honolulu via United Jet #190
	4:25 p.m.	Arrive Los Angeles Leave Los Angeles date of your choice via American Jet; arrive Kennedy or Newark

It was the first time I'd ever flown first class. The stewardess gave each of us a printed dinner menu enclosing a fresh red rose. The menu read: " '21' Club Service—Fruits de Mer with

'21' Cocktail Sauce. Prime Steer Beef with '21' Sauce Borde-
laise. Major Bibb Limestone Lettuce with '21' French Dressing.
Parfait Glacé.''

I couldn't eat.

"I'm tired, Jim," I whispered.

"Then go to sleep, Babe," he said.

He put his jacket over me protectively, and I quickly fell
asleep. We didn't speak again until we'd landed.

While Jim checked in, I read the hotel's literature at the front
desk. "The New Fairmont Hotel and Tower, atop Nob Hill
. . . For a spectacular view of downtown San Francisco and the
San Francisco bridges, with the Marin, Oakland, and Berkeley
hills in the background, ride the outside elevator to the Crown
Room, 26 stories high in the sky . . ."

This was the farthest I'd ever been from home. I'd spent a
summer with my grandmother in Maine and traveled with my
mother through the southern states to visit my brother in Florida, but that was all the traveling I'd done. Jim had traveled
throughout the States, Europe, and Russia. He'd spent two
years fighting in Korea during that war. He told me we would
see the world together. But as the Fairmont's outside elevator
ascended to take us to our room, I didn't feel excited by San
Francisco's lights. I simply felt far from home.

I took a bath and dried my body slowly, studying myself in the
mirror that stretched the length of the bathroom wall. My skin
was blue-white under the fluorescent light, and my hair looked
yellow-green. I had a small waist and a woman's hips, but the
arms and chest of an adolescent boy. The white peignoir with
its deep-cut front hung from my bony shoulders limply.

Jim was sitting on the edge of the white double bed wearing
blue cotton pajamas when I finally entered the room. He
looked at me and laughed. "Take that off," he said, "and put
on something else. You look like a fool in that thing."

130,047 ——

It was as if I weren't there, or as if I were dreaming. I wished it were a dream that I could wake from, to find myself at home in my own bed.

Why doesn't he kiss me? . . . Why isn't he touching me? . . . Why is he swearing at me? . . . Why doesn't he speak to me? . . . Please get off of me, you're too heavy. . . . Please get up, I can't breathe. . . . Please don't be so rough with me. . . . You're hurting me. . . .

I wanted to scream, but I bit my lip.

"Where did you learn that?" he said angrily.

"What?"

"To move like that."

"Move?"

"Only whores move like that."

I stopped struggling.

"No," I said to myself, softly, when it had ended.

"No, what?" he said, as he turned away from me. But before I could reply he was asleep.

I don't remember much about the year I was a wife. It's as if I left the memories behind, with most of my other belongings, the day I left. Or as if, by slamming the door behind me, I woke from a terrible nightmare, which I tried to forget. Now, fifteen years later, I must return. And remember.

· · ·

My memory of our honeymoon in Hawaii is a blur. I can see only hazy outlines of two disparate people, together on an island far from home. Drinking papaya juice and eating fresh coconut meat on the beach. Having big dinners at good restaurants every night. Gaining six pounds in ten days. Learning some words of Hawaiian—*Mele Kalicke Macka:* Merry Christmas and Happy New Year. Watching surfers riding the waves at dawn from our balcony. Shopping and sightseeing all over Oahu. Making breakfasts in the kitchenette of our suite. Going to the laundromat in my bikini. Stopping at a campsite far from Waikiki and falling from a narrow reef, knocked down by an unexpected wave. Jim catching me by the leg before I was washed away. Having my bleeding, coral-scraped back bandaged by the troop leader at the nearby Boy Scout campsite. Jim telling me earnestly, "That means no more sex for a while;

you can't lie on your back." Depositing two hundred dollars at a savings bank in Honolulu to start saving, Jim said, for our second honeymoon in Hawaii in ten years. Inquiring about a boat trip to the outer islands and the ticket clerk looking at the two of us and saying to Jim, "For you and your daughter?" and Jim getting angry at her for saying that and at me for laughing. Being embarrassed by the way Jim bargained with merchants and made demands of waiters. Reading Anne Morrow Lindbergh's *Gift from the Sea* while Jim slept, with his back to me. Feeling as if I were dreaming.

Jim's father picked us up from the airport when we returned from our honeymoon in early January and drove us to the small house where we were to begin our married life. For the length of the hour's drive, Jim's father hardly spoke. He must have been afraid to warn us: The house wasn't ready. The carpet in the living room had not been laid. The furniture had not yet been delivered. There was nothing to sleep on but the bare floor.

On seeing that his clear instructions, his firm commands, had not been followed, Jim went into a rage. He became someone he hadn't been before: a terrifying man—as my father had been whenever he got drunk—violent in his behavior and in his language, profane. But Jim was even more frightening to me because he *hadn't* been drinking.

I sat on the rolled carpet watching him, hugging my knees, and shaking with fear. "That's it!" he finally shouted. "We're not living here! A man in my position shouldn't have to live in a place like this anyway! We're going back to Summit Avenue where I belong."

Like a fly caught in a web, I was too frightened and stupefied to struggle or speak.

•   •   •

On Sunday afternoons, or sometimes after dinner in the summer, my family used to go for long rides in my father's gold

Hudson convertible "to see how the other half lives." When the weather was warm we'd drive with the top down—my father at the wheel, my mother in the front seat on the other side, and my younger sisters and I in the back seat, bare-chested and tanned brown, white-blond sun-bleached hair blowing in the warm wind—toward the posher parts of our county. We'd drive slowly past the big houses and their sprawling lawns and play guessing games as to how much each house might be worth, who lived inside, and what it must be like to live there. It's possible, although I don't remember doing so, that we drove down Summit Avenue then and admired the wide, tree-lined street, its rows of stately mansions, its cleanliness, quietness, dignity, exclusivity. "I wonder what it's like to live *there*," my mother might have said, pointing to the large white house on the right. Ten years later I would have an answer.

• • •

Jim had bought the house on Summit Avenue and moved in with his retired parents several years before we met. It was too large for three people, and too much work for his elderly parents to cope with. But Jim felt the address was good for his image as a successful attorney in this success-conscious, three-piece-suited upper-middle-class town.

Jim was what might be called a self-made man, living the American Dream. He was a child of the Depression from a modest background. His father had been a hardware salesman until his retirement, his mother an assembly-line worker in a garment factory. His older brother had joined the navy after high school and left home. Jim was a "good boy"; he'd been an acolyte in church. He was a "bright boy"; his parents invested in him. They sent him to a military prep school and to college. After the Korean War, in which Jim had served as a sergeant in the army artillery, he lived with his parents while he attended law school. Jim was the favored son, the big investment, the ticket. Summit Avenue became his domain, but his parents' payoff. In return for the privilege of having arrived with him at that address, however, Jim's parents functioned as his live-in servants. His father was the gardener, maintenance man, and errand boy; his mother, the housekeeper, cook, and laundress.

The three lived together there continuously, if not always happily, for four years. There had been, I later learned, terrible arguments between Jim and his parents. They had even tried to take him before the Ethics Committee of the Bar Association to have him disbarred. I never learned why.

When I moved in to Summit Avenue I didn't bring much with me. Just the few clothes from home that I could call my own (by that time my mother and sisters and I all wore the same size, and our wardrobes were communal), my own books, scrapbooks, family photographs, diaries, poetry. Everything fit, with room to spare, into one of the walk-in closets in the master bedroom, which Jim and I shared. Jim's parents slept in separate bedrooms at the far end of the second-floor hall.

I tried not to intrude on their established way of life. I didn't want to interfere. Jim found a part-time job for me in town, working as a secretary in a small insurance agency, to keep me, he said, "out of Mom and Pop's hair." While I was at work Jim's mother did the housework, but when I got home I took over the kitchen duties, in an effort to do my share.

"Let me teach you how to cook," Jim's mother said soon after I moved in.

"Thank you," I said, as tactfully as I could, "but I already know how. I've been cooking for my family since my mother went back to work when I was eleven." I didn't add that I'd been studying cookbooks religiously for years.

She seemed insulted. "Well, Jimmy likes things done a certain way. *My way.*" She showed me how she prepared asparagus, "one of Jimmy's favorites," by boiling it in a large potful of water for twenty minutes, then pouring all the water down the drain, burning some butter in a frying pan until it was black, stirring in some breadcrumbs, and pouring this all over the platter of soggy spears.

"I think I would do it a little differently," I said after she finished her demonstration.

30

She left the kitchen then without a word, but when Jim came home from work she complained to him that I was "pig-headed," "ungrateful," "insolent," and "stubborn."

The kitchen became my private sanctuary. While Jim's parents sat in the study watching TV, I'd work alone in the large kitchen happily. I made my favorite recipes, which Jim and his parents seemed to enjoy eating. But every day Jim's mother would complain to him that I was "antisocial" because I spent so much time in the kitchen.

Perhaps, I thought, *in this respect she's right.* I simply didn't know how to converse with these people, who were so much older than I, so different from anyone I'd ever met before, so hostile toward me, so possessive about Jim. His mother also frightened me. She had a temper as fiery as the color of her hennaed hair and a stare that made me shiver. Jim's father was for the most part a docile man who shuffled along behind her like a shadow, nodding his assent to everything she said.

As politely as possible, I continued to avoid them and tried to keep the peace. Jim did his best to please everyone. But the tension in the house increased, and the knots in my stomach grew thick. I felt sick to my stomach every day, and one morning I fainted in the shower. Jim took me to his doctor.

"Raise your arms," the doctor said. He felt my breasts. "Are they sore?" I said they were somewhat, and wondered what that had to do with stomachaches. He examined me internally. "Did it occur to you that you might be pregnant?" he said. It hadn't. Jim and I had been married less than six weeks, and we hadn't made love often. At the time I thought it took more planning and effort than that to get pregnant.

When the tests came back positive, Jim and I were elated. He wanted children, he said, more than anything else in the world; and he wanted them soon, because he felt he was getting too old. I was thrilled at the thought of a life growing inside of me, delighted with the prospect of becoming a mother, pleased to be the bearer of Jim's happiness.

After he learned I was pregnant Jim lost all interest in sex. He told me that for us to have sexual relations "might harm the unborn child" and that sex was "only for procreation anyway." He felt that sex for any other reason was "dirty," "disgusting,"

31

"vulgar." I disagreed with him but didn't argue. Without any personal experience to go by, how could I? I'd simply always thought that sex was meant to be wonderful, something worth waiting until marriage for. So I'd waited—excitedly, expectantly, silently, the way I used to wait for Christmas as a child. But with Jim, I felt as if I were still waiting.

From that day in February 1965, Jim and I shared the same king-size bed but slept apart. He didn't approach me, didn't touch me. Yet to other people he'd complain, in front of me, "My wife is a cold fish. We live like brother and sister."

When Jim's mother learned of my pregnancy, she became even more hostile. She waited until Jim left for work one morning and followed me into the kitchen. She pointed to my stomach, waved her finger at me, and began screaming, "God is going to curse that baby! God is going to curse that baby!" I did not reply. Instead, I turned the faucet taps on full and tried to drown her voice with the sound of water.

I phoned Jim at work to tell him what had happened, and he later asked his mother whether what I'd reported was true. She told him I was lying. And he believed her.

When Jim's parents began eating their meals in the basement at a small table they'd set up by the oil burner, telling the neighbors I forced them to do this, and when, every day, before Jim left for his office and I left for my job, they told us we'd find them dead when we got home, slumped over the front seat of their car in the garage, the car motor running, the garage door closed, Jim seemed to behave as if these threats and accusations were part of the script of a bizarre play he'd starred in all his life.

Jim had other worries. He was, it appeared, deeply in debt, and his parents were among his many creditors. They had given him all their savings, approximately twenty thousand dollars, plus their Social Security, and now, they said, he was "forcing them out on the street."

Sometimes Jim's friend Jerry was called in to referee. He would take me aside and speak sweetly, timidly, as if he were afraid of me. "Be reasonable," he said to me once. "Can't you see what this is doing to this dear old couple? Their lives are falling apart. You should have more respect. . . ." I told Jerry I'd be happy for Jim's parents to stay and for Jim and me to go to the small house. I told him I'd never said anything about their leaving. He didn't believe me.

Finally, in April, Jim's parents packed to go, telling the neighbors, "She kicked us out." Jim gave them a car and his yacht, in part payment of his debt, and they pulled it across the country to California, where they planned to live in a retirement village not far from their other son and his family. I left my job at the insurance office and stayed home to keep house and wait for the baby. I was certain everything would get better.

While they were away, Jim's parents telephoned occasionally. They said they were enjoying the retirement village and the sunny California climate and they got to see their three grandsons frequently. Jim and I listened on two of the Summit Avenue house's five phones.

"But why haven't you been answering my letters, Jimmy dear?" his mother said, in a tone one would use to reprove a two-year-old.

"What letters, Mom?" he said defensively.

"Why, the letters I mailed to the house."

When he'd put down the receiver, Jim turned to me. "What have you been doing with Mom's letters?"

"We haven't received any letters—"

"Are you calling my mother a liar?"

"None of her letters have arrived here."

Jim glared at me. "I'll tell her to write to my office."

So from then on Jim's parents telephoned him and corresponded with him at his office, and he dictated his replies to his secretary. Nothing of what they said was shared with me.

Our life without Jim's parents settled into a married-couple routine. I would wake at eight and make breakfast of bacon and eggs while Jim got ready for work. We'd eat together in the breakfast room and Jim would tell me what chores he expected me to do that day. After he left the house a few minutes before nine, I'd watch "I Love Bob" in the study until nine-thirty. The Bob Cummings show made me laugh.

Then I'd begin the household chores, which lasted all day. Although we didn't use all seventeen rooms, they still got dusty and dirty; and his mother had left many of them in disarray. The house became for me a mammoth master, and I its sole slave. I scrubbed it, polished it, dusted it, vacuumed it, painted it, redecorated it, and made new draperies for it. Then I'd cook dinner for Jim and me. Once, in mock-television-commercial fashion, I showed Jim our freshly scrubbed refrigerator when he got home from work. "Note the drawers," I said playfully, "see how they glisten, and the shelves, how they shine!" Jim ran his hand along the top edge of the door, then put his hand up, as if to stop traffic. "It's still dirty," he said soberly.

I remember spending an entire afternoon polishing all twenty-four pairs of Jim's shoes.

One day I asked whether I could have some help with the housework. Jim said he would think about it. For my twentieth birthday, in mid-May, he gave me two new vacuum cleaners. "You wanted something to help you with the housework," he said.

I had little time for socializing, no time for fun. My closest acquaintance in the neighborhood was the Scottish live-in maid who worked for the people next door. She and I would talk with each other as we hung our wet wash on adjacent lines. *She seems to like living on Summit Avenue,* I thought, *but then, she gets days off—and gets paid.*

In the early months, before my pregnancy became obvious, sometimes door-to-door salesmen would come to the house and ask, "Is your mother in?" When I'd say, "This is my house," they'd be apologetic. But so would I. I'd feel as if I'd told a lie.

My one big outing each month was the standing third-Thursday-at-three-o'clock appointment I had with my obstetrician. I'd put on makeup, fuss with my hair, wear my best maternity dress, and drive to the doctor's office with the anticipation of a lover on her way to a secret rendezvous. Then I'd sit in his crowded waiting room pretending to read a magazine but really studying the faces of the women around me. They all seemed excited, expectant. I was sure we were all in love with him.

When my turn came, I'd sit on the edge of his examining table, nervously. And then when he walked into the room, looking like Cary Grant's identical twin, and reached for my hand and stroked it tenderly and said, "How are we today?" with a broad smile, or "Tsk, tsk, we *are* getting fat, aren't we?" and shook his head, I'd practically swoon. Each month, after examining me he'd say, "Everything's fine. You're going to have a big, healthy baby." Then I would go home to wait.

. . .

Jim was often generous with his money, hospitable to the neighbors and his client-friends. He liked to buy gifts for people and present them ceremoniously. Frequently he would come home from work with unexpected gifts for me—a string of pearls, a new hair drier, a dozen pairs of stockings, new pots and pans—things I neither needed nor wanted. He called me Babe and told me daily that he loved me, but except for passing kisses when he left for and returned from work, he never touched me.

Once he paid me a compliment. We were on our way home from a dinner party attended by his contemporaries—professional men and their wives, all in their mid-to-late thirties—and he turned to me and said, "Everywhere we go you always handle yourself beautifully." And once he made me laugh. I met him at the door one day as he came in from work with, "Hi, I'm the downstairs maid!" He pointed to my basketball-size stomach and remarked, "Looks like you've been doing a bit of upstairs work, too."

Although I don't remember ever seeing Jim read a book in the whole year I lived on Summit Avenue, he seemed to know everything. He was, I thought, a genius, and I was in awe of that. I'd ask him about other countries, about politics and history, and he would answer my questions fully and patiently. Compared with him, I felt, I knew nothing.

35

Sometimes I would help in his office when one of his secretaries was out ill, and I'd be amazed at his ability. He remembered each detail of every case without having to check the files. He handled his clients deftly and with unquestionable authority.

"My clients are all little people," he once said to me. "They need someone to direct their lives. Some lawyers would prefer a few big clients. Not me. I'd rather have a lot of little ones who look up to me."

Sometimes in the evenings we would go for walks, and it was on one of these walks that we chose names for the baby. We agreed to accept each other's choice—I would choose the boy's name and Jim the girl's.

"If it's a boy," I said, "I think I'd like to call him Cary Alexander."

"All right," Jim said. "And if it's a girl, I like the name Whitney."

"Whitney? Isn't that a boy's name?"

"Not necessarily."

But something—whether it was the pressures of his work, his debts, or his heavy responsibilities—was making Jim angry, and he seemed to need to vent his anger on me.

The arguments would start over nothing, then billow like poisonous fumes throughout the house. If I tried to walk away, he would follow me into each room, shouting at me and pounding me with words as if they were bricks. He never struck me physically, but the words hurt more than anything he might have done with his fist. Always, in every argument, the theme was the same: "You are an abortion," he would say, "the product of two miserable people! You are a crazy woman, and I'm going to have you put away! I'm going to take that baby away from you and give it to my mother so she can raise it the way I was raised!"

One night in the early summer he came home with photocopies of custody judgments in which the custody of very young children was given to the father. He threw these papers at me saying, "See, this proves I'll be able to take the baby away from you."

I tried to read the papers, but I couldn't understand the legal language. I tried to ignore his threats, but they were unremitting. I tried to understand what was troubling him, but it was beyond my twenty-year-old grasp. I felt overpowered, helpless, trapped. Where could I go where he couldn't follow me? What can a pregnant woman do?

As he battered me with words, all I could do was cry. And as I did, he'd take my tear-contorted face and press it against the nearest mirror. "Look! See that face? It's the face of a crazy woman!"

Sometimes I'd simply crumple into a heap, sobbing. Then Jim would phone a neighbor or one of his client-friends and ask him or her to come over. "My wife is having another one of her attacks," he'd say. "She's not well. No, it's not the pregnancy; it's her head." The chosen person would come quickly and gently suggest I get up and go to bed. Jim would give me one of his sleeping pills and tuck me in, and in the morning he'd behave as if nothing had happened.

It was as if he had been drunk the night before and had no memory of his drunken behavior when he woke the next day. I'd experienced this with my father all my life. But with Jim I couldn't transfer my hurt and hatred to the contents of a bottle. Whatever it was that made Jim change was not something that he consumed, but rather something that consumed him.

Sometimes at night, sitting up in bed and watching TV, Jim would suddenly start to cry, and when I asked him what was wrong he'd say his mind was filled with terrible memories, like a horror movie that played incessantly. He saw the people he'd killed in Korea. He saw their blood, their bullet-riddled bodies. While the eleven o'clock news reported on the war in Vietnam, I sat beside my husband on our king-size bed and listened to him speak of his memories of the war in Korea.

Sometimes he cried because, he said, he was afraid of death. He was afraid his high blood pressure was killing him. He complained of pains in his right arm, "the first sign of a heart attack," he said.

At other times he told me he was haunted by the memory of his mother working "with all those other poor women in that sweaty factory. She did that for me," he said, weeping. "If it wasn't for Mom, I'd be nothing. She made me what I am. I owe everything to her. Now look what I've done to her—I've sent her to a retirement village to die."

He worried about his law practice, his loan payments. Money. He owed more than one hundred thousand dollars. He had trouble sleeping. Each morning when I cleaned the ashtray on Jim's side of the bed I counted more than twenty cigarette butts in it, knowing I had emptied it before we turned out the light the previous night.

He took pills every day. Blood-pressure pills. Sleeping pills. Librium.

In the corner of our bedroom was a cabinet full of guns. Jim wasn't a sportsman; he didn't hunt. We lived in a relatively crime-free community. When I asked why he kept them, he answered, "Just in case." The rifles stood barrel-up behind a glass door. A dozen handguns were heaped in the drawer below. Boxes of ammunition were stacked nearby. One of the pistols was gold-plated. I asked Jim where he got it. He said, "From a friend in the Mafia, for doing him a favor." I never touched the cabinet again.

In September, one month before the baby was due, Jim and I went separately to a marriage counselor whom Jim knew because he had an office in Jim's building and to whom Jim often referred his clients for help.

For the first time, I confided in someone about our marital problems. I had been too embarrassed to tell my friends, too ashamed to tell anyone from my church, too afraid I might upset my mother by telling her. But in the course of three visits, I told the marriage counselor everything—about our arguments, Jim's constant threats of divorce and taking the baby from me, my feelings of helplessness and fear.

The man took notes as he listened. When I finished my unpleasant task of recounting the events of the previous nine months, I waited anxiously to hear what he had to say. I thought he might have an answer, a cure for the sickness that was pervading our marriage. When he looked up from his notebook his expression was intense, the look of a man who takes himself and his profession seriously. He spoke slowly, deliberately, as if he were speaking to an idiot or a child. He said: "The first year is always the hardest."

Lindy and I met in our kindergarten class play. I was the star, Goldilocks, and she the baby bear. She had a small, sturdy body and only two speeds: slow and asleep. That may have been one of the reasons I liked her. She was the only person I'd ever known who was slower than I. For as long as I could remember my mother had said I was the slowest thing on two legs. Lindy was living proof my mother could be wrong.

Lindy and I walked to and from school together almost every day for about six years. At eight-fifteen in the morning I would arrive at her home, and sometimes I would find her in bed—still sleeping.

"Oh, Lindy," I'd moan, "you're going to make us late again! C'mon, please wake up!" I would rub her back to wake her the way my mother woke me and repeat the things my mother said to me: "Rise and shine, rise and shine . . . brand new day! . . . Let's not be late for school. . . . Here are your clothes. . . . That's it. . . . Hurryhurryhurry."

Lindy would grunt, roll over, open her eyes halfway, and in slow motion start to rise and, in her fashion, shine. I would watch as she slowly traded her faded green ski-pajama top for a new blue pullover. I'd bring her her loafers and socks while she groped in the closet for a skirt. Slowly, she'd brush her teeth, wash her face, and comb her hair. "Okay, let's go," she'd say sleepily.

As we wound our way out of the house, dodging toy trucks and baby bottles, Lindy's mother would run after us and hand both of us a slice of cinnamon toast to eat on our way to school. Most of the time we walked the remaining mile and a half in silence.

In that respect I felt Lindy was the best kind of friend for me. She seemed to like solitude and silence as much as I did. Once in a while we would talk, though, sometimes even have discussions, such as the time we decided our mothers were trying to make us look ugly: My mother gave me permanents on the smallest-size rollers, which made my hair frizzy and silly-looking ("If I was meant to have frizzy hair, I would have been born with it," I told Lindy), and Lindy's mother made her wear her big sister's clothes although they never fit right. "It's a conspiracy," we muttered. "They're jealous."

Lindy's mother was very beautiful and also very religious. She had been converted ("born again," she said) sometime between her fourth and fifth child, I calculated—a calculation based on her children's names. In order, they were: Veronica, Lindy (Caroline), Brent, Walter, Jeremiah, Zechariah, and Esther. Lindy said if her mother ever had another baby she'd probably call it Deuteronomy. At times Lindy was droll.

Often I stayed at Lindy's for dinner. One night Lindy's mother took roll call in the kitchen before dishing out overcooked hamburgers, homemade applesauce, and canned peas. Three of the noses she counted did not belong to her; two of her own children were missing.

"Where's Brent?" she asked Veronica, her deputy.

"Next door at Keith's. He said he wouldn't be home for dinner."

"And where's Walter?"

"He's in the bathroom," a chorus answered.

If Walter had been in a neighbor's bathroom, he would have heard his mother call him. "Wal-TERRR!" She had an ear-piercing way of emphasizing the last syllable of her children's names whenever she called them. And she was always calling one of them.

Walter came in, squeezed between Jeremy and Zach, and before anyone could raise a fork, Lindy's mother said, "Let's all bow our heads. Dear Heavenly Father," she began, with a sweet soft voice she reserved for her husband and God, "we thank you for this food which we are about to eat . . ." I opened my eyes a crack and scanned the table. Esther was finger painting her high chair with catsup, while Walter was playing war with Zach, using peas as pellets in their slingshot-spoons. Their mother's eyes were tightly closed as she continued to pray. "Please bless this food to our bodies and us in thy service. We ask this in the name of your dear Son, our Lord and Savior, Jesus. Amen."

The idea of God coming down and invisibly blessing dried hamburgers and canned peas was strangely thrilling to me. God had never blessed the food at my house; he was never invited to. And if he had ever arrived uninvited, he would have felt unwelcome. I felt unwelcome, too, so I stayed away. My parents seldom asked me where I went, and they never told me when to be home. Was it that they trusted my judgment, I wondered?

Lindy's mother loved children, even other people's. She never minded how many strange small faces sat at the enormous oval table in her oversize kitchen, as long as her own children were accounted for. The cooking wasn't as good as my mother's, I thought, but there was a kind of joyous disorderliness there that I found as delicious as exotic fruit. Such as the time Veronica made three pumpkin pies, forgetting to add the pumpkin, but everyone happily ate the pies anyway.

So I spent more and more time at Lindy's house—after school, on Saturdays—and finally I began to go to church with Lindy on Sundays. On the way to church in her tomato-red Volkswagen bus, Lindy's mother led in singing, "Jesus loves the little children, all the children of the world," while chaos reigned in the seats behind her. "Red and yellow, black and white, they are precious in His sight. . . ." Lindy gazed sleepily out of the window. I tried to learn the words of the songs.

Almost every Sunday we were late for church, but when Lindy's mother entered, always breathless and embarrassed, with her small flock in tow, the people in the pews smiled benignly, understandingly. There was warmth and kindness there such as I'd never felt before.

I had been to only one other church, when I was much younger. My father used to drop my sisters and me there and drive off. The small church was built of cold stone; the people inside sat rigidly, solemnly. The minister wore what appeared to me to be a black Halloween costume and kept his back to the congregation most of the time. I never knew when to stand, sit, or kneel. I always felt tempted to run out while the minister's back was turned, pulling one sister by each hand, but the big front doors were kept tightly shut and two old men stood guard by them to prevent such escapes.

Lindy's mother's church was not like that. It was large, plain, warm, and made of wood. It was filled with friendly people and singing. The minister wore a business suit and spoke to the people instead of to candles. He said simple things that even I could understand, such as "Suffer the little children to come unto me, and forbid them not; for of such is the kingdom of Heaven."

Although Lindy's family moved away when I was in the seventh grade and we lost touch, I didn't stop going to Lindy's mother's church. In time it became my own. Every Sunday morning while the rest of my family slept I got up and dressed and walked two miles to the big, wooden church in the next town. When I returned, my parents never asked me where I'd been or why. Was it that they knew, I wondered, or they didn't care?

I went to that church faithfully, hungrily: to the Sunday school classes, the morning worship services, the evening youth group meetings, the evening services. I went for the music—Bach in the morning and gospel songs at night—for the Bible lessons, for the warmth of the people, for the messages of love and peace: "For God so loved the world that He gave His only begotten Son that whosoever believeth in Him should not perish but have everlasting life." I went to escape the strife at home and find a haven with the promise of Heaven.

I studied the people in the pews around me: old couples with almost identical profiles sitting close together holding hands,

young couples with radiant faces glancing at each other lovingly, mothers cuddling their little ones serenely. To them, in this
church, God was real. Not cold and remote like the farthest
star, but as close and vital as one's own heartbeat. This God was
an all-knowing, all-loving, all-forgiving, ever-present *Friend,*
who was worshipped, not with repetitive phrases read from a
book, but with simple, spontaneous language spoken from the
heart.

"God knows your heart," Pastor Holbrook said. "He wants
to cleanse it and make it whole. He wants to come into your
life and give you peace and joy and eternal life. . . . Won't you
say, 'Yes, Lord, I believe you died for me; here is my heart, fill
me with your Spirit'? . . . If you haven't already done so, in the
quietness of your own heart, why don't you say, 'Yes, Lord, I
believe,' tonight?"

And as the congregation sang, "Amazing grace, how sweet
the sound, that saved a wretch like me," I said, *"Yes, Lord. Yes.
Yes."*

From that night on I woke each morning at six to read the Bible and pray before getting ready for school. I spoke to God
as if He were my parent, asking Him for guidance, help with
my homework, love for my family, strength to be a good Christian, more faith.

I wrote to my brother at marine boot camp and told him
about my religious conversion. He told me never to write to
him again. My mother was glad that I'd found God, but she
said it wasn't for her. She said she didn't want to go to Heaven;
she'd feel out of place there. My father called me Sister Bonnie
and asked me questions about God and the Bible—whenever
he was drunk. My sisters went to church with me, occasionally.

One Sunday morning we went to church together as a family.

"There will never be peace in the world," Pastor Holbrook
said, "until there is peace in each country, peace in each city
and town and village, peace in each family, peace in each indi-
vidual heart. . . . Christ freely offers that peace to those who
will believe. . . . It is a peace that passes understanding . . ."

My father sat beside me, solemn and erect, listening.

44

God, please touch my father's heart, I prayed. *Please open his heart to you. Please make him stop drinking so that we can have a happy family. Please, Lord, please hear my prayer . . .*

My father stood and sang the hymns with a deep, sure voice. I hoped he'd leave the church a changed man.

"That Pastor Holbrook is a gentleman and a scholar," my father said in the car going home. But he never went to hear Pastor Holbrook again. And he kept on drinking.

• • •

I told Jim all of this before we were married. We'd even gone to my church together every Sunday. Jim told me he believed as I did, and I never doubted his word. *Why would anyone lie to me?* I'd always thought. *What could anyone gain by lying to me?* But after we were married, after we learned I was pregnant, Jim admitted he'd lied.

"Why," I said, "why did you lie to me about this?"

"Because you wouldn't have married me otherwise," he said.

Religion, then, became an issue in every argument. He told me we would go to his church, which I found ritualistic, impersonal, and cold. I said I'd prefer to go to my own, where I could feel spiritually fed. For him this was a clash of wills, which he was determined to win. To me, it was a question of betrayal. He tried to make me change my beliefs, deny my faith; I told him they were as fixed as the color of my eyes. He didn't say I was "stubborn and willful," which I couldn't have denied. He didn't say I was "odd" or "different from most people," which I'd always suspected. He said I was "mentally ill," he was going to have me "put away," and then he would take my baby.

W ould you prefer to have your baby here or in the hospital?" the doctor said, soon after he started examining me.

It was a little after three p.m. on the third Thursday in October 1965, and I was there for my monthly office visit. The baby wasn't due for ten days.

"In the hospital," I said, "when the time comes." The white sheet covering my raised knees hid the doctor's facial expression, and I couldn't tell from the tone of his voice, either, whether he was joking.

He stood up from his stool and helped me to a sitting position on the examining table.

"Well then, you'd better get over there right away," he said. "You're already almost three fingers dilated. It won't be long now."

My sister and I had spent the morning shopping for baby things, walking for hours through the major department stores in a nearby shopping plaza; and apart from mild cramps in my lower abdomen, which I'd ignored, I hadn't felt anything unusual that day. If I hadn't had the doctor's appointment, I thought, how would I have known I was in labor? I had asked friends who'd recently given birth to tell me what the warning signals were and how they felt, but each one just smiled at me mysteriously and said, "You'll know, don't worry."

I wasn't worried. My mother had always said she loved having babies—she'd had five, one of whom died soon after birth—because it was the only time in her life when she could get away from the housework and cooking and be on her own for a few days, when she could stay in bed all day and have meals brought to her bed on a tray. Since no one in my family, during the course of my childhood, had ever been ill enough to need hospitalization, I grew up thinking that having a baby was a bit like taking a vacation and that maternity wards were holiday resorts.

"We're going to the hospital," I whispered to my sister in the doctor's waiting room, and the other women waiting there could tell from our excitement that my time had come.

. . .

All I can recall are the bright lights on the ceiling and the white-coated people standing by my open legs. "Good girl, good girl," I heard through a drugged haze. "Take a deep breath now. . . . *Push* . . . that's a GOOD GIRL . . ." I remember I didn't scream or cry. I don't remember any pain at all.

Two hours after I drove myself to the hospital, my eight-pound baby was born.

When I woke from the anesthetic, the doctor was beside me. "You are the mother of a beautiful girl," he said.

"Nooo," I said, in sleepy disbelief. It all seemed too easy, too quick. And a *girl?* Jim had said the baby would unquestionably be a *boy;* there had been no girls born on his side of the family for more than thirty years.

"Then shall I take her home with *me?*" the doctor teased.

"Oh, no," I said, "she's *mine.*"

"And the next time you have a baby, young lady," he added, "make sure you stay very close to the hospital—or it might be born on the sidewalk."

As he left the room, I smiled and closed my eyes.

Jim came from court as soon as he could, bringing a delicate bouquet of pink rosebuds in a porcelain music-box vase shaped like a cradle. He sat beside my bed, holding my hand, weeping with joy. "Thank you, Babe," he said. "You've made me so very happy—I don't know how to thank you— She's so beautiful—"

When I saw the depth of Jim's emotion, his immeasurable pride and happiness at the birth of our child, I forgot all that had gone before.

In an otherwise empty diary for 1965, I made this entry:

"*Thursday, October 21*—The day that changed my life! . . . Whitney Lee is a tiny pink bow which has bound her daddy and mommy into a deeper, stronger, wider, fuller love." On the page I drew a picture of a bow, and added, "I love her so."

The night before my wedding I'd asked Kathy about love. How did you know when you had it? What did it feel like? Where does it begin and how does it grow? How is it shared and cared for? I didn't know. Kathy loved Carl. She knew.

But when the nurse first brought Whitney to me to be fed, I knew. It was as if this perfect little being with large, dark-blue eyes and wisps of white-blond hair was the embodiment of love. She was there because of me; she needed me as no one else had ever needed me before. As I touched her skin and studied her—this separate life, once part of my body—I knew I would cherish her forever, I would kill to protect her, I would die for her if need be. *This is love,* I said to myself as I rocked her in my arms to the Brahms "Lullaby" coming from the cradle music box, *now I know.*

Perhaps it was because I was the eldest daughter at home and I remembered my sisters as infants and the care my mother took of them; or because I'd played with dolls until I was eleven, feeding, dressing, and caring for each one as if it were alive; or because I'd babysat for other people's children for years; or for all these reasons put together, motherhood came easily to me. I never felt nervous or unsure in handling my baby. Just as I knew my hands were incapable of speed and dexterity, I knew they were supremely capable of handling my child securely and confidently. I'd never felt so confident about anything before. It was as if I'd been a mother all my life.

And I was blessed with a good baby. The hospital pediatrician who came to my room the day after Whitney was born told me she was "perfectly healthy." My diary entry for that day adds, "What a good eater she is." The adjective people used most often to describe her was "placid." She seldom cried or fidgeted or fussed. She was content to be held close, to be rocked and fed and sung to, to look around the room as far as her newborn eyes could see, to sleep and dream (if indeed babies do). Her contentment flowed into me and mine into her, as if our bodies were still attached by a life-sustaining cord, only this cord was intangible, invisible, mystical, and by it we sustained each other equally.

Jim phoned me at the hospital every morning and visited each day. We walked together down the corridor of the maternity ward, walking slowly because of my stitches, to stand by the plate-glass barrier and admire our daughter sleeping in the tiny white crib among the rows of others. She was the second-largest baby there, the blondest, and, we thought, of course, the prettiest.

Jim brought with him news of home—how well he was looking after the dog and cat, where he'd gone for dinner the night before, how much he hated being in the big house alone. And more news: "Mom and Pop are coming back from California."

"That's nice," I said. "For a visit? To see the baby?"

"No," Jim said, "to stay. I bought them that little house that was for sale around the corner. They'll be moving into it next week."

"Why didn't you tell me—"

"I just did."

———

I was in love—with my newborn child, who taught me, word-lessly, the meaning of the word Love; with my new exalted position and its lifetime title of Mother; with Life, because I felt I'd played a part in making it. I was so in love sitting there in that hospital bed fifteen miles or so from Summit Avenue that I didn't even mind the fact that Jim's parents were returning.

· · ·

Tuesday, October 26, 1965—Mother and daughter came home from hospital. (I fit into the size 9/10 corduroy dress!)

Thursday, October 28, 1965—Whitney Lee one week old! Very blond hair, very blue eyes. Looks like her daddy; has her mommy's nose. Eats very very well, hates to be changed. Sleeps 3–4 hours between feedings. Very good baby. (Mom weighs 138—must lose 18 pounds.)

Thursday, November 18, 1965—Whitney Lee four weeks old to-day. Healthy and thriving. I fed her cereal and bananas last night and she slept six hours straight for the first time (10:30 p.m.–4:30 a.m.). (I am still trying to lose weight—trying to ex-ercise and diet every day. Weight—135. Measurements—38-26-38.) ... Weather getting colder and colder; each day looking more like winter.

· · ·

Without asking Jim's permission I put an ad on the bulletin board at the local high school to get a girl to help me with the housework. The baby, I felt, was my first priority; I could no longer spend my entire day cleaning. The girl that I hired was sixteen—four years younger than I—and from a large family in a neighboring town. She needed an afternoon job, she said, to earn money for college. I picked her up from high school at three and drove her home by five, and while she was helping me in the house—with the ironing or vacuuming or dusting or whatever chore I hadn't completed that day while Whitney napped—I'd sit and rock the baby.

50

"Why do you hold her all the time?" another young mother once commented to me. "Put the kid down. You're going to spoil her."

"It's impossible to spoil a newborn infant," I said defiantly. "There's no such thing as giving them too much affection—"

Jim admired Whitney at arm's length. Like many large men, he felt awkward and clumsy about holding a small and seemingly fragile baby.

"She won't break," I said to him. "Babies are really quite sturdy—"

But still he preferred to watch me hold her and rock her and feed and change and bathe her. He demonstrated his love the only way he knew how, by buying her gifts—fuzzy toys, a gold chain, a sterling silver cup and spoon. He never took a turn feeding her in the night, but I didn't mind. *This is my job,* I thought; *he has his office. He can't afford to be tired in court.*

My life revolved around my baby, as though we were dancers whirling gaily in the center of the floor and the room around us was a blur of bright colors. I hardly noticed that Jim visited his parents every day after work and spent more and more time there, that he went out in the evenings with his friend Jerry instead of me.

When we did go out, Jim's mother would babysit readily, quick with advice on how I could be a better mother.

"Why aren't you breast-feeding?" she said soon after her return from California.

"Because they gave me an injection right after the birth that dried up my milk," I told her, "without ever asking me—"

"Any mother who doesn't breast-feed doesn't love her baby," she said. "I breast-fed Jimmy until he was two . . ."

Standing there with her bright red hair and her large-flower-pattern dress, she became part of the background blur of the room, and her words were drowned by the music that my child and I danced to.

• • •

Up to the day my daughter was born I'd felt almost invisible. Somehow I was unaware of myself as a physical presence taking up space and capable of giving and receiving corporal pleasure or pain.

But with the birth of my baby at twenty, a whole new dimension was added to my life: my body. Suddenly I felt in touch with it—and not only in touch with it, but electrified by it, proud of it, in awe of it. *Look at what my body can do!* I wanted to shout, *Look at me! Aren't I beautiful? I am a woman now! I made a baby!*

The empty space where the baby had been ached to be filled again. So when Jim was in a good mood one evening, I danced around him teasingly and wooed him into bed. For the first time, I got on top of him, and I moved to the sound of the primitive music I'd just begun to hear. And for the first time, my entire network of cells seemed to explode in a frenzied chain reaction, from my body's core to its farthest extremities. I saw only dazzling lights. I heard nothing. I forgot where I was or whom I was with. For as long as it lasted, nothing mattered except the sensation itself.

It was, of course, unexpected, unintentional, even unnameable to me then. All I knew was that this was the most pleasurable physical experience I'd ever had; and as soon as I came down, breathless and flushed, from wherever I'd been, I wanted to go there again.

At first Jim was alarmed, and then he was angry. He said that the woman should never get on top, that that position emasculates men. He called me a slut and a whore.

But my newly awakened woman's body had a mind and a will of its own. I knew what I'd felt was good and natural, and I knew that I'd always want more.

•   •   •

Jim began having dinner with his parents every night. Not invited to join them, I stayed at home, alone with the baby. When he returned, at nine, ten, or eleven o'clock, he was invariably enraged. He behaved as if he were drunk, but he was always totally sober. The litany began: I should get out, go back to my mother's and leave the baby behind; if I didn't leave voluntarily he'd have me "put away"; the house was *his*, and I didn't belong there, the baby was *his,* and he wanted his mother to raise her; I was no good, and he didn't want his child to know me— I was a religious fanatic, I was mentally ill.

One evening Jim brought home with him an insurance policy on my life, equal to his total indebtedness of one hundred thousand dollars. I looked at the collection of guns in our bedroom, listened to the hatred in his voice, saw the malevolence in his eyes, and I became terrified.

Whenever his car drove up at night my whole body would shake uncontrollably. I couldn't shout, *Man your battle stations, girls!* and run giggling with my sisters for cover. Except for my newborn baby sleeping sweetly in her crib, I was all alone.

When the baby was awake and changed and fed, I'd sit with her in the rocking chair in her room and whisper softly, as if the question were a lullaby, "What should we do? What should we do?" and she would look at me contentedly and coo.

. . .

He said it so often—"You're mentally ill"—that I began to think he might be right. Where was the honor student, the scholarship winner, the girl I had been quietly proud to call me? I looked for her in the mirror but didn't see her. "Look at that face," Jim said repeatedly, "it's the face of a crazy woman!" *Perhaps so,* I thought, *but you'll never take my baby.*

I lost interest in eating and became drawn and thin. I had difficulty sleeping in the same room with him. Sometimes in the night I would slip away and try to sleep in the smallest of the three spare bedrooms at the other end of the hall. The bed in this room was narrow and soft, and I'd try to hide there, safe and secure beneath the warm eiderdown, until the baby woke for her morning feeding. But every time I did this, Jim would come into the room, like a prison commandant in blue pajamas, and wake me from a sound sleep by shouting, "This is physical desertion! This is grounds for divorce!"

Our first anniversary, on December 19, passed without celebration. What was there to celebrate?

"Get out," Jim said.

"I have nowhere to go."

"Go back to your mother's."

"I won't do that."

"Just get out and leave the baby here."

"Never."

The week before Christmas Jim sold my car, removed all of the charge cards in my wallet, closed our joint checking account, and announced he would no longer give me money for the house or myself.

"Now what are you going to do?" he said.

"What are *you* going to do?"

"Divorce you and take the baby."

• • •

Saturday, December 26, 1965—The saddest Christmas of my life. I was left alone with the baby in the house most of the time. When Jim did come home, he stayed only long enough to start an argument, get me upset and leave. He said he was with his parents and friends; told them I was sick, "mentally ill" . . .

• • •

While Jim slept in our king-size bed, I sat in the rocking chair in Whitney's room. "What should I do?" I prayed aloud in the darkness, rocking, rocking. "Dear God, what should I do?"

On Monday morning, after Jim left for his office, I called a taxi to take me to my mother's. I asked my sisters, who were home from high school for the holidays, to mind my baby for the morning. I walked to the bank where my mother worked and asked if I could borrow her car. Then I drove to a local lawyer, a friend of my mother's, and sought his advice.

"Do you have any witnesses?" he asked me.

"No."

"Too bad. If you did, you'd have a clear case of mental cruelty. But since you can't prove it—"

"What can I do?"

54

"Well, there's no law that says you have to stay with the guy and continue to live like that—"

"He says he's going to take the baby."

"Impossible."

"Are you sure?"

"Positive."

"Then I can leave and take my baby with me?"

"Yes. But if *you* leave *him,* you forfeit your rights to alimony. That's obviously why he's forcing you out."

"I'm not interested in his money—"

"But he'll still have to support the child."

"He can't take her away legally? He showed me copies of judgments where—"

"Not a chance. No judge would take your baby away from you."

"Thank you."

I drove my mother's car to Summit Avenue and hurriedly packed a few of the baby's and my things: the second-hand Smith-Corona typewriter Jim had bought for sixty-four dollars so I could do work for him at home; the new Singer sewing machine he had given me to make draperies for the house; the Hoover portable vacuum cleaner, one of the two I received for my birthday; my hair drier, tennis racket, ice skates, and jewelry box; the baby's carriage and cradle, diapers and bottles; some of my clothes and the baby's—nothing more would fit in the car—and tried to leave the memories behind. My only regret as I drove away from Jim's big house was that I'd ever lived there at all.

My parents were the children of immigrants who had settled in the same town during the early years of this century. My father's father was a Scotsman, born in Johannesburg, South Africa, in 1887, who—the story goes—lost his family during the Boer War and came to the United States as a stowaway when he was in his teens. He met and married a girl from Glasgow named Jessie and started his own business as a house painter, the income from which his frugal wife amassed beneath the cushions of their sofa.

My father used to talk about his childhood whenever he wanted us children to know how lucky we were. He said his mother fed him oatmeal porridge every morning for breakfast, and if he didn't finish every spoonful in the bowl, he'd see it again for lunch. He told us that for Christmas every year his mother gave him underwear and oranges—and then only if he'd been good.

But if Jessie skimped on breakfasts and Christmas gifts, she was generously saving for her children's future. She dressed and groomed her beautiful dark-haired daughter in order that she might marry well (which my aunt did); and she sent her promising young son to college and to law school so he'd be sure to succeed.

I have only one image of Jessie in my memory, which could

56

be just the memory of an old dream. She is sitting in my mother's chair in the living room of our home. She is large, immobile, formidable. Her face is stern, her mouth is pressed to a thin horizontal line, and her arms are as thick as a man's.

My father's father, whom we called Pop, survived his wife by several years. After Jessie's death in 1949, he took a trip to Scotland and returned with gifts for all of us—kilts and tam-o'-shanters in the family tartan for my sister and me, cashmere pullovers for my brother and parents—and a new bride for himself. She was a short, round, jovial widow named Nellie.

Pop was a quiet man, tall and thin, who reminded me then of a smiling Abraham Lincoln without hair. He spoke with a thick Scottish burr, which my sister and I loved but sometimes had difficulty understanding. Whenever we would tease him, "You talk funny, Pop," he'd just laugh. We'd never dream of talking to our own father that way; we were too afraid of him.

Before Pop died we visited him and Nellie about once a year, usually for Thanksgiving dinner. I remember the smells of the house most of all—the warm, moist smells coming from the kitchen, of roasting turkey, boiling turnips, and fresh-baked pies; and the cool, damp smell of the house itself, like that of a dark library or an old church. It was the same two-family house in which my father had grown up, and I could sense he dreaded going back.

The summer my youngest sister was born, my other sister and I stayed at Pop's for a week; and we found—in the course of our clandestine explorations—that Pop had a secret studio in his attic, filled with clean canvases, tubes of oils, and dozens of completed paintings of many-masted ships on stormy seas. All day, in his white overalls and work shoes, Pop stood on a wooden ladder painting other people's houses. But at night, we discovered, when he came home, he stowed away in his own attic, where he stood at his easel in the dim light of one dangling bulb and painted what he remembered of the sea.

My mother's father was an artist, too, in his spare time; and he too painted his love for ships and the sea. He was born in 1871 in the port city of Danzig, then the provincial capital of West Prussia, had been an officer in the German navy, and had sailed around the world for fifteen years before he married. He met his bride—a petite, fair-haired girl named Agnes, seventeen years younger than he—through a friend at a dance in New York. Agnes's family was also from Germany.

I have no memories of my mother's father because he died when I was two. But I have a photograph of him holding me in his left arm, with my mother standing on his right, close to him. He has a strong build and squarish face, with a dimpled chin and straight dark hair. His arms are muscular and his fingers stubby. In this picture he looks proud and happy. And my thin blond mother, then in her early thirties, looks exactly like me today.

When my mother's father died in 1947, my grandmother, then sixty, took stock of her life. She had loved her husband single-mindedly and could not conceive of remarrying and sharing her life with another man. He had left a small life insurance policy, but she found she had little else to live on—no savings to speak of, no pension benefits from the factory where he'd worked, negligible Social Security payments, no salable assets (they'd lived in a rented house), no marketable skills, no education beyond high school, and too much pride to become dependent on her only surviving child and son-in-law, my parents.

All that my grandmother had was forty years' experience as a housewife—caring for her family, slaughtering her own chickens, canning her own vegetables, making her own jam. In forty years she had prepared roughly 43,800 meals, made about 51,100 beds, washed countless dishes, ironed innumerable pieces of clothing, and worked every day of the week; but she had never been employed. When Grandma became a widow, she knew she had to get a job.

So she decided to do what she was best at, the only work she really knew. She went to an employment agency that specialized in domestic help for the well-to-do, and she became a chambermaid.

Grandma took her holidays at the end of every year to spend Christmas and New Year with our family. She'd arrive at the station carrying fancy plaid suitcases and wearing a handsome gray dress with matching bag and shoes, looking more like a relative of the wealthy people she worked for than like a relative of ours.

Grandma didn't consider herself a servant then any more than she had when she'd been a housewife. True, her address had changed, and the furniture she dusted was not her own, and now she got a paycheck for polishing the floors instead of a pat on the cheek, but to her it was basically the same: She worked for a family and considered herself an essential part of it.

When Grandma came to visit, she approached our home as if it were an ironing board piled high with just-washed clothes; she seemed determined, with all the pressure of her indomitable will, to smooth out every wrinkle. "Do this," she'd tell my mother authoritatively, or "Do that." Sometimes, though, the pressure of her iron will was more than the fabric could bear. When Grandma's back was turned, my mother would make faces at her mother, sometimes sticking out her tongue. We children watched these women from the sidelines, the way we watched our parents playing badminton in our backyard.

• • •

Whenever Grandma came to visit when I was very young, I'd sit beside her on the sofa and take one of her hands in mine. Her fingers, bent like twigs with age, would always be busy knitting or crocheting, except when I held her hand. I'd study it and play with it, turning it and prodding it. I'd press one of my hands against hers, palm to palm, to measure the difference in size. I'd tap the rows of wormlike veins as if they were piano keys, and then push them from side to side to see how far off course they could go. I'd count the brown dots on her pale skin and sometimes try to connect them. I'd follow each thick, bent finger to its neatly clipped and polished tip.

Grandma never minded my peculiar fascination with her hands.

When I held her left hand I played with her rings, and she would promise that her diamond engagement ring would be mine when she died. It's the small solitaire set in pink gold that

I've been wearing on my right hand for more than ten years.

Between visits Grandma would write letters or send cards—birthday cards with crisp five-dollar bills inside, valentines, Halloween cards, Thanksgiving cards—and each greeting would close in a sloping, curlicue script—so different from my mother's straight, vertical handwriting—"Lots of Love, Grandma." Sometimes she would enclose a recent photo of herself taken on the grounds of her employer's estate. From the way she'd be posing by the rock-garden wall or leaning against the wishing well, you'd have thought that the place was her own.

But it was at Christmas that Grandma outdid herself. She bought us dolls and toys and books and clothes and shoes. For years, when we surveyed our separate hills of gifts beneath the tree, we thought that Santa Claus must have considered us extra good.

If my father stayed sober through the holidays, he and his mother-in-law withstood each other with cool humor, and Grandma waved good-bye to us on New Year's Day. But if he didn't, Grandma would go sooner, before she'd even made the German herring salad to bring us all good luck in the New Year.

S hortly before I left Summit Avenue, my grandmother had retired and moved into her own apartment. It was the upper half of an old two-family home that sat in a row facing a similar row of well-kept houses along a clean tree-lined street in a town not far away. Most of the people in the neighborhood were, like my grandmother, white-haired and retired. If they had small grandchildren, they seldom came to visit; the sound of children's outdoor play was never heard. The silence there was broken only by the occasional clatter of dishes in a neighbor's kitchen, the barking of a watchful dog, or the songs of summering birds.

My grandmother's apartment was roomy for one person: She had a bright kitchen large enough to contain her new dinette set; a good-size bathroom with a closet filled with cleaning apparatus; a room she called her sitting room, where she kept her desk and sewing machine; and her bedroom, the largest room, with three front windows overlooking the street below.

In her retirement my grandmother occupied a good deal of her time in much the same way she had throughout her life—by cleaning. Every morning that she felt well enough—after waking at seven, dressing, and consuming a carefully prepared and presented breakfast of boiled eggs, toasted rye, marmalade, butter, and coffee—she would proceed to clean, polish, dust, or wax everything in her home. Housework to her was more than a necessary activity; it was her art, her primary mode of self-expression. A stranger, observing the results of my grandmother's efforts for the first time—the glittering whiter-than-white bathroom wall tiles, the almost invisible windowpanes, the freshly swept carpets, the new-looking old furniture—might conclude, and rightly, that the person who lived in this apartment was not only compulsively clean, but also exceedingly proud, self-reliant, and almost militaristically fond of order.

It was into this clean, quiet, orderly world that I went with my baby the day I left Jim. Jim had ordered me to return to my mother's house, but I felt I couldn't do that. I didn't want to burden my mother—recently divorced and still supporting my younger sisters—with any more problems than she already had. My grandmother, on the other hand, had just been released from the hospital after another in a series of heart attacks and was confined to bed rest. She needed someone to look after her. I thought she might need me.

She agreed I could stay until we, respectively, "got on our feet." She refused to accept money toward her one-hundred-dollar-a-month rent; instead, she said, I could do her shopping and buy all of the groceries. And, if I used the telephone by her bed, she said, I was to note the number and date of the call on the pad on her bedside table, so she could identify my charges when her bill came in.

Borrowing a fold-up bed from my mother's neighbor Alice, I converted my grandmother's sitting room into a bedroom for myself and my baby. I placed her cradle at the head of my bed, so I could easily reach out and rock her back to sleep after she woke in the night for her feedings. The largest things I had taken from Jim's—the baby's cradle and carriage, a small suitcase containing some of our clothes, my typewriter, sewing machine, and vacuum cleaner—occupied less than one-quarter of my grandmother's sitting room. I assured her I'd confine my things to that space—and that I would be neat.

It was a temporary arrangement, to be sure. My grandmother made it clear that she did not intend to be bedridden long; that I was a guest on a short stay; and that her place was too small for three people, one of whom was a soon-to-be-crawling infant.

Somehow I couldn't think beyond the present. All I knew was that I had escaped Summit Avenue that day, with a few of my possessions, my life and sanity intact, and most of all, my baby. I knew Jim could and would easily find me. I had no intention of hiding from him; and he knew that without a large family or a car or any money, I wouldn't be able to go far. I told myself I needed some physical distance from him, at least temporarily; a time to think; peace.

Whitney cooed contentedly, seemingly oblivious to the fact that her tiny, old-fashioned wooden cradle was in a different room, another house, another town. After I had changed and bathed her, fed her, and rocked her to sleep, I said good night to my grandmother and went to bed, too. Unlike Jim's king-size bed, this borrowed bed was narrow and the mattress was thin. The springs made noise when I moved, so I lay motionless, afraid I might wake the baby. There in the quiet darkness I searched my heart. *Was I wrong to leave him? Did I have a choice? Did I feel any guilt or remorse? No,* I answered myself. Although I had no thought of what the future would hold, for the moment I felt only relief to be away from Jim's hateful threats and hostility, safe in this womblike narrow bed, listening to my baby's peaceful breathing.

I didn't hear from Jim that night. The next day, Tuesday, he phoned my mother and demanded to know where I was. She told him and gave him my grandmother's new unlisted telephone number, but he didn't phone on Tuesday either. The following day, however, he arrived without phoning. He came while I was out with the baby, but my grandmother told me about it upon my return: From her bed she'd heard the doorbell ring repeatedly; too weak to go downstairs to see who it was, she went to the window by her bed and watched; Jim's black Cadillac and a police car were parked in front of the house; after many minutes of insistent ringing, she saw Jim and another man in a dark business suit get into Jim's car and drive off, followed by the policeman.

My grandmother relayed this story to me in quiet horror. "This is *terrible,*" she said. "Terrible! A *police* car! What will the neighbors think?!"

I telephoned the police.

"Your husband stopped me on the road," the patrolman said. "Told me to come with him to 'preserve the peace.'"

I explained to him that my seventy-eight-year-old grandmother was ill and that we didn't want any trouble. "Please don't come again," I begged him. "It's very upsetting to us both."

The next day, Thursday, Jim returned, again with the other man, his new law partner, and this time two policemen. Frightened and unsure of what to do, I let them in, and all four men heavily ascended the stairs into my grandmother's apartment. Without greeting her, Jim peered into my grandmother's room, where she lay, horrified, in bed. Then he inspected the other rooms, studying everything, while I stood by helplessly, shaking. When he saw Whitney asleep in her cradle, Jim picked her up, waking her suddenly. Startled, she began to cry, and he quickly put her down.

"Where is my ring?!" he demanded, while the baby continued crying.

"What ring?" I asked, surprised that he should break the ominous silence with this odd outburst.

"The diamond ring my mother gave me. You had it in your jewelry box."

"Then it must still be there," I said.

"Give it to me!"

"I'll let you have it when I get the rest of my things."

His face was livid, enraged. He seemed bloated with rage, huge. Abruptly, he turned and left, followed by the other men. My grandmother was so angry, she refused to speak to me.

• • •

My attorney had told me I had "every right" to return to Summit Avenue for the rest of my things. "It's a sure thing he's not going to bring them to you, so you'll have to go get them yourself," he said. "Break in, if you have to. You're still his wife—"

The next day, after leaving Whitney with my sisters, I drove with my friend Patti to Summit Avenue, where I found that Jim had had all of the locks on the doors changed. None of my keys fit. So I did as my attorney instructed and broke in. With the heel of my shoe, I broke a pane of glass in the door leading from the back terrace to the dining room; then I reached my hand in and opened the door from the inside. Patti waited for me in her car.

I walked slowly through each room, stunned by what I saw: The whole house had been transformed, furniture rearranged, paintings that I had chosen removed from the walls and replaced by others I'd never seen. Except for the new draperies I had made, there was no trace of my taste or decorating efforts anywhere.

I went upstairs. All of my things were gone. My closet in the master bedroom was empty. Everything I had brought with me into that house nearly a year before—my personal treasures worth nothing to anyone but me: my favorite books, childhood diaries, a notebook of poetry, family photos, my Katharine Gibbs portfolio containing samples of all the work I'd done that year (marked "A+—very neat"), my high school yearbooks, honors, diplomas—everything was gone. Gone too were my hats and handbags, shoes, belts, scarves, coats, sweaters, dresses, everything that had been hanging in the closet or carefully folded on the upper shelves. It was as if I'd been obliterated, as if I'd never lived there.

The baby's room was left just as it had been, however; with the rocking chair and pretty white crib and matching dresser and hutch all ready and waiting, as if for her permanent return. I removed the clothes from her dresser drawers—the sweaters and booties I'd knitted, the rest of her nighties, rubber pants, diapers, undershirts, and dresses, and began to leave. Passing what had been Jim's parents' bedrooms, I noticed Jim's mother's haircurlers on her vanity and her bathrobe hanging behind her door. I didn't need to see more. *She is back,* I thought. *How quickly they've worked. How well this was planned.*

• • •

Although I was only twenty, and I wished I had a strong, wise father I could turn to for help and guidance; although I had no money or car or job; although all of my earthly possessions, my worthless/priceless, sentimental mementos had vanished, I knew, forever; although my present home was temporary at best, I was not despondent. I was in love, still deeply in love with my baby. I was buoyed by a tenacious faith that all would in time be well. I was optimistic, hopeful. I was young. "No judge would take your baby from you," my attorney had assured me, and I believed him. And as long as Jim couldn't take Whitney, I knew there was nothing he could do to break my heart or my spirit.

Such a good and happy baby, all gurgles and giggles and smiles. "We'll make a new life," I told her enthusiastically, and her eyes widened brightly as if she understood. "I'll make money at home somehow, so we can stay together. I'll make all our own clothes. I'll take new photographs, write new diaries and poetry. Everything will be fine, little pumpkin. You'll see."

That afternoon I wrote a poem, a long, simple, singsong love poem to my baby entitled, "To Whitney Lee, Ten Weeks Old, January 1, 1966." The last lines read: "My little babe, I love you. And please know/I'll never, never ever let you go."

• • •

The next day, Sunday, I returned to my old church, where the people had known me since I was twelve. They welcomed me genuinely, without inquiry, and made a fuss over Whitney. I felt reunited with a large and loving family.

I began to read the Bible again, taking special comfort in the psalmists' words of praise and promise: "Yea, the sparrow hath found an house, and the swallow a nest for herself, where she may lay her young, even thine altars, O Lord of hosts, my King and my God. . . . For the Lord God is a sun and shield: the Lord will give grace and glory: no good thing will He withhold from them that walk uprightly." I prayed for strength and guidance and increased faith.

———

66

The following day, while the baby napped and my grandmother watched her favorite afternoon TV programs and I sat in the kitchen making cards to post on bulletin boards at the local university ("TYPING—Term Papers, Theses—accurate, prompt, efficient service—call . . ."), the doorbell rang. *Jim?* I wondered as I hurriedly hid my cards and went to the door, bracing myself for another confrontation.

I was relieved to see it wasn't Jim. It was an old, shrunken man in a worn storm coat. "Yes?" I said, thinking he was some sort of salesman or solicitor. In a strange, flat, expressionless voice the stranger asked my name; and I told him. "This is for you," he said, pulling a thick sheaf of papers from his briefcase. Without another word, I took the papers and the man quickly turned and walked away.

"Who was that?" my grandmother asked when I'd reached the top of the stairs.

"I don't know," I told her, and returned to the kitchen, where I sat alone at the table and read—in disbelief, as if they'd been delivered to the wrong person by mistake—the papers I'd been handed. As I read I wrote in the margins "NO" and "UNTRUE" beside the statements and accusations in Jim's complaint.

He claimed that upon my departure he "immediately sought to have the Defendant [me] and the child return to the marital abode" but I "refused to return to the marital abode with the said infant child and refused to allow the Plaintiff [Jim] to in any manner visit with the infant child." His complaint continued:

The said mother of said child is morally unfit to be entrusted with the care, custody, education and maintenance of said child . . . for the following reasons: She has failed to maintain a proper home for said infant child; she has on occasions threatened to inflict forceful and serious physical injury upon herself and said infant child; she is emotionally unstable and unfit so as to be entrusted with the care and custody of said infant child; she has no means with which to adequately maintain and care for such child; she has and will place the child in unfit and unsavory environs wherein to raise said child; she has threatened to abscond with said child from the state and to thereafter forever conceal said child from Plaintiff.

Wherefore, Plaintiff demands judgment: That he be granted custody of said child together with her care and education; that the Defendant be enjoined from interfering with or taking the child from the Plaintiff's custody . . .

Attached to this complaint was a nine-page affidavit in which Jim attempted to substantiate his claims. I read on, making notations such as "FALSE!" and "NEVER!" in the margins:

. . . the defendant has evinced various characteristics which force me to the belief that she is unable to comprehend the world about her and which have driven her to her present mental and physical condition, the totality of which make it unsafe for her to have the custody of the infant child of the marriage. . . . Upon her leaving, the defendant extracted every piece of silver, silverware, and various gifts and articles of value that I had in the home. . . . the defendant returned on or about December 31st, 1965, and forcibly entered the home, broke a window, deranged the home and removed more articles of personal property belonging to myself, and also some of my mother's clothing. . . . Defendant's early childhood was poor and because of same, there has remained an imprint upon her personality which has in great part caused her present condition. . . . Defendant is presently under psychiatric treatment where a character neurosis has been diagnosed, in that defendant cannot adjust to people and life. Defendant borders upon schizophrenia and her many unprovoked outbursts and carryings-on clearly attest to the instability raging within her.

I continued reading:

The defendant has for some years been a member of the Reform [Reformed] Church. . . . She has taken to the preachings of this church with such fanatic and irrational abandon that it has manifested itself within her as a disease. . . . After we returned home [from our honeymoon] she would without provocation fly into rages and tirades against me. . . . During defendant's pregnancy, she further evinced characteristics which I fear make evident that she should not have custody of the infant child. . . . her tirades became more frequent and intense. . . . After the birth of the child . . . defendant refused to allow me to hold the infant. . . . Several times the defendant flew into rages when the baby was near and her flailing arms and carryings-on nearly resulted in physical harm to the child. . . . She began threatening that

68

she would take from me the one thing I cared for, the baby. . . . Aside from these carryings-on, the defendant on many occasions when in a fit of rage would physically assault me. . . .

Due to the aforementioned, I respectfully request that this court grant to me the custody of said child. Aside from the loving care and affection that I shall afford the child, I shall make and obtain for the child every necessity and care for all of her needs. . . .

Attached to Jim's affidavit were several others: one from a new neighbor, one from Jim's friend Jerry, one from Jerry's wife—all describing me as "nervous, distraught, and disturbed," and all prepared by Jim and signed in the presence of his law partner on December 30, the previous Thursday. Three days after I left. The day before I returned to Summit Avenue to get my things. *How quickly he works,* I thought. *How well planned.*

The last legal document was headed "Order to Show Cause With Restraints." I read on:

Upon reading and filing the verified complaint of . . . the plaintiff herein, and it appearing that defendant has unjustifiably separated herself from plaintiff and has taken with her the infant child of the marriage . . . and that defendant threatens to abscond from the jurisdiction of this court with said infant child, and it further appearing that immediate and irreparable harm will occur to the plaintiff and to the infant child of the marriage, and good cause appearing therefore: It is thereupon ordered that the defendant herein show cause why the custody of the infant child . . . should not be granted to the plaintiff pending the final hearing in the above matter, and further answer said complaint and abide by the order of this court. . . . It is further ordered that the . . . County Probation Department forthwith make an investigation of the parties and the facts and circumstances surrounding the within action . . . and file with this court said report of investigation as soon as same is completed.

I tried to make sense of what I'd just read. It seemed the judge who signed this order, a man before whom Jim tried his own clients' cases regularly, had read Jim's accusations and believed them. Why else, I wondered, would he use words such as "unjustifiably separated herself," "threatens to abscond," "immediate and irreparable harm"? *Judge, I wanted to shout, how can you believe this? You've never even seen me. You've never seen my healthy, happy baby!* I felt as if an animal trap had just clamped shut on my leg.

You must be calm, I told myself. *Think this through. Read the order again. The judge is ordering you to explain ("show cause"?) why you should keep your baby—*

Whitney stirred in her cradle and began to cry a soft, muffled cry. *Judge, do you hear that sound? She's saying she's had enough sleep and she's getting hungry. She has another sound to tell me her diaper is wet or dirty. I know all of her sounds, each one of her moves. No one else could understand her and love her the way I do, judge, because she is part of me, still a part of my body. If you take her away from me, I'll bleed to death. I'd rather you took my arm or my leg. Here, take the leg that's caught in this trap and let my baby and me go free—*

"Did my pumpkin have a good nap?" I lifted Whitney up and she cuddled her head into my neck. "Shall we say hello to Great-grandma before we have a bottle?" Her face suddenly went red and she grunted. "On second thought, perhaps we should check your diaper first—?"

After Whitney was fed and changed and propped up in her infant seat in front of me on the kitchen table, shaking her plastic, heart-shaped rattle and kicking her legs almost in time with the beat, I began to draft a long, entreating letter to the judge, explaining why I left Jim, that I never intended to "abscond" with my baby, that I had never caused her harm and could never cause her harm. Simply and plainly, as if I were addressing him in person, I wrote that I had no intention of every denying Jim his paternal right to know, love, and enjoy his daughter, but that I as her mother should not be denied my right to provide her maternal love and care; that nothing should break that bond—

I never sent this letter. When I spoke to my attorney later that afternoon, he instructed me in the proper legal procedure—to reply to Jim's affidavit point by point.

•   •   •

The cold months of January through March 1966 passed in a bitter storm of legal papers: affidavits, accusations, answers, denials, points and counterpoints. My attorney, a busy, preoccupied man in his late fifties who seemed worried about my inability to pay him, commented one day while I was in his office, "What's all this fuss over a *baby?*" He shook his head. "I don't get it. . . . Give me a good real estate deal any day. Now, how much did you say he's been paying in child support?"

"Nothing, so far."

"Well, we'll have to do something about that. Give me an itemized breakdown of your estimated weekly expenses—"

I prepared this list for my attorney. The weekly total for food, clothing, diaper service, pediatrician, drugs, and miscellaneous expenses came to fifty-eight dollars. In his answering affidavit Jim labeled this figure a "fantastic exaggeration." He contended that fifteen dollars per week would be "more than adequate." Nevertheless, he waited for the judge to rule before he paid anything.

I sold Jim's diamond ring, the one his mother had given to him and I'd inadvertently taken out of the house with me in my jewelry box. I sent our savings passbook to Hawaii to withdraw the two hundred dollars he'd deposited on our honeymoon, "to begin saving for our return trip in ten years." I did typing at home for college students and for my mother's neighbor Alice, who owned her own publishing company and always needed to have edited manuscripts retyped. Even without Jim's financial help, I managed to support myself and Whitney without getting into debt.

In early February a judge awarded "temporary custody" of Whitney to me "until the further order of this court" and granted temporary visitation to Jim on alternate Saturdays and Sundays between one and four p.m. and "at reasonable times during the week" provided Jim gave me "at least twenty-four hours of notice in advance of such visitation." The judge further ordered Jim to pay forty-five dollars per week in child support, "until further order."

From that point on, Jim came to my grandmother's apartment three to five afternoons a week, always with either his parents or another man, usually his law partner or one of his client-friends. Jim never came alone to see his child. If the baby was sleeping when he came, he would pick her up and wake her abruptly, which made her cry; then he'd shout at me to see to it that she was awake for his visits. If his mother was with him, he would quickly pass Whitney over to her and admire the two of them as though they were a fine painting of the Madonna and Child. If his mother was not with him, Jim would handle the baby briefly, gingerly—as if he were afraid she might spit up on his suit, or fall and break—and leave soon after. If I told Jim I could not be home at the specified hour he chose to come the next day, he would say, "Well, the baby must be here; I'm giving twenty-four hours' notice!" When he came the next day at the hour I'd said I couldn't be home, he would remove my note on the front door—"*I am not in. My grandmother is resting. Please do not ring bell*"—ring the doorbell repeatedly, and leave.

"When is this going to *end?*" my grandmother demanded. "How long do I have to put up with this? You said you came here to help me. Do you think this is doing me any good?"

All I could do was apologize and promise to look for a solution.

At the end of February I was served with more papers, more affidavits—from Jim; from the witnesses he had brought with him on his visitations; and from three medical doctors who stated that since the baby was "normal, healthy, and thriving," weekend visitations with her father, away from her mother, would do her no harm.

Then one Tuesday afternoon the assistant chief probation officer came to my grandmother's apartment to interview me. He was a small man, near retirement age, I guessed, soft-spoken and gentle-mannered. I imagined he had never married, that he lived with an unmarried sister.

We sat at my grandmother's kitchen table, while I held Whitney on my lap, and we spoke for over an hour. At the end of the interview, he asked me to put into writing all that I'd said to him that day—in effect to write an essay on why I should have custody of my baby—in order that he might incorporate this document into the probation report to be submitted to the court.

Grateful for the opportunity to speak for myself without a legal intermediary, I prayed for the right words to express my thoughts, and proceeded to write from my heart. "Dear Mr. Penfield," my letter began, "It is with pleasure that I answer your request for a letter explaining why I believe I and not Jim, should have custody of our five-month-old infant, Whitney Lee. First, and I believe most important, I love her with all my heart. I love her unconditionally; I love her because she *is*—she is my child, and I am her mother. I love everything about her. I love to hold her, feed her, bathe and dress her, talk to her, play with her. One look at Whitney Lee would prove to anyone that she is an extremely well-cared-for child. I give her at least one bath a day; clean, fresh clothes every day; regular, nutritious meals and vitamins every day; and all of my love and attention. . . ."

Late into the night, while Whitney and my grandmother slept, I wrote and rewrote. When it was finished, the letter came to seven single-spaced typed pages. I read it again and again, searching for errors I might have missed. I felt proud. Of all the things I'd ever written, this, I thought, was the best. I sealed the envelope with a lick and a prayer and mailed the letter the next day.

Because Jim was attempting to make a case of my alleged mental instability, I was ordered by the court to be examined by a psychiatrist in the county psychiatric hospital. When the day of my appointment came, I wore a new turquoise suit I'd just finished making, dressed Whitney in a pretty pink dress, borrowed a friend's car, and drove to the hospital, praying all the way.

"Well," the doctor said, without looking up from the papers on his desk, "can you tell me why you are here this morning?"

"Yes," I said. "The court sent me here because my husband is claiming I am an unfit mother—mentally unfit—and he's trying to get custody of our child—"

Whitney sat quietly on my lap, content to look around the doctor's small, institutional office.

"This child?" the doctor said, pointing his pencil at Whitney.

"Yes."

"Why does your husband think you are mentally unfit?"

Slowly and calmly, I tried to tell him about the year I spent with Jim on Summit Avenue and about Jim's constant threats, from early in my pregnancy, that he could and would take the baby from me. "I think he expected me to give up without a fight," I said, "give him the baby and go. Since I *am* fighting, he must make a case, so he's saying, among other things, that I'm mentally—"

The doctor, appearing to be deep in thought, broke in. "Tell me," he said broodily, chewing the end of his pencil, "what do you think about baseball?"

This must be a test, I thought, *to see my reaction. Perhaps people who are truly mentally ill become angry or violent when they're interrupted like this. Or maybe they laugh at such silly questions.* Gathering my thoughts quickly, I continued speaking as if I were still discussing my reason for being there. "I seldom think about baseball," I answered. "I prefer to play games rather than watch them, and I haven't played baseball since I was a child. When I did play—with my big brother—I liked baseball very much."

"Oh," he said. "Good. Now, tell me—"

Whitney peacefully rested in my arms, drinking her bottle, while the examination went on.

· · ·

On the first blank page at the back of my white bridal Bible—the Bible inscribed sixteen months earlier, "To my beloved wife on this our wedding day . . ."—I noted special verses under the heading, "For Comfort and Encouragement (Pending Custody Hearing)": Psalm 31:13–16, Psalm 34:19, Psalm 35:17, Psalm 37 ("claimed"), and Isaiah 43:1–3: "But now thus saith the Lord that created thee . . . Fear not: for I have redeemed thee, I have called thee by thy name; thou art mine. When thou passest through the waters, I will be with thee; and through the rivers, they shall not overflow thee: when thou walkest through the fire, thou shalt not be burned; neither shall the flame kindle upon thee. For I am the Lord thy God, the Holy One of Israel, thy Savior . . ."

Although the pretrial legal battle continued unrelentingly and I never knew when the case would ultimately go to court, although my nervous and digestive systems were weak, my faith was strong. God would never allow any judge to take my baby from me; I knew this as surely as I knew there was a just and benevolent God. I knew Jim couldn't win this case; it would be the first case he would lose.

As my grandmother's health improved, I did my best to keep out of her way. I found a full-time babysitting job for an interior decorator, a divorcée with three young children who lived in a large, Tudor-style home less than two miles from my grandmother's apartment. Every morning Kaye would come for Whitney and me at about eight, before she left for work, and when she returned from her last appointment between five and six in the evening, she drove us back home.

When Jim insisted on visiting Whitney at four-thirty every afternoon, I gave him Kaye's address and the directions to her home; but Jim refused to visit Whitney there. "The court says you are to be *here!*" Jim insisted, when he returned Whitney to my grandmother's the Saturday afternoon I informed him of my new job. "If I give twenty-four hours' notice, you are to be *here* at *that time!*"

"I don't think that's what the court meant," I said.

"We'll see about that!" he shouted, getting into the front seat of his parents' car beside his mother. His father, behind the wheel, drove away.

I brought Whitney upstairs and removed her snowsuit. Once again, I noticed, either Jim or his parents had cut the elastic on the new, white tights I'd put on her. The pink dress she wore was in disarray and the back buttons undone. Her diaper, which was sticking well up above her rubber pants (which were on backward) and was fastened to her undershirt on only one side, was wet and dirty. She had had diarrhea. I never knew what they fed her. *Look at this, judge!* I wanted to shout. *Why don't you come here and look at this? The sight of this baby in such a state is worth ten thousand words!*

. . .

In the spring, there were more affidavits, more assertions: I was "thwarting" Jim's efforts to see his child, I was a religious fanatic, my family was "unsavory." My grandmother began receiving telephone calls at all hours. In the middle of the night, she told me (I slept too soundly to hear it from my room), the phone rang and woke her; then, when she answered it, the person at the other end hung up. Her number was unlisted. Only my family and Jim knew it.

When the probation report was submitted to the court, I received a copy and read it carefully. It was fifty-eight pages long and painstakingly detailed. There were reports of interviews with, and copies of letters from, all of the people Jim had found to testify against me. There were also a few, brief, character-reference letters from people from my church, stating that I was a fine person, a good mother, but they didn't know Jim well enough to comment on him.

I turned to the psychiatric report and studied the final diagnosis: "The patient shows no evidence of any hallucinations or delusions. She is oriented as to time, place, and person. Her memory for the recent as well as for the remote past in intact. School and general knowledge is in keeping with her education. Intelligence seems to be somewhat above average and judgment is fair. Impression: No psychiatric disorder."

And then, there, at the end, was my letter to Mr. Penfield. Every word, all seven single-spaced typed pages, had been put into the report. As I read the letter again, my eyes filled with tears. Seven pages out of fifty-eight. One voice trying to be heard above the others.

"My plea to keep my child is not a selfish one," my letter ended. "If I were to think selfishly, I would not want the responsibility or the 'burden' of raising a child on my own—I

76

would not be fighting so hard for her. My concern is and always has been for the baby—her life, her welfare, her happiness. I feel an almost animal instinct to care for her and protect her—protect her from the harm that I know Jim could cause her if she were to be raised under his roof, even for a few days out of the week.

"I love her. I do and always will give her the best care. I will teach her the love of God, high morals, and a bright outlook on life. I am not an unfit mother. I am the best mother in the world—for my baby."

• • •

The custody suit, which Jim had initiated in early January 1966, never went to trial. Not long after the probation report was submitted, Jim dropped the case, agreed to my having custody, and paid for a speedy divorce.

• • •

October 2, 1966, 9:30 a.m.—I don't know why it is, but every time I'm in an airplane I think a little more clearly, a little more ethereally, as though the congestion of everyday life and thought is below me for a while. Today, at this moment, I'm in an Eastern jet, flying first class to Birmingham, Alabama. Almost two years ago I flew on another jet first class, wearing the same white wool suit and white mink collar—my wedding suit. But instead of south, I was flying west with my new husband to California and Hawaii. A lot has happened since then. Tomorrow in Alabama I'll be divorced. It's the same white wool suit, but a different person in it. I've learned a lot, I've matured a lot. I'm no longer the totally naive nineteen-year-old girl on her way to a Hawaiian honeymoon. I'm a woman now, with a woman's feelings and desires. I'm a mother of a darling baby girl almost one year old. I'm a businesswoman now—not by choice, for my heart is in the home. I have my own apartment, my own furniture, my own car. "Independence," I guess it's called.

I sold my engagement ring—the platinum ring with the heavy, rectangular diamond that I'd never grown to like—for one thousand dollars, to buy a secondhand Volkswagen. I found a small but comfortable apartment in a two-family house in my hometown; and with half of the one thousand dollars I received from the divorce settlement, I bought furniture for my new home, including a pretty white crib, identical with the one Whitney had at Jim's, which he'd refused to relinquish. I got a full-time secretarial job, and while I worked I left Whitney in the care of my friend Wendy, who had a four-year-old boy of her own.

It grieved me to leave my ten-month-old baby and return to office work. I missed my baby more, I was sure, than she missed me. I hated working in an office, sitting at a desk indoors all day, taking letters I felt I could write better, trying to fight my boss's attempts to stroke my legs whenever he gave dictation with his office door closed. I hated typing under pressure, rushing to complete the papers he needed before he caught the next plane. I wanted to be with my baby, hear her babble and laugh, teach her new words, feed her lunch, watch her tentative steps, see her grow.

Every day at my cold steel desk in that airless, sterile office, I felt a kind of homesickness in the pit of my stomach, as though I were a child at my first week of summer camp. I wondered what I could do to make enough money to be able to stay at home during the day with my baby.

One day my boss brushed past my desk and tossed a letter back at me, laughing, "Look what you did!" With a red pencil he'd circled a word I'd grossly misspelled. "Accelerate," he said, "E-X-C-E-L-L-E-R-A-T-E! Is that the way they taught you how to spell at Katy Gibbs? You've got more beauty than brains, cutie!"

While I listened to his laughter recede down the hall as he sauntered to the men's room, I painstakingly straightened the papers on my desk with shaking hands. I waited until I got into my car to cry.

"Home-again-home-again, jiggety-jig!" I bounced my heavy toddler in my arms as I carried her up the stairs to our apartment, and we both laughed. By the time we got home it was almost six, time to fix supper and get Whitney ready for bed. We shared simple meals—baked macaroni and cheese, tuna casseroles, meat loaf, mashed potatoes, and peas. Whitney ate enthusiastically, delightedly. Mealtime was a game she loved to win. She loved her bath, too; sitting in the big tub surrounded by floating, brightly colored plastic toys, which she would try her best to sink. She seemed secure in the love she received from everyone; her placid nature never wavered; she appeared to be thriving.

Jim's visitations, too, were going smoothly. One week he had Whitney from Thursday at six p.m. to Saturday at one, and on alternate weeks from Saturday morning at eleven-thirty until Sunday at four-thirty. He always arrived for Whitney on time and returned punctually with her. And we managed to hand her back and forth peaceably. Since our divorce, we seemed to make a greater effort to communicate amicably with each other, particularly with regard to Whitney's growth and progress. During the week we spoke on the phone, and Jim would tell me what Whitney had done while she was with him and how well his law practice was doing. *Things have worked out well,* I thought as I listened to Jim's reports; *I knew everything would turn out all right.*

I became worried, though, when I noticed that Jim was losing weight. He'd been a large man, like my father, over two hundred pounds. Each week now he appeared to be thinner than the week before, and whenever he reached for the baby, his hands were visibly shaking. "Are you all right?" I asked him one evening on the phone. "You don't look well to me." He didn't answer. I thought perhaps he might have cancer and not know it. One day, after he left with the baby, I was feeling so sorry for him I cried.

• • •

The world I created for Whitney and me was peaceful, tidy, and quiet. I spent my time after she went to sleep either reading or sewing. I made café curtains for our sunny yellow kitchen, as well as for the baby-blue bedroom we shared. I made fully lined draperies for our living room out of an olive-green-and-mustard-colored Early American print, to match the mustard-colored carpet I bought at a remnant sale and my new olive-green love seat Hide-A-Bed.

Except for work all week and church on Sundays, I seldom went out. I didn't date. All the love I had to give I gave to Whitney. But there were times, too, alone in my narrow bed, when I ached to know what it would be like to have this love replenished by a loving man.

Then one Sunday in late November, almost two months after my divorce, I saw Steve in church, sitting with his parents and his sister, my friend Jenny, and her husband, Tim. Steve, the handsome high school football hero, the family rebel who seldom went to church and smoked Camel cigarettes in the toolshed because his mother wouldn't allow smoking in the house. Steve, whom I'd worshipped secretly, with the hopeless infatuation of a kid sister's friend. Once, when no one was looking, I went into Jenny's family's front hall closet and hugged Steve's football jacket, pretending it was him.

I stared at Steve's perfectly masculine, exquisitely strong profile and didn't hear a word of the sermon. *Where had he been?* I knew he had dropped out of college, joined the army, and been stationed in Europe for two years. I knew he'd returned, and at his parents' urging, finished his degree. *But where had he been recently? What exotic place had he flown in from that he should look so tanned and—?* Steve turned and caught my eye, and smiled, knowingly.

After church he said hello, and I introduced him to Whitney. "I'll call," he said with a sure small nod instead of saying goodbye; and I knew he would.

It would have been like any other Friday night when the baby was at Jim's—I was home alone in my living room curled up on the love seat in my flannel nightgown and terrycloth robe, reading—except that Steve was coming home again the next day at noon, and I found it hard to concentrate on my book. My mind was wandering. Then the doorbell rang and I jumped. It rang again. I called down the stairs, "Who is it?"

"It's *me.*"

"STEVE!" When I opened the door to the cold December night, Steve lifted me high off the floor with a bear hug. He growled. "Steve, what a surprise! Do your folks know you're back?"

"No, and you're not going to tell them. I'll see them tomorrow."

"Oh?"

"I drove up nonstop, just to be with you—"

"You've been driving for *twenty-four* hours?"

"Yep—and there's no goddamn heat in that car—"

"No wonder you look blue." I hugged him again, then held his cold face in my hands. "You're freezing! Why didn't you wear a hat?—Here, let me help you with your jacket. . . . Are you hungry—?"

"A sandwich and some coffee would be great."

"But coffee will keep you awake—"

"That's okay, I don't want to go to sleep just yet."

I watched him as he ate his sandwich silently. Steve never spoke much; it was difficult to know what he was thinking. It was as if he expected his eyes and hands to say everything for him.

While Steve took a hot bath, I prepared the bed, opening the love seat in the living room and covering the thin mattress with clean sheets and two wool blankets. *It isn't wrong,* I told myself, as I removed my robe and nightgown and waited for him, shivering, under the covers.

And I was right. It was good, very good.

While Steve was away in Florida, completing a six-month training course for his job, we spoke on the telephone every night at eleven o'clock when the rates went down. My phone bill went as high as sixty dollars a month, but it was my only extravagance. His parents, who had always treated me like a daughter, seemed to assume I would one day soon become their daughter-in-law. Once a week the baby and I had dinner with them at their house; and as I told Steve's mother his latest news, his father took Whitney on his shoulders and pranced around the room playfully.

. . .

"She's too adorable," Wendy warned. "She's irresistible, you know. Whenever I take her out with me, people tell me they want to take her home with them—"

. . .

In February I bought Whitney a new, blue snowsuit.

"Show Daddy how cute you look," I said to her when Jim came at six on Thursday to take her for the weekend visitation. She went to him in her crisp blue snowsuit like a spaceman, weightless.

"Hi, Babe!" Jim babbled to the baby over and over. "Hi, Baby. Hi, Babe. Come to Da-da." He was the thinnest I had ever seen him, bent, and trembling. As Whitney toddled across the carpet to him, he kept his head bowed.

"Are you all right?" I asked him, worried. He looked too weak to lift her. His face, which couldn't seem to face me, seemed white-gray.

"Come to Da-da," he repeated to Whitney as if he hadn't heard me or I wasn't even there. He lifted her with difficulty, and I wondered how he was going to manage the stairs.

"Mommm-ma-ma," Whitney said happily.

"Da-da," Jim said, patting her back with a nervous hand.

"Jim?" I said, but he didn't seem to hear me. "Here is her bag." He seemed unsteady on his feet. *How will he carry—?* "Would you like some help—?" He took the baby's overnight bag and turned quickly toward the stairs. *He looks terribly ill,* I thought. I wondered what was wrong.

"Bye, pumpkin," I said to Whitney as Jim carried her away. "See you Saturday."

82

"Mommm-ma-ma," she said as she waved to me by opening and closing her free hand.

I went through my usual routine while Whitney was away—cleaning house, preparing meals ahead to put in the freezer, reading in the evening, phoning Steve. I kept busy. On Saturday morning I did my food shopping while my wash was at the laundromat. By noon I was home, ironing the baby's just-washed dresses. As I ironed each one and put it on its small plastic hanger in the closet that we shared, I watched from the window for Jim's car. He was always on time. But that Saturday, the eighteenth of February, 1967, he was late.

I phoned my mother, who told me not to worry and to call her back in an hour, by which time she was sure Jim would have returned. I phoned Kathy's husband, Carl, who was a policeman in another town. He told me soberly that it was possible they'd been in an accident; I should check with the local hospitals, phone the local police.

I went cold. My whole body shook with uncontrollable spasms as I made each call. I had trouble forming the questions, pronouncing Jim's name, forcing the words into the mouthpiece of the phone.

I followed Carl's instructions and phoned all of the hospitals in the area, plus all of the local police stations. I phoned Jim's home and office numbers again and again, but no one answered. I waited by the window, watching for each approaching car. I waited for what seemed like years, and as I waited, I prayed.

The last call I made, in the late afternoon, was to Florida. Steve must have hung up on me and phoned his mother immediately, because the next thing I knew, she was there. Tenderly, she wiped my face with a cold washcloth and gathered me up in her arms.

"They're gone," I said dully, from a dark and distant place in my mind, as Steve's mother drove me back to her home, "—gone—"

. . .

You must go on. How does that Millay poem end, the one you learned in freshman English? "Life must go on; I forget just why." You know Jim wants you to break down. He thinks you are weak. He thinks this will destroy you. You must never give him that satisfaction. Never let go. Never.

Take the sleeping pills Steve's mother gave you. ("*One* each night," she stresses. Her face is creased.) They're strong. They blot out the nights. You must fill up the days.

Go back to work. Now you *must* go there. Your boss says, "Take your time. Stay out as long as you need to," as if you'd broken your arm or caught a communicable disease. And you lie to him boldly, "No, I'm fine. I'm fine." No broken bones. No blood. No fever. Not even a cough.

Wear your best suit. The one you bought in Birmingham to celebrate your divorce. Five months ago. Wear enough makeup to brighten your gray face and mask your swollen eyes. Fix your hair. Take your time.

It takes half an hour to drive straight to work. Without stopping at Wendy's. Turn the radio on loud so it fills every cubic centimeter of empty space inside your car and every single, separate, solitary cell of your brain. Peter, Paul, and Mary. Joan Baez. Judy Collins. *"Who knows where the time goes?"*

Ten hours sleeping. One hour commuting. Two hours eating ("You must eat or you'll get sick," your mother tells you). Eight hours working. (*Work even harder. Stay busy.*) Spend the rest reading. (What did Emily Dickinson say? "There is no frigate like a book to take us lands away—") All the classics you haven't read yet because you've been too busy working and caring for the baby—

Don't think about it. Quick, think of something else—the snow falling, the stack of filing. You mustn't break down. No tears. Not now. Not here at work where people are looking at you for signs. Here where this cold desk by the glass doors is in full view of passersby.

Make an appointment to see the new lawyer. Upstairs. Withdraw all your savings to pay the retainer. He's smart. Looks like a bulldog hungry for a fight. He knows what to do. Do what he says. He knew Jim. Never liked him. He's offering you a cigarette.

"Thank you, but I don't smoke."

He lights up. The cigarette hangs from one side of his mouth as he speaks.

"Why'd y'ever marry the guy?"

"I don't know."

Take notes. (*What does it all mean?*) Don't bother him with too many questions or requests for explanations. He might get angry and refuse to help you. Remember: You need him. Be nice. Sit still.

"This might take some time," he says. "Here's what we're gonna do—"

Sign complaint. Warrant for Jim's arrest. Answer the questions. Try to remember every detail. Don't lose your composure here at police headquarters. Remember: This is his town, where he told everyone you're crazy. They're watching you. Waiting for you to do something crazy. Stop staring at the clock on the wall. Your eyes are burning.

Don't ask questions (*What is a felony?*); they'll think you're stupid. Try to look as if you understand. ("Here's some advice for when you're in college," a teacher in senior year told our class. "Always sit in the front of the room and look smart." He turned to me, sitting diagonally in front of him. "Isn't that right, Miss Black?") Give the impression you follow what is happening. (*What is happening?*)

Do what you're told. Do what you can. Check everything. Telephone bills. Doctors. Airlines. Steamships. Travel agents. Bank. Credit cards. Postal inspector. Real estate agency. Passport office. No help. No clues.

Phone everyone.

His law partner: "I bought him out last summer—"

"But he's been telling me his practice was thriv—"

"He liquidated everything months ago."

Jerry, denying any knowledge of Jim's whereabouts, also denies his crime: "It's not kidnapping. It's his child as much as it is yours."

Neighbors: "Saw them pack a station wagon on Friday the seventeenth and drive off. The old folks went, too."

Jim's sister-in-law is sorry, but she knows nothing. His client-friends say they know nothing, but don't seem sorry.

Go home now. Park the car on the gravel by the side of the garage, as usual. "Home-again—" No. Unhook the car seat. Store it in the garage—over there, under those boxes. Tell Nick and Honey downstairs, "Everything's fine. They're working on it. Mustn't worry." They look so worried. "No, thanks, but I appreciate the offer. I have things to do tonight. I'll have a bite to eat upstairs—"

Look at your mail. Here's the registered letter you sent to Jim in care of his brother in California. Returned unopened, marked "unclaimed, no response." He never read your three simple sentences: "Jim, Bring the baby back. If you loved her at all, you would not deprive her of her own mother. Prove you really love her by bringing her back."

If only you knew his new address. (*Does he have an address?*)

Pack everything in suitcases and boxes. Her toys and clothes and shoes. Dismantle the crib. Take it all to Mom's. Just temporarily. Don't forget the plastic bath toys in the net bag hanging by the tub—and the high chair in the kitchen, the same high chair you used when you were her age. (*Imagine if this had happened to you then . . . No, you can't even imagine.*) Remove all reminders. Just for the time being.

Go to bed now. Close your eyes. Put your arms at your sides and relax. Try. Take deep breaths as if you were in lab— Pray. *Lord, what did I do wrong? Why did you let him do it? Why, why? . . . Not my will but thine be done. Amen.* You can cry now. You're alone. Think: Maybe by the time you wake up they will have been found. Maybe tomorrow.

T his is what happened while she waited for news: In March she went before the grand jury. She stood in the front of a large room in the county courthouse, a room filled with row after semicircular row of chairs, where darkly dressed faceless people sat; and she answered a few brief questions somnambulistically. Soon after, Jim was indicted for kidnapping under state law 2A:118-1.

In April the county prosecutor gave her case to the FBI, who obtained a federal fugitive warrant for Jim's arrest for "fleeing to avoid prosecution." She met the FBI agent assigned to her case. He told her it was highly unusual for the FBI to get involved in such "family" matters. He said, however, they would do the best they could. He told her he and his wife had five children; as a parent, he understood her grief. "Some day," he said, "all this will be a big, bad dream."

She went to see this agent often, every several weeks, never making an appointment in advance (afraid someone would tell her he was "too busy"), always counting on his avuncular kindness, his parental empathy, his humanity, to let her in. He treated her gently; he was always soft-spoken and kind. When she asked, each time, what they were doing to find her baby, he assured her, "We're working on it. But you must remember, you are one of many, many people in our files." When she offered to help in the search—to write letters, make phone calls, see people—he told her, "There's nothing you can do except be patient."

In mid-May she turned twenty-two. She didn't celebrate.

That spring she stopped going to church. It was not just the well-meaning inquiries; the pitying, sorrowful glances; the offerings of Scripture Verses for Consolation in Time of Need; and the "Poor-dear's" and "We're-praying-for-you's," which pulled her down like heavy clothing on a swimmer. It was the fact that one of the elders of her church, after dinner at his home, said to her, "If you should remarry, you can no longer be a member of our church. Our church doesn't recognize divorce, so if you were to remarry—Steve, for instance—you'd both be living in sin—" She thought: *My God is not so small and unforgiving. . . . And besides, I wouldn't have to bother to remarry to live in sin—* She thanked him and his wife for their hospitality, and she never saw them again. She never returned to their church.

In June Steve was transferred to Toronto. He asked her to join him up there; but she said she couldn't go, she had to stay in the country, in the state, in the county, close to the telephone and the FBI. The weekend he left she spent crying, mourning the death of their hopes for a future together. They corresponded for a while. His letters were even briefer than his portion of their conversations: ". . . I just wanted you to know that I'm thinking of you. . . . You know that if there is anything I can do, all you have to do is ask. . . . We'll always be more than friends. Love,—" Not long after his transfer he met a Canadian girl and married her.

Her stomach hurt her, sometimes so much she hugged herself around the waist and sat up in bed alone at night, rocking. She was admitted to the hospital—the same hospital where she'd given birth twenty months before—for tests. GI series. Barium enema. Others. All negative. "It's just nerves," the doctor said, smiling. Just nerves. He prescribed a vacation.

She went to Puerto Rico by herself for five days. When she got to her hotel room, which was not much larger than her walk-in closet on Summit Avenue, she quickly changed into her bikini and ran out to the beach. It was six in the evening, and the ocean was all hers. She played with it recklessly until it knocked her backward and rolled her like a shell to shore. When she stood up, coughing and wiping her eyes, she was no longer alone. He invited her to dinner, bought her a frozen daiquiri, her first drink. She didn't tell him of her baby; he never mentioned a wife. He was handsome, about thirty. She never learned his last name.

She wrote in her diary from time to time. Questions for which she had no answers, small black poems, letters to God: "Why did You let this happen? If You were to take her life, I could accept it so much better, knowing she was with You. But now I know nothing. Is she living or is she dead? Will I ever see her again? When? . . . Lord, I believe; help my unbelief."

In July she met a young man on a blind date. He was the son of Armenian immigrants, and his family spoke only Armenian at home. He had put himself through school, earning both undergraduate and graduate degrees. He believed in hard work and higher education. He said to her, "You're not as stupid as you think you are. I think you should go to college." So, at his insistence, she enrolled in the local university and started taking courses at night.

George never told his friends or family that his new girl friend had been divorced. None of them knew about her baby, her secret, her loss. When they visited his friends, couples who'd recently become parents, and the wives took her aside and told her in rapturous detail of their deliveries, she perfected a cool air of interested ignorance about childbirth. But in George's car, all the way home, she cried.

And George preferred that no one know about their affair. He lived at home with his family. He never spent the night with her.

That summer her boss suggested she find a job elsewhere "for the sake of her career." He might have said she wasn't greeting the customers as cheerfully as she used to, that her telephone voice had gone dead; instead, he phrased his comments in her interest (he was a master at human relations): He said there was no future for her with his firm. He asked what field she would most like to pursue.

"Publishing," she told him.

"Good. I have friends in publishing. I'll see what I can do."

She was interviewed by a major magazine in New York City. She told the personnel officer she wanted to work in the editorial department, to work for a writer or editor. He said that was impossible; she didn't have a degree. She told him she was attending college at night. He said that didn't matter; a girl had to be a college graduate to be hired as a secretary in the editorial department. But, he said, there was an opening in the legal department—a well-paying secretarial position they'd been trying to fill for some time—for which, he said, she seemed perfectly qualified. He sent her to the executive offices on the sixteenth floor to meet the assistant general counsel, who promptly hired her.

In late summer George helped her move. The apartment she'd shared with her baby, which had been large enough for the two of them, grew too small for her alone with her myriad memories. Even without the crib and high chair and other physical reminders, she saw her baby everywhere—giggling in her arms as they ascended the stairs; splashing delightedly in the bathtub; toddling across the hall in her new blue snowsuit, like a spaceman, weightless.

She left for the next tenants the lined draperies she'd made for the living room windows, the white burlap café curtains she'd made for the bedroom, the shelving she'd put up in the bathroom, the pegboard in the kitchen, the rag rug that fit perfectly in the hall. She no longer cared about such things.

The apartment she found was a few blocks from the county courthouse, close to the FBI, near the local university, and within a short commute by bus to New York City. She didn't mind that the neighborhood wasn't safe to walk in at night, that the signs in the liquor store across the street were all in Spanish, that few of her neighbors spoke English. The apartment was large—four rooms—and cheap—$100 per month. Since her new job paid $135 a week, she thought she could save money living there, and when the baby was found she could quickly seek a better place for them to live.

At the nearby university she took courses in art (life drawing), history (ancient), psychology (introductory), and English.

She began to read the current best-sellers. She subscribed to *Time*. She couldn't bring herself to read the newspapers, whose daily front-page photographs of wailing Vietnamese mothers only mirrored her own grief.

In the meantime, with all the willpower she could evoke, she tried to wait patiently for news of her missing child. She tried to be strong, to put the problem out of her mind and go on living normally. But regularly, rhythmically, like the filling up of the moon, each month her emotions overwhelmed her; and she was overcome by private, psychic pain.

George was good to her. He had an abundance of Old World warmth, which is often missing in American men. He felt the pulse of her grief without pressing, he touched her hurt without causing more pain. They were active—waterskiing in the summer, snow skiing in the winter, playing tennis at his club year round. He took her dancing, to Broadway shows, to dinner, for drinks. And each month, when the uncontrollable grief returned, he comforted her, telling her she was strong, his "Supergirl," rocking her in his arms like a child. He made love to her slowly, generously, often. He knew how far away it took her, how much she needed to get away.

October 21, 1967, was Whitney's second birthday. She didn't know how or where her child's birthday was being celebrated. She didn't know what her daughter looked like—or even whether or not she was alive.

Every day that she could get a seat, she read the whole way into Manhattan on the crowded commuter bus, never speaking with anyone. She read in *Time* about the war, about the coronation of the Shah of Iran, about the growing popularity of Indian gurus, about the antiwar movement, about the "New Cinema" and its heavy use of violence and sex, about the first heart transplant. And then, when the bus arrived at the terminal, she walked alone among the pressing, rush-hour crowds to her office on Madison Avenue.

Few of the people who streamed from the buses and walked the sordid stretch of Forty-second Street to Sixth Avenue seemed to notice the screaming marquees (SEXATIONAL!

SEXCITING! LIVE SEX ACTS ON STAGE!), or the urine-soaked vagrants sleeping like fetuses in filthy doorways, or the staggering old drunks badly needing a shave, or the staring young junkies on speed, or the bag ladies begging for some change to "buy breakfast," or the tired prostitutes in microminiskirts tottering along the street in spike heels. Most of the people seemed to walk to work without seeing any of the things for which Forty-second Street is world famous. But she never learned how. All of it—the rancid fried-food smells; the anxious traffic noise; the sidewalk litter thick as fallen leaves, the broken bodies and blank faces of those who had, for reasons she didn't know, let go—seemed to slap her in the face each morning and sting. Yet she deliberately took the same route every day, as if it were a self-inflicted object lesson in The Other Side of Reality.

Sometimes, on Fifth Avenue, she would be stopped by tourists and asked directions in German, and she would have to explain, through sign language, that she couldn't help them. And occasionally someone would very kindly ask her whether she needed directions, because she "looked lost."

On Madison Avenue she looked at other women enviously. She studied the cut of their hair, the measure of their stride, the size of their handbags, the shade of their nails. She wanted to learn how to walk down the avenue like them—confidently, jauntily.

But, she found, New York—which she had sought for its promised blessing of anonymity and for its dearth of reminders of homes, babies, and families—only served to further erode her self-confidence and sense of identity. No longer her parents' child, Jim's wife, or Whitney's mother, she groped helplessly for an answer to her unspoken question: *Who am I?*

She felt fragile, hollow, empty—a pinpricked egg with the insides blown out. What else could she do, she wondered, but reinforce and decorate her shell? So she tried to make a mask, create the costume of a young, pretty, new identity. She had her hair done at Sassoon, she bought new clothes, studied fashion magazines. But, she soon found, no amount of makeup could make her eyes smile; no deodorant, mouthwash, or perfume could cover up the scent of sadness she knew she exuded;

none of the newest fashions were light or bright enough to lift her spirits or her shoulders; and every pair of shoes she bought—even the most dainty—were too heavy. In her heart, all she really wanted to be was Whitney's mommy.

No one at her office knew about her baby. It was her new policy not to let anyone know. If nobody knew, she thought, they couldn't pity her, question her, or remind her. The man she worked for was brilliant but unfriendly. He seldom said more than three words to her all day. The first, mumbled as he turned the corner into his office, as if on the last lap of a foot-race, was a one-syllable word: "Gmng." The second, repeated twice—once at eleven and again at about three—was "Caw-fey." And the third, at the end of the day, was "Gnite." For most other communication he used his buzzer. One buzz: Pick up the phone. Two buzzes: Come into my office. Three buzzes: Come into my office and bring your shorthand pad.

He usually buzzed three times and spent hours dictating, mostly acquisitions agreements. These long and complicated documents, involving many millions of dollars, went directly from his brain to her pad to final typed form in one day. When he dictated, often with his eyes closed, he indicated every comma, capital, and period. When he paused to think, she sometimes passed the time by sketching his face in her shorthand pad: short, wavy hair; receding brow, rippled with parallel lines; closely set eyes; rounded nose; thin, tight mouth, like a slice across his face; small chin . . .

"Are those your daughters?" she asked one day during a break in dictation, pointing to the large framed photograph on the bookshelf near him of three pretty little girls with long, fair hair, sitting close together, arms around each other.

"MnHmm," he said flatly, without opening his eyes.

"You're very fortunate—" she said, and then she caught herself.

"Yeah, sure," he said. "Now, where were we—?"

She was never fond of the man, but that day she hated him.

She spent Christmas Day at her sister's. Her sister had been preparing for the holidays for weeks—decorating her apartment with ornaments she made herself, baking special Scandinavian Christmas breads and cookies, planning the dinner menu, which included wild-rice-stuffed Cornish hens *à l'orange.* There was a full house—immediate family, her sister's in-laws, friends. She tried her best to be controlled; but when her sister's baby joyfully tore the wrapping from his first Christmas toy, she had to leave the room and stay away. She later learned that she'd upset her sister's holiday.

• • •

Hope became a palpable substance she chewed and swallowed daily. She knew that one day—one day soon—she would be reunited with her baby. She was as sure of this as she was sure of her mother's love or the existence of God. And even if she hadn't been so sure, she would have been convinced by those who repeatedly reassured her it was true—her mother, George, the FBI agent assigned to her case. It was, she knew, and everyone who knew said, "just a matter of time." So every night she went to bed hopeful, thinking: *Maybe tomorrow.*

Sometimes, though, she couldn't wait that long. She would see her baby, still a toddler, on an island with tall, swaying palm trees. Her own hair would be long, longer than it had ever been, and as she ran to greet her infant and sweep her up in her arms, her long hair fluttered in the air like a flag. The joy! Her child was well! Her happy baby hadn't grown or changed! Time had stood still! It was over! *It was all over!*

After such nights, the days became bad dreams.

Jim seldom entered her conscious thoughts. It was as if the worst thing she could do to him was to blot him out of her mind utterly, to exterminate, annihilate his memory. But in her dreams he appeared uninvited, standing a few yards away, facing her. Quickly, she'd reach for her father's half-filled vodka bottle on her mother's kitchen table, and, as she and her sisters had done as children, poor its contents down the drain. Then, before Jim knew what was happening, she'd grip the bottle by its throat, crack it against the kitchen sink, breaking its base into jagged pieces, sharper than sharks' teeth, and lunge at Jim's face, aiming for his eyes. She was a cat, quiet, fast; and

94

she caught him completely unaware, because he'd always seen her as a dog. Before she saw his face bleed, she'd wake up, shaking.

As time passed, she grew more desperate and groping. She went on hoping, but, in addition, she sought fresh opportunities for action. And, like a starving person who steals stale bread with a clear conscience, she sometimes resorted to harmless lies.

After work one day, when her boss had gone, she approached the most approachable attorney in the legal department, who was working late.

"May I speak with you, please?" she said. "I need some advice."

He offered her a chair.

"My sister has a serious problem," she said, without meeting his eyes. "Her husband took her baby and disappeared last year, and our family can't afford private detectives, and she doesn't know what to do, so I'm asking everyone I can think of whether they have any ideas—"

If she had been a waitress who'd spilled soup on the sleeve of his suit jacket, the expression on his face might have been the same. "Well," he said, leaning over his desk and smiling forcefully, "I think your sister should try to find him herself. If she's as pretty as you are, she could become an airline stewardess and fly around the world looking for him . . ."

"Thank you," she said sincerely. "I'll tell her," she lied.

She thought his suggestion was a wonderful idea. It gave her something to plan for, something to *do*. Hopefully, she went for interviews at several airlines. She wrote on their applications "divorced," "no children." She waited, hopes high. But she was rejected, without explanation, by all of them.

That April she read in *Time* about the assassination of Martin Luther King and of the riots that followed. In May she turned twenty-three. On the same day, her grandmother, who was eighty, had another heart attack and died. In June the Vietnam conflict broke a record by becoming the longest of America's wars, with a total of more than 2,376 days and 25,068 U.S.

dead; and Senator Robert Kennedy was assassinated. From the window in her boss's office she could see the crowds below, standing four abreast, in lines that wound along many city blocks, waiting to enter St. Patrick's Cathedral and file past Bobby Kennedy's coffin. And she saw the policemen, too, poised on every available ledge of every building in the area, holding rifles pointed toward the street, prepared for trouble.

. . .

One day that summer a young woman came to the office to visit. She had worked as a secretary in the legal department and had left eighteen months earlier to have a baby. She brought her baby with her. Numbly, the young mother whose child was missing watched from her desk as this baby toddled up the hall. His tentative steps, the shape of his head, the color and length of his hair, the little nose, the large blue eyes—they were all the same as *hers,* her own baby's. Was it that this baby matched more closely than any other child she'd seen since hers was taken the baby of her memories, photographs, and dreams? Or was it that she'd been carefully avoiding all contact with children, that for months she hadn't seen any babies, especially those who might remind her of her own? She stared at him, frozen, appearing, no doubt, to be as afraid of babies as some people are of dogs, until his mother picked him up and said her good-byes.

It was then, for the first time at work, she broke down. Sobbing in the ladies' room, she told one of the secretaries she worked with—a woman who for several years had been trying to start a family and who spent the first day of her period each month in the ladies' room in tears—about her missing child.

Within days, everyone in the office seemed to know.

Shortly after this incident, her boss called her in to his office.

"You don't appear to be happy here," he said. It was, perhaps, the longest statement he had ever made directly to her. She wanted to respond to it with: *Neither do you.* "You do your work all right, but you don't seem to enjoy it," he said.

"Yes," she nodded, "that's true."

"Why do you think that is?"

"I think this type of work is uncreative, unfulfilling—"

"But it's more than that, isn't it? I know you have problems—"

"Problems?"

"I heard about your problems—and I, ah, think you might be happier elsewhere—"

"Yes," she said, "that's quite possible." *But where?* she wondered. *Where?*

One thing was clear: She hated secretarial work—sitting for hours at one desk in an airless office, when she'd rather have been physically active, preferably outdoors; being dictated to as if she were a faceless, soulless recording machine; being told how to punctuate each sentence as if she were devoid of all intelligence; having to ask permission to be excused to go to the ladies' room, as if she were a grammar school student; answering the phone, "Mr. So-and-So's office" so often she'd almost forget she also had a name; being the convenient scapegoat for his mistakes—"Oh, my girl forgot to remind me about that meeting!"—and never the recipient of his praise; having to type under pressure every day, forcing her hands to move faster, faster, faster, until her stomach ached from the tightness of its knots. Although her eyes had no trouble reading the clear outlines of her shorthand notes, her hands wanted to go their own way and type another message in rebellion: "I should have been a pair of ragged claws/Scuttling across the floors of silent seas . . ." Her hands would have been better employed rubbing backs in hospitals, or grooming horses, or stirring soup, or kneading bread, or gripping a tennis racket, or bathing a baby . . .

Somehow, when she was growing up, she never thought she'd need a career. At that time, when most young girls were given a choice of three—nursing, teaching, or being a secretary—she wasn't interested in any. When asked to write an essay in eighth grade on What I Want to Be, she was the only student in the history of the school who wrote—glowingly and voluminously—about wanting to become a housewife and make a happy home for her husband and children.

Now, however, she knew she had to have a career in order to support herself and her baby (when she returned) comfortably. And she knew that that career would require a degree. So, instead of returning to Gibbs's Placement Service, she phoned the personnel office at her university. They had an opening, the personnel director told her, for an administrative assistant for a fund-raising firm hired by the university to raise money for a new dental school. Her office would be on the campus; her tuition would be free. Would she mind spending hours doing research in the university's library? they asked her. Would she have any objection to being in an office alone four days a week? How would she feel about writing detailed reports on the meetings she would attend in her boss's absence? Was she, at twenty-three, too young to accept so much responsibility? She told them the job sounded ideal, and they hired her immediately.

Since she was no longer commuting to New York City and didn't need the convenience of an apartment on the bus route, she moved again, this time to a small garden apartment in a nice town with good schools, pleasant shops, and well-kept children's parks. She was sure her baby would be found while she lived there.

During the week she ate lunch in the university cafeteria with the undergraduates, who played Botticelli over tuna on rye, and she took as many courses after work as she could. It was a quiet campus in a middle-class suburban setting, where, at the height of other, larger universities' angry antiwar demonstrations, the navy recruiter in full-dress uniform sought enlistments with impunity.

George and she continued to see each other about three times a week. Although they'd been dating steadily for more than a year, they never discussed marriage. When she raised the subject, George would say, "Wait and see what happens about the baby." She couldn't understand that he couldn't even say, "I love you," because to him it meant, "Will you marry me?"

The baby. In October 1968, the baby turned three. She was no longer a baby.

On the nights she didn't see George, after work and after class, she would return to her small apartment and lie on the living room carpet in the dark, listening to the same side of the same Judy Collins album over and over. Softly, sadly, in the darkness, she sang along: *". . . I really don't know life at all."*

For dinner she ate tuna straight from the can. On Saturdays she slept till noon. She never returned to church, she stopped reading the Bible, and her daily prayers were reduced to the one-word question "WHY?" She got straight A's in all her courses; she worked hard at her job. She kept busy. She kept in touch with her lawyer and the FBI, but they never had any news for her. She kept away from children.

Thanksgiving. Christmas. New Year's. The same painful holidays, the same tears. A new semester at school, new courses to get lost in, one of which was child psychology. She quickly chose the topic for her term paper: "The Effects on Young Children of Maternal Deprivation."

A man and his teenage son moved in to an apartment above hers, and sometimes the son, Tom, came down to visit her. He would come in with an armful of acid-rock record albums because his father didn't have a stereo, and then he'd try to talk over the noise. He told her his parents were divorced, his mother had remarried, and she didn't want him with her, so he lived with his dad, who traveled a lot on business. Tom would lean back on the love seat and look around her apartment, rolling his eyes. "Look at this place, man," he'd say, "just *look* at it! Curtains, carpet, desk, books. This is a *home,* man, a real HOME. It's warm like a home—it even *smells* like a home. Y'know what my old man and I have upstairs here? A *cave.* We live like *animals.* One room with two single beds on opposite sides of it. That's it. I come down here, man, and I feel like I've come *home!"*

Sometimes he'd reach into the breast pocket of his plaid flannel shirt and offer her a marijuana cigarette. Terrified, she'd refuse. She was afraid she might like it, that it would dull her pain, and she would want more and more and more. She was afraid Jim would somehow find out and accuse her of being an unfit mother, a "drug addict."

It had been almost two years since her baby was taken, and, she realized, in all that time she'd lived not only in hope but in fear. She had a suspicion that although she didn't know where Jim was hiding, he was somehow keeping tabs on her. So she lived ultracircumspectly, careful not to do or say anything or go anywhere that might one day be held against her, that might jeopardize her right to have custody of her baby. She was only twenty-three, but she lived a life devoid of spontaneity; she lived like an old woman.

When Tom came to visit, he told her about his ambitions and dreams. He was going to be a famous writer; he had it all worked out: First, journalism—reporting on rock concerts; then feature articles for music magazines; then books, "the big time, man." Then he'd retire at forty and live on an island in the Mediterranean.

Often, late at night, she'd hear him typing upstairs, faster with two fingers than she could type with ten, the articles he was submitting for publication. When the first one was accepted, and he proudly presented her with a clipping, she wrote a poem to him and put it in his mailbox the next morning:

> Some day, when the world
> knows you better than I,
> when your works
> will be published abroad,
> I'll say with a sigh,
> I remember him when,
> and I'll sit in my room
> and applaud.

· · ·

When the fund-raising firm she worked for decided to pool its accounts in one central office in Newark, she had to leave her office on the tranquil campus and drive to Newark daily, passing the unhealed wounds of the race riots of two summers be-

100

fore—the jagged, broken glass, boarded-up stores, burned-out lots—hoping her car wouldn't fail because she'd be too afraid to get out. There was anger in the air there, hotter than a simmer, that made her afraid, for the first time in her life, because her skin was white. Black men in passing cars with bumper stickers reading BLACK IS BEAUTIFUL hurled hateful words in her direction. She wanted to shout back at them, "What have you got against me? I don't hate you. I've never done anything to harm you—or any other black person." She might have added that she'd never known any to hate.

In the corner of America where she grew up, there were no blacks. No black homeowners, no black schoolchildren, no blacks in church. (In Sunday school the children sang, "Red and yellow, black and white, they are precious in His sight," but there were only white children there.) There was no racial prejudice or hatred either. How could the people hate what didn't exist for them?

From the window in her office she could see nothing but gray. Gray buildings and gray sky met in a blur where there should have been an outline. She stood at the window stretching her legs, pretending the window was open and she was filling her lungs with fresh air. It was a game she played; the window was sealed shut with thick layers of old paint, and the air outside wasn't fresh anyway. She looked out to where lower Manhattan was shrouded in gray in the distance, and beyond it to where the Hudson joined the ocean, and thought, *Somewhere out there. Somewhere.*

Since the move to Newark her job wasn't the same. She missed the autonomy she'd had at the university, the earnest students, the old brick buildings, the trees. In the new office the women were treated more like secretaries. Everyone smoked except her, and the smoke made the air in the room gray. Most of the time she tried not to breathe.

For two days she'd been typing the same letter to each of the two hundred people on a carefully compiled mailing list, inviting them to a special luncheon at a ritzy country club, where the governor would speak on the urgent need for another dental school in the state. Part of the fund-raising psychology, she learned, involved sending perfectly centered, individually typed, hand-stamped letters of invitation to luncheons such as this. It seemed that the very rich only read originals.

She didn't write the letter, it was dictated to her. But she did take the liberty of placing a comma before the "and" connecting two independent clauses in one of the sentences. She had to leave her mark.

She was inserting a fresh sheet of letterhead into her machine when her telephone rang.

"Good morning, Hansen Associates."

"Bonnie?"

"Yes." It was her lawyer, Mr. Lundy. It was the first time he'd phoned her.

"I've got good news. They've found him."

"*They've found him?*" she echoed, voice out of control. All of the typewriters in the office stopped clicking; her heart stopped beating. "*Where?*"

"In Rhodesia."

"Rho-de-sia," she repeated slowly, feeling each syllable. She'd never heard of Rhodesia; she'd never read about it in *Time*. She tried to find it on the world map in her mind, but it wasn't there. *Near Malaysia, perhaps?* It sounded as if it should be near Malaysia. The other women in the room had stopped their work and turned to stare. *Control*, she told herself, *you must have control.*

"But there's a problem, Bonnie." Her lawyer's voice was gentle, concerned. "The FBI can do nothing more now. There's no extradition with Rhodesia. It's out of our jurisdiction. You'll have to go there yourself. Do you think you can handle it?"

"Oh, yes." Her stomach felt as if she'd swallowed broken glass. "Anywhere—I'll go anywhere."

"All right, then, This is what you should do—"

• • •

Do what he says. Do what you're told. Don't lose control.

As you make each call you draw boxes around the words on your shorthand pad and then more boxes around the boxes.

PASSPORT OFFICE   GEORGE PICK-UP
"BE THERE TODAY"
BANK LOAN—MOM $$$$ TRAVELER'S CHECKS   TWA
NEW YORK—LONDON—JOHANNESBURG
ROUND-TRIP $1,045
BABY'S BIRTH CERTIFICATE

Tell your boss the news. Why does he look so worried? Tell him it shouldn't take long—just a few days—you'll be back as soon as you can. He'll hold the job. Good, good. Thank you. Good-bye.

Pack. What? Three dresses, matching shoes, makeup, curlers, underwear, stockings, nightgown, bathrobe. What else? Oh, a book: child psychology.

Look up Rhodesia in your desk encyclopedia. ". . . formerly Southern Rhodesia . . . 150,333 sq. mi.; pop. c. 3,857,000 . . . S. central Africa; cap. Salisbury . . ." *Africa.* Remember: when you were ten, playing Sheena of the Jungle, dressed in leopard skin, carrying a rifle over your right shoulder? And at fifteen imagining yourself as a missionary in a plain cotton dress, carrying nothing but the Gospel's good news to barely literate tribes along the Congo? You are going—as if again—to *Africa.*

George lies to his mother, says he's spending the night at Paul's. He sleeps beside you restlessly, his entire body twitching nervously. You lie awake, motionless, numb, thinking: *TO-MORROW.*

W hy are you shaking, Mommy?" I say as I move closer to her, putting my arm around her slim shoulder, as if she were a little sister afraid of the dark. "You should be happy—"

"I'm never going to see you again," she says softly. She fixes her eyes on her hands in her lap, not wanting me to see what her voice betrays.

"Don't be silly," I say, squeezing her shoulder. "I'll only be gone for a few days. One small suitcase, see? I'm just going to pick up the baby and come home. I'll be right back."

"No," my mother says, shaking her head, "you won't."

George paces anxiously in front of us. From time to time he looks at his watch, then studies the Departures and Arrivals board above our heads. He looks as if he hadn't slept—although I know he did—as if in all the pacing of the morning ten pounds had melted from his already thin frame.

Of the three of us, I am the most calm; almost, in fact, serene.

At last, it is time. Nervous hugs. Quick kisses. I-love-you's exchanged like fragile gifts. George says "I love you" to me for the first time; and I think without thinking: *Too late.* I take my seat and check my watch: 10:10 a.m. The captain says: "Takeoff

104

will be in five minutes." I listen to my watch's ticking. *Six hours to London. Soon . . . soon . . .* I close my eyes and take deep breaths. My heart, like this plane, has outstretched wings.

A small fat man in a black suit sits wrapped in a furtive silence in the aisle seat to my left, an empty seat between us. Several times during the flight I see him pull from his pants pocket a folded wad of bills, nearly an inch thick. He holds the money in his small puffy hands nervously, fearfully, as if none of it were his to keep, and his life depended on getting it all quickly to its proper destination.

Someone taps me on the shoulder from behind.

"Hi," he says, "I noticed you're writing."

"My diary," I say, glad to break the flight's long silence.

"Would you happen to have a spare pencil? Thought I'd do the crossword to kill time. I've already read all of the magazines."

"Sure. Here—"

We introduce ourselves. Vince is a young and handsome black man in a conservative business suit. A computer instructor for Fords.

"Where're you headed?" he asks.

"London, first."

"Ever been there?"

"No, never. I've never been overseas."

"You must be excited. You look real excited. Where're you staying?"

"I'm not sure yet. I thought I'd find a hotel near the airport. I'll only be in London until tomorrow—"

"And then?"

"I'm going to Africa," I say. The words emerge proudly. I feel strong and brave: lioness reclaiming her cub. No longer caged in uncertainty.

His eyes brighten. *"Oh?* Vacation?"

"No, personal business."

"Really? Where?"

"Salisbury . . . Rhodesia."

"Oh," he says flatly.

Have I said something wrong? "And you?" I say to keep the conversation going. "Where are you headed?"

"Home. I live in Italy with my wife and two kids. Just been back to Philly for my mom's funeral."

"Oh, I'm sorry."

"Look, if you have any trouble getting a hotel, let me know. Here's the number of my club in London where I'll be staying. I'm sure I can get a room for you there."

Vince insists on carrying my suitcase out of Customs and waiting with me until I am sure of my accommodation. We walk together past the crowd of people standing patiently behind a barricade, preparing to greet their arriving friends and relatives with quiet handshakes and hugs.

"Vince, look," I say, motioning toward a young man in the front of the crowd holding up a placard bearing my name. I hurry ahead toward the man and tell him who I am.

"Well, *hullo*," he says heartily, as if I were an old friend. "Am I glad you're here! I felt like a right fool waving this thing! My name is Rick Craig-Wood. Stan cabled us today"— *(Stan cabled? After I rushed past him in the hallway at work yesterday, telling him, breathlessly, I was flying to Africa via his "motherland"?)*—"told us you were coming and asked us to look after you. Stan's an old friend of the family, you know. Went to Cambridge with my eldest brother—"

"Stan didn't tell me he—"

"Well, that's Stan for you. Always was full of mischief." Rick reaches into his pocket, and I realize he is about to tip the black man beside me holding my suitcase.

"This is Vince," I say quickly. "We met on the plane. He offered to help me find a place to stay."

Rick withdraws his hand from his pocket and extends it toward Vince. "How do you *do?* That's very kind of you, but she won't be needing a hotel. She'll be staying with my family."

Miniature cars. Shoulder-to-shoulder brick houses. Narrow, twisting roads. Ancient trees with gnarled, protruding roots. Damp and drafty home; warm and gracious family. I tell them why I am going to Salisbury. They give me kind warnings: "Rhodesia is a dangerous country. . . . Be careful. . . . Be prepared—"

At Heathrow the next afternoon, I check my bag with South African Airways.

"Your visa, please."

"Visa?"

"You must have a visa to enter South Africa."

"But no one told—"

She looks impatient. People are waiting in line behind me.

"I won't be leaving the airport in Johannesburg. I'll be taking the next plane to Salisbury—"

"I'm sorry, madam."

"But I must get to Salisbury immediately—my baby was kidnapped and—" I'm surprised to hear myself say this. I feel unconvincing, as if I'd told a lie, as if I'd *meant* to imply my child had just been taken, when the truth was she'd been gone for more than two years.

Heads turn in our direction. My eyes cloud with tears. My suitcase has long since disappeared, borne off on a black conveyor belt.

She is unmoved, as if she'd heard it all before, seen it all. "I'm very sorry, madam, but you cannot take this flight without a visa. You will either have to obtain a South African visa or wait until the next direct flight to Salisbury—"

"When will that be?"

"This Tuesday. Now, if you don't mind waiting to one side, I'll see that your bags are retrieved—"

Cables to lawyers in Salisbury and home, to George and my mother: . . . LEAVING LONDON TUESDAY 3-25-69 ARRIVING SALISBURY WEDNESDAY 26TH . . .

Monday in London. The city is old, bleak as Dickens's descriptions, cold. It is snowing lightly. (*Snow? In London? In March?*) I walk along Belgrave alone, shivering. I am dressed for Africa, in a thin, spring suit. I hail a taxi: "How much would it cost for a tour of the city?"

"Oh, 'bout twelve pounds, love."

How much is twelve pounds worth? I wonder. *However much it's worth, it's worth it.*

With unsteady hands, I take photos of London's landmarks with George's good camera, forgetting his hurried instructions ("depth of field"? "ASA"? "F-stop"? "infinity"?). None of the pictures will come out.

We stop at the Tower of London to see the crown jewels.

"Care for a sandwich?" the cabby says, pointing to a sandwich stand on a cobblestone street across from the Tower.

"Oh, yes, thanks, I'm starved."

"What sort would you like?"

"Ham and cheese, please."

"Whoah, you must be hungry. You'd like *two* sandwiches, would you?"

"No, thanks, one will be plenty."

"Ham or cheese?"

"Both."

"Never heard of such a thing."

He buys two sandwiches for me—"Lunch is included in the fare," he insists—one ham, one cheddar cheese, combines the fillings to make one sandwich and presents it to me ceremoniously: "For milady," he says, bowing deeply, theatrically.

Rick's mother insists on my returning to their home in Surrey for the night and on taking me to the airport the next day. She is a large-hearted, motherly woman and she waits with me until my flight to Salisbury is called. "Aren't you forgetting something?" she says gently, eyes twinkling. I look at her handsome, open face searchingly. "Children like gifts," she says. (*Children like*—? Suddenly, I feel frightened. It's been so long since I've been with children, I can't remember what they like. Or what they are like.) "You wouldn't want to re-enter your little girl's life empty-handed?"

Together we go to the airport's best shop, and I buy an infant-size Winnie-the-Pooh teddy bear and a Mother Goose story book to take to Whitney.

Terminal 3. Gate 6. Four forty-five.

"Good-bye, my dear," Rick's mother says.

"You've been so kind—like a mother to me. I don't know how to thank you—"

She hugs me and we kiss good-bye.

"Would you care for a drink?" the stewardess says.

"Yes, please. Orange soda."

"Orange squash with soda water?"

"No, thank you; just plain orange soda."

"I'm sorry, but I don't know what you mean—"

Sixteen hours to Salisbury. Often I check my watch, watch the hands move, listen to the steady ticking. I write to George and my mother, try to read. The plane is almost empty. When the lights go out, I stretch out along three seats, but cannot sleep.

From my window in the morning I see Africa clearly. I see mountains, lakes, rivers, clumps of green. Unlike the man-made patchwork design one sees from the air across most of America, the terrain below seems untouched, natural, raw. I search for signs of people, hunt for game, but find none.

I am heavy and light, cold and hot, brave and afraid, too numb to move from my seat, too excited to sit still until the taxiing stops.

The airport looks like a whitewashed fortress, so white in the dazzling sunlight it hurts my eyes. For an instant I imagine a gunman standing ready behind the white parapet with a hidden rifle pointing in my direction. My imagination, like a technicolor motion picture playing in my mind, causes me to tremble as I gather up my things, smooth my hair, straighten my light-blue dress. I tell myself I'm not afraid, I've never been afraid to die. *Lioness shot trying to reclaim her cub . . .*

Perhaps I am delirious. I'm not even sure I can walk. *Daddy, would you carry me?* GOD, PLEASE GIVE ME STRENGTH.

A large black man in a blue uniform studies my passport, then stamps it hard. "We are expecting you," he says.

Who are "we"? And who am I that "they" should be expecting—?

A small man in a rumpled suit rushes through the almost empty airport lobby toward me.

"Mrs. Jason?"

"Yes? I haven't answered to this name in more than two years.

"I'm Frank Clarke of Winterton, Holmes and Hill, your solicitors. I've come to fetch you."

When I was ten, playing Sheena of the Jungle, wearing leopard skin, Africa was green and lush. Animals roamed freely in the bush; they ate from my hand. This Africa now is brown and dry. It stretches as far as the eye can see and then is sewn along a straight seam to the azure sky.

From the airport to the city the narrow macadam road, like a frayed black ribbon on a faded beige dress, follows the gentle curves of the earth's body, swerving neither left nor right. There's not an animal in sight.

Mr. Clarke leans toward the steering wheel, driving silently, soberly. His hands are like a workman's. His suit is shabby. *Is he the office messenger?* I wonder. The old car rattles, as if to signal its demise.

"I must tell you," he says at last—

Anything, tell me anything. Something.

"—you're not at all what I expected."

". . . . . ."

"I was expecting someone . . . older . . . ah . . . someone very different from—"

"Why?"

"I read your husband's al—"

"Ex."

"—your ex-husband's allegations. The papers came in this morning, and they . . . ah . . ."

"Yes?"

"—paint a very bad picture indeed."

"Papers?"

110

"He's taking this to court. Mrs. Jason, I—"

"Please call me Bonnie."

"—I don't want to upset you, but it's very bad."

". . . . . ."

"He says you are mentally ill—a religious fanatic. He says you beat your baby, that your mother had an affair with the judge who awarded you custody, that your brother committed incest with you . . ."

Mr. Clarke looks across at me to study my reaction to his news. He is not a messenger. He is a man of authority.

"When can I see my baby?"

"I'll see what I can do."

The city of Salisbury is clean, modern, white; its tall white buildings glisten in the sun. Mr. Clarke parks his car and we go straight to his office. He orders tea as we pass through the reception area toward his office, which is the largest, at the end of the hall. Mr. Clarke, I deduce, is probably the most senior partner in the firm. I glance about his room: worn carpet; old (World War II?) dark-wood office furniture; ancient telephone with a strange, shrill ring.

"Frankly—" Mr. Clarke says as he lights a cigarette nervously. A black man in a khaki-colored uniform softly enters the room carrying a tray. Mr. Clarke takes no notice of him. "Frankly, I'm worried that this case could be a long-drawn-out one—" He takes a deep draft on his cigarette. The black man gently places the tea tray on a nearby table and silently leaves the room. "You could be here for one, two, or three months." He looks at me anxiously, as if waiting for a response. I look back at him, speechless, drained, exhausted, numb. "How do you take your tea?" he says, reaching for the pot.

There is a knock on my hotel room door. I call out, "Yes?" A man answers, but I cannot understand what he says. He knocks again, and I begin to tremble. *Is it Jim? Or has he sent someone?* "Who is it?"

"Dee bed, mah-dem. I come to turn down dee bed."

"No, thank you. Not tonight. Please."

I rush to the toilet in my bathroom and become ill.

In the darkness, in my bed, I listen to the chimes of the church across Salisbury square. *I am here,* I silently reply to the chimes. *I am here.*

"When can I see my little girl?" I ask Mr. Clarke the next morning.

"I am making arrangements," he says. "Perhaps tomorrow."

Tomorrow.

Mr. Clarke takes me to the American consulate. There I learn how Jim was found: He'd made a mistake—a "slip of the tongue," the American official says—had mentioned to someone at the consulate that the FBI was "after" him. They thought he was a "crackpot," but decided to inquire of Washington anyway. The answer came back in due time: Yes, indeed, he is wanted. *They didn't "find him" at all,* I realize. *Jim virtually—unwittingly—turned himself in.*

"I've seen your daughter," the American official says to me. "Your ex-husband brought her in with him." He stares at me. "She is very pretty," he says, "just like her mommy." I feel weak and dizzy, too weak to hold back tears. "I'm sorry," he says, handing me a tissue. "I wish there was something we could do for you. But you must understand, you are both American citizens—we can't take sides—" I thank him and leave.

Mr. Clarke plans my life, paternally. Offers me work in his office to keep me busy. Offers to find me free accommodation for the duration of my stay. Promises to make me "as comfortable as possible here." I sink into his arms, figuratively.

That night I write to George requesting him to sublet my apartment and sell my car to pay my monthly bills. I tell him, "I am being strong, you mustn't worry."

It is arranged. Mrs. Clarke takes me. The living room seems filled with people, but I don't see them. *Where is she?* Jim is there; I see him peripherally. I cannot look at him. He does not exist for me.

"Mrs. Jason," a pleasant, dark-haired woman with a British accent says, "would you like to come with me?" She leads me to another door and calls outside for Whitney. "Boom-Boom!" *Boom-Boom?* "There's a lady here to see you." *A lady?*

There, in a cotton sundress, is my baby. No, not a baby, a little girl. I want to run to her, lift her up, hold her close; but I am afraid I'll frighten her. *There will be time,* my heart says, pounding; *proceed slowly.* I walk slowly toward her on the lawn. She is pale and chubby. Her white-blond hair is cut short, like a boy's. Her face looks like photos of my brother's son. She resembles my family. She cocks her head quizzically as I approach. *Does she recognize me? Does she remember me?*

"Hello," I hear myself say cheerfully.

"Heh-wow," she answers lightly.

Do you know who I am, honey? I crouch down to bridge the distance between our faces. *What should I say?* "I came a long, long way *just* to see *you,*" I tell her, smiling. Gaily, she scampers away. "Would you like to play a game?" I call to her. "I know a lot of games." She runs back to me. "Do you know how to play hide-and-seek?" She shakes her head. "Well, this is how it's played—"

Like two small children, neighbors, friends, Whitney and I played outside for the full hour of my allotted visitation. We giggled and ran—hiding, counting, finding. "I know where you are!" I called out to her. "You're behind that tree—" She squealed delightedly. *I found you, honey. Thank God, I've found you.* She seemed happy, healthy. She didn't know me.

When my time was up, the dark-haired woman came out to inform me. "I must go now," I said to Whitney.

"*No!*" she said. "We didn't finish our game!"

"I'll see you again very soon. All right? And next time, I'll bring you a surprise from London—"

"Good!"

"May I have a kiss good-bye?" I said, crouching, face to face. She leaned forward and kissed me.

It wasn't until the house was no longer in sight that I let go. Mrs. Clarke reached over from the steering wheel and held my hand.

Mr. Clarke arranged for me to check out of my hotel and move in with the family of Alwyn Pichanick, one of the partners in Mr. Clarke's law firm, Winterton, Holmes and Hill, who offered to let me stay with them rent-free until my case went to court. From the Pichanick's home on Monday, March 31, I wrote to my mother of my second visit with Whitney:

Yesterday Mrs. Edwards (Mr. Clarke's secretary) and I drove to J's home. We arrived ten minutes early and waited outside for the baby to return from Sunday school. J. and his parents were not supposed to be present, but as can be expected from them, they were there. . . . Mom, my little girl is just precious! I bought her a teddy bear in London and promised it to her on Friday. When I brought it with me yesterday she said, "I has enough toys" (obviously a direct quote from you-know-who). But by the time I was about to leave (my *hour* was up), she was begging me to stay and have dinner with them. She also said, "Maybe I can stay with you some night?" and I assured her *she will.* I haven't told her yet that I am her Mommy; I thought at this point it would only upset her. . . .

She still has her happy, carefree personality, and I'm sure that the transition from one parent to the other will not cause her harm. She is *very* bright and cute (and seemingly well aware of both). Yesterday she snuggled up beside me on their living room sofa while I read to her from the story book I brought her. She seems to stare at me, as if to say, "You look like me!" . . . She is very warm, very affectionate, very responsive and outgoing. I'm sure that the overwhelming love which I feel for her is transmitted when we're together. . . .

Mr. Clarke tells me that J. is now trying to say that *I* was having an affair with the judge who gave me custody! At first, he said in his allegations (hideous things—37 pages worth) that *you,* Mom, were having an affair with the judge, but after seeing what I look like now, I guess he thought he could change it to *me.* (Who knows, maybe tomorrow he'll say we *both* were. Lucky judge!)

Mr. Clarke also said something to the effect that J's approach now is to make things so difficult for me (nothing new) that for either physical, emotional, or financial reasons I'll have to give up and go back home. Mom, I can't let that happen. . . . I don't care if I have to fight this out for the rest of my life, I must stay until it's over. . . .

• • •

"Joymount," the Pichanicks' home, was even more grand than the majestic homes along Summit Avenue. It sat alone on the top of a hill five miles from Salisbury center. From my room I could see clearly, like a short strand of pearls on the horizon, the small white cluster of buildings that composed the capital city.

In between lay virgin brush—scrubby trees, patches of parched grassland, untouched Africa. On Sunday afternoons I could feel the reverberations across this stretch of earth of distant drums that I could barely hear. Like healthy heartbeats, the tribal drums made the land seem vibrant, glad to be alive.

Five full-time African gardeners kept the grounds at Joymount in showcase splendor. There was a rose garden; a multiflowered, three-tiered rock garden; an herb garden; a vegetable garden; a goldfish pond; and a clay tennis court with thick vines of passion fruit climbing up its fence.

Inside the large brick house, the rooms were warm and spacious. From the foyer a wide staircase opened like a fan and created a central balcony, which led to six second-floor bedrooms. The living room had a large fireplace (used occasionally, when the weather dropped below sixty degrees in winter), comfortable plush furniture, and an immense Oriental carpet in delicate pastels. Adjacent to the living room was a dimly lit billiard room, seldom used, whose wood-paneled walls were filled with old framed photographs of famous cricket teams; next to it, a small library with floor-to-ceiling bookshelves contained every book on cricket ever written.

The kitchen was as large and well equipped as that of a well-run restaurant. Sue Pichanick, an American, born in New York but raised in Rhodesia, was a graduate of the London Cordon

Bleu Cooking School. She taught her full-time African cook, Albert, everything she knew; and the meals he prepared were excellent.

Because the dining room was too formal for everyday use, the family ate most meals at a smaller table in the large, cheerful room that the four Pichanick children also used as a playroom. I was given a place at this table and was made to feel part of the family.

After breakfast on weekday mornings, Alwyn and I drove to the office, where I shared a room with his secretary, Joyce, and worked with Mr. Clarke on my case. Our answering affidavit, refuting once again all of Jim's allegations, came to forty-nine pages.

Mr. Clarke arranged for me to have weekend visitations with Whitney at Joymount, in addition to three one-hour weekday visitations at Jim's home in the Salisbury suburb of Highlands. For the weekday visits, Mrs. Clarke drove into town to take me to see Whitney at Jim's.

On the first of these weekday visits, Tuesday afternoon, April 1, there was a dramatic change in Whitney's behavior toward me. She would not come near me. She refused to take my hand. She rejected the crayons and coloring book I brought for her, saying her "na-na" (grandmother) didn't allow her to play with crayons. She said she was not allowed to kiss me anymore—she could only kiss her "da-da" and "na-na"—and I must not kiss her. She said that she couldn't sit on my lap anymore—only on her da-da's and na-na's; that she couldn't accept the toys I offered because her da-da bought all her toys; that she didn't love me, she only loved her da-da and na-na; that she couldn't go in my car because I was going to take her away. I walked beside her silently, listening, trying not to reveal my horror in either words or actions.

We stopped at the edge of the goldfish pond to admire the fish. Whitney pointed to each one as it swam into view and began to count them for me: "One . . . two . . . free . . ." Suddenly, Jim's mother shouted from the back door, "Get her away from there! We don't allow her near there—she could fall in and drown! Boom-Boom, come in now, it's time for your tea!"

I turned and looked at the old woman for the first time in

116

years. "I came to see my child!" I said, groping for my rights; but Whitney had already started toward the house obediently.

"Please tell her I'm her mother," I said to Jim in the living room while Whitney was in the kitchen having tea. It was the first time since my arrival that I'd confronted him. Jim and his father, sitting on the sofa side by side, looked like brothers, old and broken. Though Jim was only forty years old, he looked like sixty.

"Well, I, ah . . ." Jim fumbled, aware of Mrs. Clarke's presence. "Well, I don't . . . ah . . . think this—"

"Then *I* will tell her," I said, leaving the room.

When Whitney had finished her tea and we could go outside again together, I asked her, "Where is your mommy, honey?" I crouched beside her, holding my hands tightly together so she wouldn't see them shaking.

She pointed toward the kitchen.

"Your na-na?" I asked, and she nodded. *(I will take that baby from you and give it to my mother to raise—)* I felt dizzy. The white house, the flower beds, the yard, began to spin. "Your na-na is your mommy?"

"I has *these* many ma-mas," Whitney said, jutting two fingers in front of my face. "Na-na is my ma-ma and Hedda is my mama."

Hedda? Their African cook? A neighbor? A friend? Jim's Rhodesian fiancée? Mr. Clarke told me Jim had a fiancée . . .

Now. No! *She must know.* Now? *Now.*

"*I* am your momma, honey," I said slowly, gently, looking straight into her pure blue eyes.

"*NO!*" She backed away. "You tried to *kill* my ma-ma! You *tried!*"

Once again I felt the cold, steel teeth of a trap clamp shut on my leg. *How could they do this, too? And what could I do to stop it? Take her and run? Where? How far? Without a car or money for two tickets home? Without a passport in my pocket (because it was being held by my attorneys, as Jim's was being held by his)? Go home alone—before more damage to this child was done? After so many people had extended themselves to make it possible for me to stay to "see justice done"? What was the answer, the antidote, the cure? All I could think of was:* Patience and Love.

. . .

*Easter Monday afternoon—April 7, 1969—*The room is dark with the draperies closed. Whitney is asleep in my bed. So pretty and sweet and still! . . . Yesterday, for the first time, she called me Mommy. She told the Pichanick twins, "That's *my* mommy!" We went to a kiddy park this afternoon, and she insisted that *her mommy* join her for the train ride. And when I took her to the ladies' room, she called out, "Mommy, I'm finished!" . . . When I tucked her in for her nap just now, she asked that I come sleep with her. Oh, this poor child—how I pray she comes out of this all right!

. . .

When I wasn't working in Mr. Clarke's office, or writing to George and my mother, or visiting with Whitney, I kept busy. I explored my new surroundings, beginning with the city. At lunch hour I wandered alone along the sidewalks of Salisbury, enjoying the brilliant weather, window-shopping, studying the passersby. Like the topography, I thought, the Rhodesian people shared a certain unaffected, natural, and timeless quality. The "Europeans," as the whites preferred to call themselves, appeared devoid of any sense of fashion—whether by choice or necessity—that might have pegged them to a specific season, year, or even era. The women wore simple cotton dresses and low-heeled sandals; the men, either lightweight, dark-colored business suits or crisp tan or gray safari suits, sometimes with short trousers and thick knee-socks—a costume conceivably worn by the earliest settlers several generations before. The Africans, too, wore Western dress—simple styles, subdued shades, serviceable clothing.

What fashions the dress shops displayed were already passé by New York standards. And the newest record albums available in Salisbury's music shops were also out of date. I felt as

118

if I'd fallen back in time; it was a past time, a slower time, an almost-timeless time.

On the days when I wore my navy minidress and matching navy opaque hose—one of the three outfits I'd brought with me—I noticed I would cause a stir. Young girls stared at me as if mentally connecting my appearance with something they'd seen in a foreign magazine. African workmen stopped what they were doing to confer among themselves: Is it possible for a European to be born with blue legs? They looked at me with pity, as if I had three arms.

Because, I learned, of the trade embargo placed on Rhodesia after its breakaway from Britain in 1965, many items that I'd always taken for granted, such as name-brand cosmetics and toiletries, were unavailable in Salisbury's shops. At first I was annoyed by the salesclerks' too-frequent response: "No, I'm sorry, but we haven't had that in stock since UDI"; but gradually I grew to anticipate the answer, and after a while I no longer asked.

Many items previously imported were now produced locally, and the words "Made in Rhodesia," stamped or sewn onto them, were chauvinistically displayed. Most of the "Made in Rhodesia" merchandise, particularly clothing and shoes, was, I thought, admirable. But some of the efforts could only be called sincere. The "Made in Rhodesia" bras seemed to be made of cardboard. And the "Made in Rhodesia" pantyhose, the newest make-do item, manufactured locally since shortly after my arrival, were as thick and lifeless as the support hose my grandmother used to wear.

Few of the younger European women, however, bothered with pantyhose. Their bare legs were honey-tan from hours spent outdoors, sunbathing or playing tennis. These women looked healthy, physically fit, and beautiful in a simple, unadorned, unselfconscious way. The younger European men, too, looked tanned, rugged, and handsome; they had the attractively craggy faces of outdoorsmen, sportsmen squinting in the sun.

Many of the older Europeans I noticed in Salisbury—except for the leather-faced, weather-worn farmers in the city on business for the day—looked as if they'd never left England. Pale-skinned and over-dressed, they carried their "brollies," along with their heavy briefcases or black leather handbags, although the rainy season, I was told, wasn't due again for months.

Nearly all of the African women I saw on the streets of Salisbury carried infants on their backs, wrapped in large bath-size towels tied securely at the mothers' waist and breast. The African babies seemed to thrive on the security and warmth of being held close to their mothers' bodies and moving with their every movement; I never saw one that was fretful or crying.

When an African family walked together, it was often the woman who carried the biggest load. She usually had a baby on her back, a box or basket filled with goods on her head; with one hand she carried a bag or valise, and the other held the hand of a toddler. The husband often carried another child in his arms. These African couples appeared to love their children dearly.

To a limited extent I explored Rhodesia itself, observing, without going far, its startling physical beauty: the paradoxical terrain; the passionate sun; the delicious, clean air; the sky, blue as a Siamese cat's eyes every day, and each night, like a canopy of black dotted swiss.

"People should pay admission to see this," I said one night to a Rhodesian friend, looking up at the sky.

"Only an American would put it that way," he replied.

In spite of all the uncertainties, each day I felt stronger and more healthy. I ate well at the Pichanicks' home and slept most nights from nine to six. Weekends were filled with little children and outings. Thanks to the people at Winterton, Holmes and Hill, I never felt homesick or lonely. June, the receptionist, and her husband, Les, sometimes took me out with them to dinner. Joyce, Alwyn's secretary, and her husband, Louie, invited me to their flat to see slides of their travels and took me on weekend day-trips when I didn't see Whitney. Nigel, a young attorney with the firm, for whom I sometimes worked, often asked me to lunch. Alwyn and Sue gave me a home. Mr. and Mrs. Clarke became like parents to me.

One Sunday soon after my arrival, after spending the day with the Clarkes and their five children—swimming, sunbathing, and playing tennis—I returned to the Pichanicks' home and was sent straight to bed by Sue.

"How are you feeling?" she said, sitting on the edge of my bed, feeling my sizzling face with her hands.

"Cold. And a bit nauseous."

"You got too much sun, my girl." She inspected my skin. "This looks like first-degree burns. . . . Is it very sore?"

"A little."

"Well, if you should feel sick in the night, please call for me. I'm a light sleeper, I'll hear you. Promise me you'll call?"

I felt as protected and cared-for as a child.

• • •

Saturday, April 19, 1969—After dinner (about 8:00) Whitney was tired, so I put her to bed and she insisted I sleep with her, so I excused myself and went to bed. She snuggled and cuddled all night (her insecurity seems to show up at night. She says she sleeps with her father every night), and she was very affectionate. She called me Mommy all the time, and we got very close.

Monday, April 21, 1969—Visitation at Clarkes'. W. very warm and close.

Wednesday, April 23, 1969—Visitation at Clarkes'. When we returned W., she said to her father, "See, I told you she would bring me back!"

Friday, April 25, 1969—Nigel drove me to J's where we picked up baby at four. She didn't cry. We drove to Pichanicks' and Nigel drove off shortly after. Whitney said to me in front of Sue's children, "Why don't you leave me alone and go away? I want to stay with my daddy for ever and ever." She had a lot of difficulty sleeping Friday night because she was so confused. On Saturday we played outside with the twins while Sue, Alwyn, Jenny Lynn, and Keith went to a wedding.

Monday, April 28, 1969—Visitation at Clarkes'. W. refused to speak to me. Mrs. Clarke asked her why. She said: "Because my daddy told me not to." I have no doubt that if and when I win this miserable case, I shall bring home with me a very confused, upset little girl who will be a problem for some time.

. . .

When we were young my sisters and I were not allowed to play indoors on nice days. "Out, out," my mother would say, "it's a sin to waste good weather!"

We played with our neighborhood girl friends in the woods that began where our backyards ended. These woods were for us a magical place, a place where adults never entered. One day it was Sherwood Forest and we were Robin and his men; another day we were Indian squaws (in cowboy boots), tiptoeing among the trees silently, stealthily, Indian-style. We climbed the trees, pretending to be monkeys; built secret hideouts, pretending to be bandits; fed squirrels from our hands. We picked wild berries and mashed them to make baby food for our dolls. Our dollhouses were hollow trees.

We played in the woods almost every day, from the time we finished breakfast until the twelve o'clock whistle sent us home for lunch, from after our afternoon naps until dinner, from after dinner until dark. We played there for years, from early childhood until the onset of puberty, never tiring of our imaginary world, our limitless repertoire of made-up games, our own wonderland without fences or walls, furnished only with trees. In the woods we were happy and utterly free.

The Rhodesian children I met spent their days outside, and the way they played reminded me of my childhood. One weekend at Joymount when Whitney was with me, the children—Sue's four, my one, and Sue's neighbor's three, ranging in age from ten to three—produced a play from their collective imagination, which they called "The Magic Paint Pot." It was the

122

story of how the colors of the flowers came to be, and they p‹ formed it for me alone, as if I were an audience of hundreds.

They took it all quite seriously; they'd made their own props put together their own costumes, helped one another with makeup, carefully memorized their lines. Whitney was a pixie, assistant to the fairy queen; Dennis, one of Sue's twins, a little bird, the forest messenger; Sharon, one of Sue's neighbor's daughters, the ugly witch who tried to foil the plan; Jenny Lynn, Sue's eldest, the beautiful fairy queen; and all the rest were flowers, waiting for the fairy queen to paint them.

On another occasion, one evening when Sue and Alwyn were out, the children amused themselves by putting on a review, performing singly, in turn, at the bottom of the fan-shaped staircase in the foyer while the other children watched attentively from the stadiumlike stairs. One would dance, another sing, another recite poetry from memory. . . . At the end of each performance, the rest applauded enthusiastically.

Whitney was enthralled by these productions, as if she had never seen a group of children play. "Look at what the children are doing," she said to me excitedly once, as though she were no more a child than I. Awkward and unsure at first, watching the others and imitating their every move, she gradually entered this imaginative world and slowly began to share its freedom and joy.

• • •

The case, which was originally scheduled for April, was postponed at Jim's request for "more time to prepare." Meanwhile, my visits with Whitney grew increasingly difficult.

By mid-May, Whitney had become not only almost totally uncommunicative but also hostile toward me. She would slap me and push me away from her, shouting, "Why don't you go away and leave me alone!" and "My daddy's going to burn your house down with you in it!" and "You're *not* my mommy!" At times I wondered what I was fighting for, why I was staying.

I wrote to George in desperation: "If it was a billion dollars we were fighting over, I'd gladly tell him to keep it all and I'd be on the next plane home. But what good is my life if I can't live with myself? I must do all I can; I must."

I stayed. Not out of pride or principles alone; not only out of motherly love, which at times I thought was weakening; but mostly out of fear. I was afraid—because of what I knew, had heard, and seen—of the harm I felt Jim could do the rest of Whitney's life if she remained with him. And I was afraid, too, of the self-hatred that would torture me for the rest of my own life if I left without her.

• • •

The network of people working on my case formed a bridge that spanned nine thousand miles. George and I kept in close communication by letter, tape, cable, and trans-Atlantic telephone; George and Timothy Dunn, a young attorney in Mr. Lundy's office assigned to assist on my case, were in almost daily contact either by phone or in person. Mr. Lundy and Mr. Clarke corresponded frequently and voluminously regarding the legal documents required from the United States for the imminent Rhodesian trial. I saw Mr. Clarke every day; and occasionally he corresponded with George.

From what we could discern, Jim worked on his side of the case full-time. One afternoon when Whitney and I were visiting the Clarkes, Mr. Clarke asked Whitney, "What kind of work does your daddy do?" She answered, "My daddy goes to town every day to see that she—" she pointed to me "—won't take me away from him." Mr. Clarke told me he'd heard that the young attorney working on Jim's case at another law firm in Salisbury was on the verge of a nervous breakdown because of the demands Jim was placing on him.

Before Jim went to Johannesburg to engage an additional counsel, Mr. Clarke insisted on obtaining Jim's passport as a safeguard against his fleeing the country with Whitney. "Look at this," Mr. Clarke said to me after calling me into his office. I studied the passport carefully and saw that between February 1967, when he left the United States, and March 1968, when he settled in Rhodesia, Jim had traveled (with Whitney and his parents? I had no way of knowing) to the Netherlands, France, Portugal, England, Jamaica, Colombia, Brazil, and Senegal.

I thought of Whitney as a baby, spending a whole year living in different cities, different countries; absorbing, breathing, tasting her grandparents' and father's fear because they knew they were "fugitives from justice"; because Jim knew he was wanted by the FBI for "fleeing to avoid prosecution." And I thought—bitterly—of the FBI, who had assured me repeatedly they were "doing all they could." They told me they'd checked passports, but how could they have, I wondered, as I stared at Jim's passport in my shaking hands, when Jim took this one out in his own name, during the same month that he disappeared, holding the baby in the photograph, without a disguise, using his own handwriting?

"Where did he get that kind of money? And what would make a man go to such lengths?" Mr. Clarke asked rhetorically. He knew I had no answers.

The trial was finally scheduled for mid-June. As Mr. Clarke wrote in a characteristic letter to George:

The proceedings commencing on the 16th June will be for the purpose of satisfying the presiding judge as to where the truth lies in the conflicting stories that are before him in affidavit form. . . . The onus in this case rests fairly on Jason's shoulders, the position at Law being that Bonnie would be entitled to have the (U.S.) Custody Order confirmed by these Courts unless Jason can show that it is inimical to the interests of the child to have the Order confirmed. This, I feel, is an almost impossible onus for him to discharge. Really the only factor that he has in his favour is that he has had custody of the child for a period of two years, and that it would not be in the interests of the child to be disturbed at this stage. . . .

• • •

Saturday, June 14, 1969—Baby confused and upset. Said: "My daddy is going to court next week to keep you away from me because you are a nasty lady. . . ."

Sunday, June 15, 1969—Mrs. Staub, the probation officer, came and baby behaved badly toward me. Mrs. Staub took notes of what baby said against me. I went for a walk while W. napped, and she awoke while I was out and cried for me, Sue said. (W. upset most of the day.)

Monday, June 16, 1969—First day of trial . . .

. . .

How does it go? "If you can keep your head when all about you / Are losing theirs and blaming it on you / . . . If you can trust yourself when all men doubt you / . . . Or being lied about, don't deal in lies . . ."

"Now, Mrs. Jason," the advocate from Johannesburg continues. The small, black-robed, bewigged man strikes a rigid, professorial pose in front of me. *He has a face that's seldom known a smile . . . pale, fragile hands, like a girl's.* "Can you recall an incident which occurred in August of 1965 in which you, without provocation, became hysterical and locked yourself in the green bathroom of your marital residence, threatening to do away with yourself and your unborn child?"

"I may have been crying and I may have gone into the green bathroom to get away from my husband, but I—"

"Just answer yes or no, Mrs. Jason."

"It's impossible to answer your questions with a yes or a no, sir, because they are made up of part fact and part fiction twisted together—"

"Are you trying to evade the question?"

"No, sir, I'm trying to be honest."

"Well, I submit that there will be witnesses called to this stand who will testify to the whole truth of these incidents."

"That won't make them true, sir."

You are a lioness. Strong. This is a savage battle you will win. You will reclaim your cub. That's why you came. Listen. Think harder than you've ever thought before. Calmly reply. You are here now. You've arrived.

. . .

126

Monday, June 16, 1969 (cont'd)—In witness box all day. Very tiring. Came home and went to bed at 7 p.m. No visitation.

Tuesday, June 17, 1969—In witness box all day.

. . .

The Rhodesia Herald, June 17, 1969

U.S. WOMAN SEEKS CUSTODY OF CHILD

A young American woman told Mr. Justice Macaulay in a civil action which opened at the High Court, Salisbury, yesterday that more than two years ago her husband, from whom she was divorced, took out their infant daughter on one of his access "visitations" in America and vanished with the child. . . . She declared in court yesterday that she finally located her husband in Rhodesia. The case is expected to go on for several days. . . .

The Rhodesia Herald, June 18, 1969

AMERICAN WIFE RESUMES FIGHT FOR HER CHILD

Mrs. Bonnie Lee Jason (24), the young American mother who has come to Rhodesia to seek custody of her 3½-year-old daughter—whom she claims was taken by her ex-husband when on an access visit in February, 1967, and brought to Rhodesia—continued her evidence in the High Court, Salisbury, yesterday. . . . Wearing a brown dress and white hat, Mrs. Jason . . .

The Rhodesia Herald, June 19, 1969

AMERICAN MOTHER COMPLETES EVIDENCE

The young American mother who is in Rhodesia seeking legal custody of her 3½-year-old daughter, who disappeared from her care in America more than two years ago, completed her evidence in the High Court, Salisbury, yesterday, after spending more than two days in the witness box. . . . Mr. Justice Macaulay asked her some questions concerning the change the child might have to go through. She said having her love would be advantageous to the child.

The case continues today.

. . .

Look at him. Look. Standing up there thin and bent. Looking like his father, only taller. See how he's aged. Watch him shift his weight, squirm from side to side, answering meekly, haltingly. Now his head is bending down, too heavy for his neck, it seems. His ill-fitting suit, too, hangs heavily, like his head. His face is pathetic, it screams for pity. Your heart goes out to him, strangely. . . . He says his wife was cruel, she beat the baby, bruising her, almost breaking her arm. He feared for the baby's life. What could he do? How sincere he is, how deeply felt his words ("I've waited all my life for you . . ."). *He seems to be about to weep. Watch him wipe his eyes and chew his lower lip. His wife, he says, was not right in the head. She said she hated him and hated the child and wanted to kill it. He had no choice: He had to take the child and go. He had to sell his practice, leave the country, break the law. But what is the law when the life of an innocent baby is at stake? . . . The judge interrupts:* "Would you please refrain from making speeches?" *The man in the stand mumbles something and hangs his head. Now your advocate is asking whether he ever planned to let the child's mother know where she was? Oh, yes, he says sincerely, when the child turned nineteen he planned to contact the mother—when the child was too old to be adversely affected by her. Oh, yes, he had it all planned; yes, that was part of his plan. . . . Poor man . . .*

But wait! WAIT! You are forgetting something!

Judge, please look at me, look into my eyes. Would I have hurt my baby? If I hated her, would I be here now? Judge, I know he seems sincere. He thinks he is telling the truth. He has convinced himself that he is right; no, more than right: righteous. Judge, Judge, how will you know? How will you be able to understand, when I was there in person, and I don't understand?

Deep breaths. Feet together. Fold your hands.

Look at him now, choking back his tears, saying he takes her to church every Sunday, sits with her in Sunday school, provides her with a home and a fenced-in yard to play in, loving grandparents who live with him. . . . Your whole body is shaking. ("I'm going to have you put away. . . . I'm going to take that baby away from you and give it to my mother.") *Look at him. So humble and sincere, but not sorry. He truly believes he has done nothing wrong. . . .*

Poor man, I feel sorry for you. And, Judge, if you believe what he is saying, I will understand. I believed him once, too.

· · ·

Jim's mother and father and fiancée take their turns in the witness stand. His parents echo all that Jim has said, with equal, heartfelt sincerity. (I see his mother pointing to my pregnant belly in the kitchen of Jim's home on Summit Avenue: *"God is going to curse that baby!"*)

Jim's fiancée is small, slightly built, dark-haired, well-dressed, soft-spoken. She sweetly tells of her close relationship with Whitney. She tells the court she makes most of Whitney's dresses—and that Whitney calls her Mommy. *What am I doing here?* I wonder. *Whose nest have I shaken from the tree?*

Jim paid for his friend Jerry to fly out from America to testify against me. Like a squirrel pinioned by a headlight beam, Jerry stands paralyzed in the witness box answering timidly the questions Jim's advocate puts to him. Jerry says "yeth" to the incident that was supposed to have taken place in the green bathroom, "yeth" to the immorality of my friends and family, "yeth" to my neglect and maltreatment of my baby, "yeth" to my mental instability. As I sit in the courtroom beside Mr. Clarke, I wonder what would drive a man like Jerry to come so far to say so little.

Now Jim's advocate is summing up: He cites several cases in which the custody of a minor child was given to the father in preference to the mother. . . . "Despite the lack of mother care from Mrs. Bonnie Jason, this child has been given excellent care . . ."

Now he is dealing with the question of "future prospects." Jim, he says, will be getting married soon; his fiancée is a "responsible, independent, level-headed girl with a *stable family background.*" If I, on the other hand, return to the States, "there is a significant probability that the child will come in contact with Mrs. Jason's family and friends. . . ."

And if I stay in Rhodesia, "probably a flat will be the only accommodation she could provide . . . she would have to work and no details have been given as to where the child would be during the day . . . she's inexperienced in relation to costs, providing a home, domestic help . . . this will lead to difficulties. . . ." He goes on:

The probation officer gave me a favorable report only because I was seen in an "unreal situation"—the luxurious home where I'm living. I'm emotionally unstable—the cause of the trouble between Jim's parents and myself was my immaturity; I was in fact "the guilty party in America. . . ."

On Wednesday, June 25, I wrote to my mother:

The trial is now finished, and believe me, I feel finished as well. . . . After court yesterday I felt so drained I thought my legs wouldn't carry me. I felt like crumbling in a heap. . . . Instead, I had to hold my head up and walk calmly out of the courtroom (where I aged ten years in seven days!) and go back to the office.

I'm afraid, Mom, I'm not the same girl who said good-bye to you at JFK on March 22. This experience has really taught me a lot, and I guess I've changed in the process. Whatever the outcome, I'll be grateful for the experience. . . . Whatever happens will be for the best.

• • •

The Rhodesia Herald, June 25, 1969

JUDGEMENT WITHIN TWO WEEKS
IN 'BABY CUSTODY' HEARING

At the end of the seven-day hearing in the High Court, Salisbury, yesterday in the action in which Mrs. Bonnie Lee Jason is claiming custody of her child from Mr. A. James Jason, Mr. Justice Macaulay said that he would give judgement within the next fortnight.

It was a tangled case and a difficult one to decide, he said. . . .

. . .

This case had become something of a cause célèbre in Salisbury. In eight days, the *Herald* devoted a total of 124 inches of space to the case. Little girls, recognizing me from my picture in the paper, stopped me on the sidewalk and asked for my autograph. Other people nodded and smiled, or pointed to me, as if I couldn't see, and whispered. I overheard one elderly woman tell her friend as I walked by, "That's the girl who beats her baby."

The Sunday paper of June 29 had a large photo of Whitney and me on the front cover, with a ten-inch article beneath:

BLONDE BONNIE AWAITS HIGH COURT VERDICT

As she hugged her three-year-old daughter last week, attractive blonde Mrs. Bonnie Lee Jason waited tensely to hear whether a frantic 9,000-mile flight from America and a seven-day Salisbury High Court battle for custody of her child had been successful. A few miles away, her ex-husband . . . was also waiting for the court's verdict. . . .

. . .

Jim and I never actually conversed. We communicated, as if we didn't speak the same language, through interpreters, our attorneys. But one day, while we waited for the judgment to be given, Mr. Clarke told me, "He wants to have a meeting with you."

"Alone?"

"Yes. He says he wants to meet you for coffee."

"Why?"

"My guess is he has something up his bloody sleeve."

"Should I go?"

"I would . . . out of curiosity."

Meikles Hotel in the center of Salisbury is as large and grand as the homestead on an antebellum plantation. It has large potted plants along the corridors, slow-moving ceiling fans, and a

131

battalion of busy black waiters in maroon jackets and fezzes. I met Jim there on Monday morning, and we sat, incongruously casual, in comfortably cushioned white wicker chairs in front of a low round table. Jim raised his arm to attract a waiter. I crossed my legs carefully, deliberately, remembering how he'd once said my legs were the best part of me.

As I opened my bag to look for my cigarettes, I tried to remember the last time we'd been alone together at a table having a conversation over coffee. *In 1965, in the breakfast nook of the house on Summit Avenue?* No, they weren't conversations; they were briefings. *In 1964, in the dining room of the Fairmont Hotel in San Francisco the morning after our wedding?* He was talking to me; yes, I could see him, I could still see him laughing coarsely across the table; but I couldn't remember saying anything in return. All I could remember was how painful it was to sit down. . . .

I smoothed my skirt and leaned back in my chair, trying to appear confident and poised. I took a cigarette from my pack and Jim quickly reached over to light it for me.

"You smoke?" he said.

"Oh, yes." (Sue had said in the midst of the trial: "Here, have a cigarette. It will calm your nerves." Then I bought a pack of my own.)

Jim had told the court I was a religious fanatic, that we'd spent our whole honeymoon in Hawaii in our hotel room, where I insisted on reading the Bible aloud to him, that I didn't approve of drinking or smoking, that I'd forced him to relinquish both of these pleasures against his will. . . .

I inhaled deeply and blew the smoke above his head.

"You wanted to talk?" I said.

"Yes. I thought we could come to an arrangement—"

The waiter came to our table with a round tray containing two small white porcelain cups and saucers, a bowl of sugar cubes, and two identical metal pots filled with steaming liquid. I took a pot in each hand and simultaneously poured into each cup the hot milk and hot black coffee for both Jim and me. My hands, somehow, were steady. *Where was the jagged bottle, the catlike attack, the waking before his face bled?*

132

"What kind of an arrangement?" I said.

"I thought you and I could come to some, some—" He fumbled for the words. His face was contorted, his eyes dull. (*"Are you on tranquilizers, Mr. Jason?" my advocate had asked him repeatedly during his cross-examination. "You seem to be having difficulty focusing on my questions."*) "—some agreement regarding the future of our child."

"What about the judge's decision?"

"If we were to present him with our own equitable and just solution, he would have to honor it."

"What sort of solution did you have in mind?"

"We could agree to joint custody—six months with you and six months with me—"

"I don't believe in cutting a child in half," I said firmly. "It wouldn't work—not with *us*. No, I'm sorry. No. I prefer to wait for the judg—"

"But she is my child as much as she is yours—it should be fifty-fifty!"

"*Oh?*" I lowered my voice and leaned forward. "What about the past two years? Did you think then—?"

"I thought about you. Every day. I couldn't sleep at night."

I saw the ashtray by his side of our king-size bed. I saw myself pick it up to empty it in the morning, but before I did, I counted the butts—three . . . eight . . . fifteen . . . twenty . . .

Who is this man, and what am I doing here with him? If only I could wake from this dream. . . .

That afternoon I learned that the judge's decision would be given the next morning at nine.

•   •   •

As soon as I learned, they were there—with their note pads, flash attachments, questions. All I wanted was to get past them, to go to the ladies' room, wash my face, blow my nose. But they were blocking the doorway to the hall. June, the receptionist, had asked them politely to leave, but they wouldn't listen. I felt exposed, invaded, encircled, dumb. They wanted quotable answers, a punchy lead. I wanted to splash my face with cold water, be alone in the ladies' room, smoke a cigarette, say a prayer.

The next morning, July 2, there was a large photo of my tearful face on the front cover of the *Herald*, and everyone in Rhodesia learned the news:

AMERICAN MOTHER WINS CUSTODY
OF HER DAUGHTER

Mrs. Bonnie Lee Jason, the young American mother who fought a seven-day battle in the High Court, Salisbury, for the custody of her three-year-old daughter, Whitney Lee, has won her case. Yesterday Mr. Justice Macaulay found in her favour. She was not in court to hear him deliver judgement.

Mrs. Jason . . . told *The Rhodesia Herald:* "I have been crying for joy ever since I heard it. . . . I shall be picking up my daughter later in the day. It is all a wonderful relief."

Mrs. Jason was still tear-stained when a reporter spoke to her. She gave the impression of not fully realising that her long suit in the High Court was finally over.

Mr. Justice Macaulay, at the end of a lengthy judgement, said the mother would be awarded custody; the child would remain within the jurisdiction of the court—that is, within Rhodesia. Mr. Jason was entitled to reasonable access and both parties would have a week to make written representations on the question of access arrangements before the judge gives a ruling on this aspect of his judgement.

Mr. Jason was ordered to pay the costs, and Mrs. Jason was declared a necessary witness. (This means her expenses from America to this country will be paid.)

Giving his judgement, the judge said . . . there was nothing in Mrs. Jason's past behaviour or in her present character, now that the strain of an unhappy marriage had been removed, to justify the view that she was incapable of being the custodian of the child. . . .

Mrs. Jason had said she would not leave the child, whatever the result of the case might be. She had obtained some temporary work and she was competent to secure a position in the commercial world and provide a flat where she and the child could live. . . .

He was satisfied that the child's material welfare would be fully and adequately catered for in this country. It was also desirable that the child should continue to have contact with her father and grandparents.

134

The child must not be removed from this country, said the judge. This called for sacrifice on the part of the mother—and she was prepared to make this sacrifice.

• • •

As the people of Rhodesia read their morning newspaper and drank their first cup of tea, brought to the bedroom on a breakfast tray by the "houseboy," nine thousand miles away my mother was receiving a phone call from George, relaying the news he'd received in my cable—that I had won the case, but as long as Jim stayed in Rhodesia I had to remain there also.

I had won the case, fairly, and I felt, justly. The battle had ended, justice was done, a young mother had fought for her child and won: To some this was a storybook happy ending. But I had no sense of victory. When Jim drove up Joymount's long winding driveway to deliver Whitney, who was crying hysterically, I wasn't sure what, in fact, I *had* won or what Whitney had gained by my winning.

"Daddy, don't go; don't leave me, Daddy!" Whitney screamed.

"There, there, be a brave soldier," he told her, clutching her tightly against his chest, capping her head with his hand, not letting go; while I stood by helplessly, hands at my sides, silently clawing the air.

The Pichanicks' children, and their African servants, who had never seen us exchange Whitney before because this process had always taken place at Jim's, watched this scene with horror. "What is happening to the little girl?" their faces asked. "Who is hurting her?" And although they never said a word, I felt I could read Sue and Alwyn's thoughts: "How much more of this must we endure?"

In the quietness of my bedroom at Joymount, long after Jim had driven off like a man who'd accomplished his mission, and Whitney had been calmed and soothed, bathed and put to bed,

I found I had to confront the truth, not the happy storybook ending.

In the three months following my arrival, Whitney had changed. No longer the happy, carefree, laughing child I played with on our reunion, she'd become increasingly somber, laconic, and angry when with me. It was as if at that first meeting we were facing one another, smiling, with our arms outstretched but not yet touching; and now, in July, she was far away, almost out of sight, with her back to me—while I stood with my hands at my sides, watching helplessly.

Nothing in the child psychology book I brought with me could have prepared me for this. I had always liked children and they seemed to like me. Except for the previous two years, when I'd avoided children because it was too painful to be with them *(Was that it? Was I out of practice, out of touch?)*, I'd instinctively known what to say and do to win a child over, soothe a bruised knee, coax peas into a zippered mouth, share a silly joke or a tall story. But none of the children I'd known had been instructed not to listen to me or speak to me, none of them had been taught that I was "a nasty lady" who had come to take them away.

Whitney's reaction was understandable but nonetheless devastating: She seemed to hate me. How else could I interpret the cold resentment in her eyes, the winter storm that settled on her face and constricted her brows in anger, the way she ignored everything I said and pulled away from me when I came near?

I told myself it would take time and love to win her back. I braced myself for a long and rocky uphill climb. But there were moments, too, when I was sorry I'd re-entered her life, when I wondered whether it would have been better to have left her with her father, to leave "well enough" alone. My feelings of inadequacy and despondency led to feelings of guilt: *What kind of a mother was I to have these thoughts? What kind of a life would she have if he was allowed to continue to twist her mind? How could I abandon her now, after the judge decided she should be with me?*

And yet, the fact remained, we were immeasurably estranged. When I looked at her I saw a blond, blue-eyed, three-

and-a-half-year-old stranger who could have been anyone's daughter. And though I ransacked my heart to find the feeling I'd had before she was abducted—the feeling that our lives were linked by an invisible, indestructible cord through which the purest form of love flowed back and forth—I couldn't find it. It wasn't there. *It will come back,* I told myself, *in time.* But at that time, at that crucial time after the judgment was given, when Whitney's whole being seemed at times to be flooded with anger, resentment, and hatred, I could only feel the unutterable fear that although I'd won this case, I'd lost my child.

• • •

It was clear I could no longer stay at Joymount. The Pichanicks had graciously allowed me to live in their home rent-free for the three months prior to the trial; and I felt deeply indebted to them, knowing that without their kind hospitality I would not have been able to afford to stay in Rhodesia long enough to fight my case. But after judgment was given, when Whitney came to live with me there, and I stayed at home to care for her, I felt I couldn't impose on the Pichanicks' kindness any longer.

I knew that I had started a new life with Whitney once before, and I managed all right then. I got an apartment, a job, a babysitter, a car; and I gradually accumulated furniture and made a home for myself and my baby—all by myself. But now I was in a foreign country where I didn't know the cost of living, didn't have any means of support, didn't know where to put my child during the day (and how, I wondered, could I prove to the courts in Rhodesia that she'd adjusted to me if I spent all day away from her and she spent most of the weekend with her father?). I looked in vain for a job, and found apartment-hunting almost impossible. I felt alone and helpless; in my blackest moments I wondered whether I shouldn't go home, without the baby, and forget the name Jason forever—for the baby's sake. The hold that Jim still had on me was inescapable. He still held the strings, and as he pulled, I jumped.

———

Then, with a sudden stroke of good fortune, I found a place for Whitney and me to live for the duration of our stay in Rhodesia. The newspaper ad said: "Centrally located furnished flat, all utilities included, £20 per month." As soon as I saw the place, I took it.

Without my even asking, my Rhodesian friends generously loaned me everything I needed to set up house: One woman let me borrow her old Singer sewing machine, another gave me linens; and my advocate's wife, Anne, brought over two big boxes of things—pots, pans, dishes, cups, saucers, spoons, forks, mixing bowls, sheets, blankets, pillows.

• • •

Two and a half years after Whitney waved good-bye to me from her father's arms as they descended the stairs of the apartment she and I shared in my hometown, we were together, just the two of us, under one roof again. But this roof was corrugated metal that helmeted a single-story, sprawling house on a scraggly patch of land on the corner of Fife and Blakiston avenues near the center of Salisbury, Rhodesia—nine thousand miles away from home.

Our living arrangements at the Fife Avenue flat were unlike anything I'd ever experienced or could have imagined. The kitchen, for example, had no hot water. To wash dishes we poured boiling water into the sink from the large aluminum kettle kept busy on the stove. I say "we" because I shared the kitchen with the house's two African caretakers, Noah and Joseph, who prepared their meals there, as well as the morning tea that they took to each tenant's room.

The stove, too, was unlike any other I'd ever seen. The day Whitney and I moved in I asked Noah, a soft-spoken, gentle-faced man in his early twenties, to teach me how to use it. Noah lifted the heavy cast-iron lid on the right that covered one of the two top burner plates and explained, "This side is hot, madam." Then he lifted the lid on the left. "And this side—is hot-hot."

"And the oven?" I said. The two doors beneath the burners looked as if they belonged on the brick wall of an old bakery.

139

Noah patiently repeated his explanation, opening the oven door on the right. "This side, madam, is hot. And this one"— he pointed to the door on the left—"is hot-hot."

I knew there would be no use asking which side of the oven I should use to bake a cake, or how long I should bake it. There were no knobs or temperature gauges anywhere; nothing so scientific. I realized that cooking on this cast-iron stove—like so many other aspects of my new life there with Whitney—would be a daily challenge, requiring patience, determination, guesswork, and good humor.

Old wooden cupboards, sagging under innumerable coats of cream-colored paint, lined the narrow passageway that led to our living room. When I asked Joseph, the other caretaker, about the white powder covering the cupboard shelves, he told me it was "mooti" (medicine) to kill the "ho-ho's" (bugs). The medicine, I later learned, was a homemade mixture of baking soda and scouring powder; and the bugs were cockroaches— the first cockroaches I'd ever seen.

Whitney and I also shared the bathroom, located across the hall from our living room, with the other tenants, who, for the most part, were shadowy, solitary old men in dark suits who kept odd hours and bathed only once a week. So at six-thirty every evening, which became bath-time for Whitney and me, we'd invariably find the old-fashioned, white-tiled bathroom utterly free.

Two large adjoining rooms—the living room and the verandah—were our own. The living room, which was also my bedroom, contained a threadbare red-patterned Oriental carpet; a functioning white-manteled, corner fireplace; a tired daybed slipcovered in red, with two wobbly tables at each end of it; and an ancient chifforobe, probably brought out from England by an early settler.

The sunny enclosed verandah facing Fife Avenue became Whitney's bedroom and playroom. We put her toys—the few that Jim had given me, and the things she and I later bought on our daily walks to town, the baby doll and storybooks and plastic tea set—on the shelves beneath the louvered windows,

140

all within her reach. And we decorated the blank walls of her room with alphabet-and-number posters we made one afternoon together—I lettering and drawing the pictures on separate sheets of white construction paper (capital A in the upper left, lower-case a to the right of it, drawing of one fat apple in the center, the number 1 at the bottom right; capital B, lower-case b, drawing of two balloons and the number 2; c, carrot, three carrots, and so on) and Whitney coloring in the drawings.

Our new home was unquestionably primitive by American standards—no telephone or television, radio or radiators, private bath, gas range, or hot tap water—but it was clean and safe, close to town, temporary, and cheap: the equivalent of forty U.S. dollars per month. And here, far more than in the comfort and anywhere-in-the-world affluence I had known at Joymount, I felt more connected to Africa, closer to its earth, more in tempo with its elemental beat. This, I thought, as I looked around the flat laughing to myself, is where Sheena of the Jungle might live.

To have a place, however humble, of our own; to be with Whitney after our unnatural separation; to function as a mother again on a day-to-day basis, despite the obvious hurdles and handicaps that confronted us; to live where time was slower, pressures fewer, and friends friendlier made me happier than I had been since Whitney was newborn. And my happiness, I could see, infected Whitney.

During these weeks Mr. Clarke and Jim's attorneys were negotiating agreements that would allow us to return home to the United States. Feeling that we would soon be uprooting ourselves from Rhodesia, I didn't work; instead, Whitney and I spent every moment of every day—except for the hours when she visited her father—together. I tried to make each day an adventure, which wasn't hard to do because so much of the city was still new to me, too, and I was anxious to explore it; and I tried to think of all the things we could do together that might please her.

At the top of my sure-to-please list was meals. Knowing how much Whitney had always enjoyed eating, how badly Jim's mother cooked, how inexpensive farm-fresh groceries were in Rhodesia, and how much fun it could be to experiment on our mysterious old stove, I spent hours planning and preparing special meals she would enjoy.

While Whitney sat quietly at the kitchen table looking up at me quizzically, I pretended I was a famous chef and she was my cooking class: "Today, ladies," I said nasally, "we will be making a delicious breakfast of Frrrench toast. Have you ever had Frrrench toast, ladies?"

Whitney, smiling as if I'd gone mad, shook her head.

"Nevah? Evah? Well, you haven't *lived* until you've breakfasted on Frrrench toast!" I leaned across the table and kissed Whitney's nose; she giggled, put her hands to her face and pulled away. "First—now watch this, this is like a magic trick— you take one fat Humpty-Dumpty egg in one hand—like this— and crack it gently—CRACK!—against the side of this little bo-ell, and then you shake your hand above the bo-ell like this, and then, presto—PLOP—magic! Raw-egg-in-the-bowl, one-handed! Now, we throw the shell away and add a little milk to the raw egg. Would you care to pour it in for me, ladies? Yes, that's it. Little more . . . little more . . . stop! Fine. Thenk-you-veddy-much. To this bowl of milk and egg we add a big pinch of sugar—PLUNK—and a dab of vanilla. Smell this bottle of vanilla, ladies, isn't it just *perfume?*"

I circled the opening of the vanilla bottle with my right forefinger and touched behind my ears while Whitney watched in open-mouthed amazement.

"And now we beat it! Here is a fork, ladies. Beat it well, but be careful not to beat it to death! Good, good, good. Now you take this old bread—old bread is best—and drop it into the mixture—see how it puffs up like a sponge?—and then you— come with me, ladies—place it in your lightly oiled frying pan which has been waiting evah-so-patiently on the not-as-hot-as-the-other burner and you count to—what number shall we count to? Nineteen you say? All right—and you count to nineteen and see whether it's ready to be turned over . . ."

"Do you like the French toast?"

"Mmmmmmmm."

"When my youngest sister—your aunt—was a little girl—a

142

few years older than you are—I used to make her French toast on Saturday mornings. Do you know how many slices she would eat?"

Whitney shook her head.

"Eight! How many is eight?"

She showed me with her fingers. "These many."

"That many, that's right."

She took another bite and chewed it thoughtfully. "You're a good cooker," she said.

After breakfast every day we walked into town, through the Children's Park, past the outdoor aviary, across Salisbury Gardens, stopping to greet the birds, play on the swings and slides, admire the manicured shrubbery and beds of multicolored flowers. One day, soon after we began this daily regimen, Whitney released my hand and walked gingerly to the top of a large flat rock that rose only three or four inches above the ground.

"Mommy," she said, "do you think I could jump from here?"

"Sure you can. It's not very high."

"But what if I fall down?"

"You won't fall, honey—"

"But what if I do? Will I hurt myself? Will I have to go to the hostpital?"

"No, silly," I laughed. I couldn't understand her unfounded fears.

"But what will happen?" she said, standing rigidly on the edge of the rock.

"If you jump, you probably won't fall; but if you do fall down, you won't hurt yourself badly. You won't have to go to the hospital. You'll just pick yourself up and try again. There's no need to be afraid."

Whitney jumped from the rock and didn't fall, then she looked at me and smiled a smile I hadn't seen on her before. It was the smile of an innocent prisoner set free. And then her hesitancy made sense to me: In the overprotected atmosphere of Jim's home, raised by Jim's mother, who was then over sev-

143

enty, Whitney had obviously been prevented from playing freely and spontaneously, out of fear of physical harm. It seemed as if she'd never been allowed to test her legs; as if she'd been carried or carted everywhere.

While she was living with her father and grandparents, Whitney's hair had been kept short, as short as a boy's; and Jim's mother often dressed Whitney in boys' clothes—short-sleeved sport shirts, boxy shorts, little boys' brown shoes and short beige socks. Although she wasn't overweight, her body was puffy and soft; and her skin seemed to me to be too pale for a child growing up in such a sunny climate. Before the case went to court, I could say or do little about this, or any other aspect of the way they were raising her; but afterward it became my campaign slowly and lovingly to transform this pudgy, pale, overprotected, androgynous child into a healthy, happy, and playful pretty little girl.

Poor little thing, I thought as I watched her run awkwardly from the cement-pipe caterpillar to the swings, *to be caught between such different people, taken by one and molded one way, then reclaimed by the other and again reshaped. Where have you traveled? What have you seen? What have they fed you and taught you? How have they shaped your life thus far? What can I do to make this transition easier for you? What else can I do but be myself?*

And who was "myself," the stranger thrust on Whitney? A stubborn, independent person of twenty-four. Strong-willed, like her German grandmother. Becoming more and more free-spirited, as her mother was when she was young. Her fair hair, bleached almost white by their daily walks in the sun, was growing long; her skin becoming golden-tanned; her face full and happy. For the first time in her life she actually admired herself in the mirror. And in town she saw, though she didn't let it show, that people turned their heads when, walking hand in hand, she and Whitney passed by. Perhaps her quantum leap into self-confidence after flying to Africa and fighting her case had landed her on the edge of arrogance. Had she become too proud?

———

Whitney and I walked for hours, sometimes stopping to see the latest exhibit at the National Art Gallery, sometimes shopping for clothes for her at Barbour's department store or for inexpensive toys at O.K. Bazaars. Jim had given me only a few of her toys, a couple of the cotton sundresses his fiancée had made, which were not warm enough for the current cool weather, and some of the boys' clothes already described. Although I didn't have much money left, I knew this wouldn't do.

"Cute little boy you've got there," strangers would say when, in the beginning, I dressed Whitney in the trousers Jim had given me.

Using the borrowed sewing machine, I made Whitney several jumpers from one simple pattern and good-quality fabric bought on sale. I bought her three turtleneck pullovers, two pretty cotton blouses, several pairs of knee socks and frilly panties—all in matching pastel colors—to wear with the jumpers during the cooler weather. I told her we'd let her hair grow long, past her shoulders, like mine.

For the most part, Whitney seemed to like her new life, her new partnership with me. Sometimes, though, she made comparisons and found my life-style wanting: "Why can't we *drive* into town in a car? My daddy has a car. . . ." ("Because walking is good for your legs. It makes them strong and beautiful. . . .") and "Why don't we have our *own* house? My daddy has a house. . . ." ("Your daddy has a *rented* house, and we have part of a rented house. We don't need as much space as your daddy does."). On the whole, however, I found her adaptability remarkable. Between her scheduled visitations with Jim she seldom mentioned him. She never mentioned her grandparents. She didn't seem to miss them.

Leisurely breakfasts, walks to the office, lunch at the open-air restaurant in Salisbury Gardens, then home for a nap—this became our daily routine. On Tuesday and Thursday afternoons we visited friends, and on the other days, from four to six-thirty, and overnight on weekends, Whitney was with Jim.

As he had when he'd returned Whitney to Joymount, Jim returned Whitney to my flat at six-thirty and would not readily let her go. Standing at the open door he held her tightly, patting her on the back, while she cried, "DADDY, DADDY, DADDY!"

"There, there, be a brave soldier, Babe—"

"Jim, please put Whitney down—"

"DADDY, DON'T LEAVE ME, DADDY!"

"But you must be a brave soldier—"

"She is not going to war, Jim. Please put her down so she can come in and stop crying. Please. You're only making things worse—"

It was impossible for me to reason with him. He just stood, clutching her, sadly repeating in her ear, " . . . brave soldier . . . brave . . ." Seeing this filled me with helpless rage. I wanted to kick him, beat him with my fists, scream in his ear, *LET GO! WILL YOU LET GO OF HER!* but there was nothing I could do to him that would not in turn hurt Whitney. Her body wrapped him like a coat of mail. And didn't he want me to hit him? Wasn't that what his witnesses, watching from his car, were waiting for? He probably had their affidavits already typed and signed. I bit my bottom lip, kept my clenched fists at my sides, and stood there facing him, helpless and immobile.

"DADDY, DADDY, DADDY, DON'T GO!"

"Please put her down, Jim." My voice became a hiss. My stomach churned with crystallized anger, like chunks of broken glass.

Pitifully, heavily, he released his grip and bent to let her feet touch the ground. Quickly, the way one whisks off a bandage so as not to prolong the pain, I took her by the hand and led her in.

Sitting in my lawyer's office, Jim's lawyer said to me, "Don't you think you should bury the hatchet now? You won the case. You got what you came for. Be big about this. Forget the past and forgive—"

I looked at Mr. Clarke, who was looking away, and then at Jim, who reminded me of Jackie Gleason's "Poor Soul" character; but the only ones in the room who were familiar with Gleason's act were Jim and I. And who was I? A young woman, a mere secretary, surrounded by three college-educated, dark-suited, professional men—lawyers—all many years older than I.

"—just have to sign these letters we've prepared," his lawyer went on, "addressed to your county judge and prosecutor back in the States, requesting them to drop charges against Jim now that you've got your daughter back and all is well—"

Jim wrung his hands and hung his head, staring into his lap. *Why did I ever marry him?* I thought. *Why? Why?!*

"—that way your husband—excuse me, I mean, your former husband—will be able to pick up where he left off instead of going to prison, which surely would be a blot on—"

George had said: *"If you let him return to the States, I don't want to be part of the picture."* My mother had said: *"That man should be punished for the harm he's done."* Whitney said repeatedly: *"Daddy, don't leave me, don't leave me!"* And I sat in my lawyer's office, speechless.

"—and certainly you realize that if Jim went to prison he wouldn't be able to pay any child support. In addition to which, Whitney would be deprived of her father's love—which, as his lordship Justice Macaulay found in his judgment, is vital to the well-being of—"

I signed the papers dropping charges against Jim, not because I had forgiven him, but because I felt I had no other choice, and I wanted to go home again. Now, all that stalled our departure was an agreement as to visitation and child support in America. The negotiations progressed frustratingly slowly. Jim was bargaining for what I considered to be more-than-liberal visitation rights and less-than-adequate child support payments. But I chose to leave these dealings in Mr. Clarke's hands and to concentrate on Whitney.

· · ·

"What kind of flowers are these, Mommy?"

"These are poppies. What color is this one?"

"ORNGE."

"Orange, yes."

"And these ones? What are they called?"

"These are daisies—they're my favorite. Do you know how they got their name?"

Whitney shook her head.

"Look at this one—see the yellow center, like the sun, and the petals radiating out of it—like sunbeams? Well, the name 'daisy' comes from *day's eye*—the sun is the eye of the day."

"Oh," she said flatly and pointed to the row to our right. "What kind are these?"

"These are snapDRAGONS!" I tried to sound dragon-fierce, and Whitney giggled. "I'll show you why. If you take one . . . and gently squeeze it—like this—between your fingers, it opens up like a dragon's mouth. . . . You try it now."

Suddenly my mind slipped backward twenty years. I heard my mother's voice say, ". . . and this is a snapdragon . . ." and I saw her pretty hand with its tapered, polished nails take one of the flowers and press it gently to open its mouth. *"But they're good dragons,"* my mother said, laughing.

"But they're good dragons," I said to Whitney.

We walked hand in hand along the winding unpaved path that cut through the park—past the aloes and canna lilies, the bougainvillea and masasa trees, past the goldfish pond and sculpted hedges, the war-memorial obelisk and the African gardeners in khaki uniforms pulling weeds—and stopped at the aviary on our way home.

"Those are parrots," Whitney said, pointing up to two small green birds sitting close together on the dowel swing suspended by nylon string in their nature-simulating cage.

"They look like parrots, don't they. But parrots are much, much bigger than these little birds. These are called Nyasaland Love Birds. Can you say that name?"

Whitney tried.

"They're called love birds because they love each other so much they can't bear to be separated. When something happens to one of them—if one of them dies or is taken away—the other one gets sick and loses all of his feathers out of grief—"

"What is *reef?*"

"*Grief* is when we're very, very sad because we've lost something or someone that we love."

"Does it make you cry?"

"Yes, grief makes you cry."

"Then my daddy has griefs. He says he cries for me every day I'm at your house. He does."

All the way home—across Moffat Street, along Rhodes Avenue to Blakiston, and up one short block to Fife—I couldn't think of anything to say.

• • •

Sometimes it was difficult to talk with Whitney. When we fell into pockets of silence, I'd think: *What do other mothers say to their three-and-a-half-year-olds when they're alone? Do they ever have to strain for words? What did my mother say to me when I was that age?* I couldn't recollect a conversation. She'd say: "Go outside and play now, girls; it's a beautiful day. Mommy has housework to do." So my sisters and I did as we were told and talked and laughed and played among ourselves. But Whitney had no siblings, and I no excuse of housework. So I had to grope and grapple for the right words to bridge the silences between us.

Certain topics, I felt, were best avoided. For example, I tried not to ask her questions about her life with Jim and his parents, as much as it might have been helpful to me to know more about their life-style and routine and how it affected Whitney. I thought that the less she had to dwell on the recent past, the better. And I never discussed Jim. I knew she loved him and was trying her best to be loyal; I didn't want to say or do anything that would force her to take sides.

I couldn't talk with her about the future because it was still utterly uncertain. Could I tell her she'd be meeting her other grandmother, her aunts and uncles and cousins soon? That we'd soon be returning to America, where she lived when she was a baby? I couldn't, because I didn't know when or whether that would be, and I didn't want to raise her hopes or apprehensions prematurely or needlessly.

If we had talked about the distant past, what our life together had been like when she was a baby, the question would surely have arisen: Where had I been since then? And, since I felt I couldn't answer that question fully or honestly without accusing Jim, I skirted this subject as well—at least for the time being. I knew that to Whitney, who had no memory of her early life with me, and whose memory embraced only Jim, his parents, and their home in Rhodesia, I was the guilty one—I took her away from him. But she seemed willing, after a while, to give me a fair trial. After her understandable anger and confusion subsided, she displayed toward me a great deal of mercy.

Our conversations, then, concentrated on the present, the "here" and "this" and "now" of our days. And when I felt unsure of my lines as a mother (*What would another mother say now? . . . I don't know*), I tried to talk to her as a sister or a friend.

One place where our communion was most sisterly was in the bath. Rather than bathe her from outside of the tub, which I felt would be treating her like a baby, I chose to bathe *with* her, so that we could face each other in naked honesty, her outstretched legs between mine, and talk quietly within the confines of the tub's walls and the privacy of the locked and bolted bathroom.

"What are those?"

"Which? These? These are breasts . . . small breasts."

"Not as little as mine."

"True. But when you get to be a big girl, you'll have bigger ones, I'm sure. Maybe like your na-na's."

"When?"

"In about ten years or so."

"Oh."

"When I was a little girl I used to take baths with my sister like this. We used to pretend we were in a sailboat. . . . Now, let's wash ourselves. Take the washcloth—"

"The flannel."

"Yes, same thing. Take the flannel . . . soap it up, like this . . . and begin with your face—"

"Why?"

"Because we must wash from top to bottom—first the face, then the neck, then the arms, then the tummy, then the back, then the bottom, then the legs, then the filthy little feet."

"Why?"

"Because if we washed our feet first—see how dirty your feet get from walking all day in sandals?—the water would be too muddy to make our pretty faces clean. . . . Now show me how you wash yourself. . . . That's it—"

Like strangers at sea in a small craft, we grew closer in the tub, and we seemed to be sailing in the right direction.

But something happened when Whitney visited Jim, especially on weekends. For every step up she and I made in our relationship, her visits with him and his parents pulled her back down again. Jim would tell her how he cried while she was gone; he slept in the same bed with her when she visited. Always when he brought her back she'd be hysterically crying, and on several occasions she was so emotionally overwrought she became ill.

Sunday, 5:45 p.m. A knock at my door: Joseph, usually so stately, tall, and strong, looks nervous, shriveled, worried: "Madam, the piccanin madam has come home. She is . . . she is—" "Where is she, Joseph?" He points to the street, and I rush past him out the door. There, by the side of the car, Whitney is bent over, vomiting into the gutter, gagging on her cries, gasping for air. Jim, beside her, stands helplessly, doing nothing, while his fiancée, like a small bird on a fragile limb, only twitters. Passersby congregate to gape. I think: *How cruel, how sick and despicable that he should allow this! That he should stand there, as if drunk or drugged, and do nothing to help her!* In my rage, as I run like a madwoman toward his car, I imagine that this, too, is part of his design: He wants me to put an end to this by giving up and giving her back to him. *He will stop at nothing.* Without a word, I scoop Whitney up and carry her into the kitchen, where I wash her face with cool tap water and try to speak soothingly above her choking sobs. Jim follows, lets himself in, and watches in feigned meekness. I am so angry I cannot speak to him. I see Joseph's handmade kitchen knife resting on the windowsill, and a terrifying chill sends shivers through my body: I imagine myself reaching for the knife and plunging it into Jim.

• • •

Listening to the Voice of America give details of the moon landing, I felt as if I were living on another sphere, farther than the moon from the planet Earth. The situation that existed in Rhodesia then curiously paralleled my own: It was a pretty bubble suspended somewhere in space. At odds with its neighbors to the east, west, and north; cut off economically and politically from the world community; far removed geographically from Europe and the United States, Rhodesia was a beautiful landlocked island, out of touch, out of time, paradisiacal and parochial. World news was available, of course, through the usual media; but what went on beyond Rhodesia's iridescent borders didn't seem to matter much to many of its citizens.

I too was suspended, cut off, and alien; feeling more and more ambivalent about going home. I felt bitter about the apparent ineffectuality of the FBI in handling my case (*If Jim hadn't virtually turned himself in,* I thought, *I'd still be home waiting*), and angry that the American Consulate in Salisbury had done nothing whatsoever to help me. When I looked at the United States from that distance then, I saw it in my mind as a middle-aged businessman, a large Anglo-Saxon man with close-cropped hair, wearing a dark suit; a powerful man, more interested in profits than people, and prepared to go to any lengths—including to the moon—to get his own way. . . . Africa, on the other hand, seemed like a large, old black woman, simple, guileless, and warm, who loved her pale foster children as much as she loved her own.

It was then that I began to love the life there. I loved cooking on my antiquated stove, taking my large basket to the market for fresh vegetables and fruit, walking with Whitney to town and to the park where we often had lunch at the outdoor café. We frequently had guests for dinner and often were invited for tea or lunch by my friends who had little children Whitney's age. Apart from the problems I had with Jim, it was a sunny, leisurely, stress-free life, conducive to health and well-being.

• • •

One morning after breakfast while I was standing at the stove—bringing soup stock to a quick boil on the left burner, then leaving the pot to simmer on the right—I heard an African woman laughing in the backyard. It was a laugh I hadn't heard before, an unforgettable laugh, the kind that makes you smile when you hear it—an earthy, deep, infectious, knee-slapping laugh, as thick as meat. When I went to the kitchen sink to wash my hands, I saw the laughing woman through the paneless window, sitting on the grass with Noah and Joseph in the shade of the avocado tree. The three were drinking tea from enamel mugs and talking animatedly in Shona. I wondered what they were saying that made the woman laugh so.

I turned to Whitney. "Let's go to the park now, honey," I said, as I brushed her baby-fine hair and buckled her sandals.

"Okay, Mommy."

We walked out of the kitchen door, in the direction of the Africans drinking tea.

"Good morning, madam, miskus," the caretakers called to us.

"Good morning," we said to them in unison.

"Madam, this is my friend Margaret," Joseph said.

"Hello, Margaret," I said. She stood to greet me. She was a robust woman, almost as tall as I, dressed in a plain skirt and blouse and wearing a knitted cap on her head. "This is my daughter, Whitney," I said.

"Hello, piccanin-madam-Whit-tenny!" Margaret said forthrightly, and she laughed her earthy laugh and slapped her hands together in delight and added, "Oh, madam, you have a lovely piccanin!" Margaret wasn't the least bit shy—as most Mashona women were in the presence of Europeans. She looked me in the eye as she spoke, and I liked her right away.

The next day, when a friend and her children came by in the afternoon to take Whitney and me swimming, my friend asked, "Who's that nanny over there?"

"Her name is Margaret," I said.

"What does she do?"

"I don't know," I said.

"She must be a prostitute," my friend said matter-of-factly. I looked at her with surprise. "There are a lot of prostitutes in town," she explained. "They satisfy the Africans whose wives and children are in the Tribal Trust Lands. The men can only afford to go home a few times a year. In the meantime, they've got to do something . . ."

From then on I saw Margaret almost daily. She arrived in the morning to join Noah and Joseph for tea, and she sometimes stayed all day.

One day as Whitney and I were walking to town, I saw Margaret coming toward us with her arm in a sling.

"Margaret," I said as she came closer, "what has happened to you?"

"Oh, madam, it is my husband. He beated me up."

"No! Margaret, why?" I asked without thinking.

"Because he is drinking too much, madam." The expression on her swollen face seemed to say, *How would you know what I'm talking about? How could you possibly know?* Then I saw my father stumble up our front stairs, grab my mother by the hair, shout slurred obscenities at her, then punch her . . .

"I'm so sorry, Margaret," I said weakly. "Is your arm broken?"

"Yes, it is broken."

"What can you do, Margaret?"

"I am divorcing him, madam. He is no good. He is always drinking too much. He does not support the childrens. I came to town to find a job because he does not support the childrens. He followed me here and beated me up."

"How many children do you have, Margaret?"

"I have five, madam. My firstiborn is fourteen years old. They are living in my village with my sister."

"How old are you, Margaret?"

"Twenty-five years, madam—I think."

"I am twenty-four."

"Do you need a girl to work for you, madam? I am very good at the washing and ironing."

"I've been doing my own washing and ironing—" She looked downcast. "How much do you charge?"

"Only one pound ten, madam, a month."

"But how will you manage with one arm?"

"I will get Joseph to help me."

154

"Okay, Margaret." A large smile brightened her bruised face. "And Margaret, you don't have to call me madam. My name is Bonnie."

"But I do, madam. Yes. You are my madam."

One day when Whitney and I were returning from town we found Margaret ironing in our living room. She was standing on a small rubber mat an inch thick.

"What's the mat for, Margaret?" I asked her.

"My legs, madam."

"What's wrong with your legs?"

"Look," she said, lifting her skirt above her knees. Thick ropes of varicose veins bulged from her calves. I hadn't noticed her legs before. "Feel it," she said.

I crouched beside her and gently ran my hand along the tracks of her veins. Her skin was smooth, taut, thick, cool. It was the first time I had ever touched black skin.

"Do they hurt you, Margaret?" I said. "I have varicose veins, too, from being pregnant with Whitney, but they're not as bad as this—"

"It only hurts when I stand too long, madam."

"What does the doctor say you should do?"

"He says no more childrens."

"That's a good idea, Margaret," I said, and we both laughed. Then Margaret became serious.

"Madam? What can I do so I will not have any more childrens?"

"Have you tried the pill?"

"No, I cannot take the pill, madam, because of my legs. And even so, I would need my brother's permission—"

"Why?"

"Because it is the custom. African women must have a father or a brother give permission before the doctor will give the birth control pills. And my brother, he would not say yes."

"That's not fair."

"Yes, madam."

"What about the loop? Do you need his permission for the loop?"

"The loop, madam?"

"It's a small device that the doctor puts inside to keep you from having more babies. It doesn't hurt—"

"Good, madam. I will see about the loop."

"Oh, and Margaret. You don't have to bother ironing my underwear. I've never ironed my underwear—"

"But I must, madam, because of the ho-ho's. There is a fly that lays its eggs in the wet washing. If the eggs get into the skin, they grow into big worms. . . ." She shook her head. "That would be very bad for you and the piccanin-madam. I must iron everything, everything."

"Thank you, Margaret. I didn't know that." We looked at each other appreciatively, as if we'd just exchanged gifts.

"I know," she said.

• • •

My friend Nigel, one of the young attorneys in Mr. Clarke's office, became like a brother to me. He often stopped by to see how I was doing and deliver my mail; and sometimes, when I needed a shoulder to cry on, I'd use his. This was paradoxical, because he was unlike anyone I'd ever known—haughty, aristocratic, and remote. But beneath his high-buttoned shell, I sensed he was a lonely man looking for a friend. He'd been an only child, born to middle-aged parents, raised in England; he'd attended Oxford, lived in India, traveled widely, and he felt at home nowhere in the world.

I used to ask him to describe all of the faraway places he had seen, which he would do for me joylessly. "The trouble with so much travel," he said one day over lunch at the outdoor café in Salisbury Gardens, "is that it makes you jaded. You keep searching for the perfect place but never find it. You become discontented wherever you are."

"Have you been to America?"

"Not 'A-*mare*-i-cah.' Softer, like this: 'Ah-mah-riccuh.' "

"Oh, Nigel. Have you been there?"

"No, I'm serious. You Americans must learn how to speak the language properly."

156

"*The rain in Spain . . .*"

"All right. . . . Yes, I've been to your A-mare-i-cah."

"Did you like it?"

"Hated it. . . . It's full of bloody Americans . . . speaking of which, where is your husband's child?"

"She's behind you . . . in the shade by that tree . . . playing with the bubbles we bought this morning."

"Look at her chase them—she can't even run—"

"She's learning."

"Frankly, I can't understand what all the fuss has been about. If I were you, I'd tell him to bloody well keep her."

"Nigel, I can't do that. You don't understand. When you have children of your own some day, you'll know—"

"*Me?*" he said, appearing to have smelled something foul. "Me, a father? Never! Can't bear the horrible little beasts. And as for you—you'd be better off without her."

• • •

While Whitney was with Jim on weekends, I accepted invitations from friends—to go boating on the lake, driving into the bush, visiting nearby game reserves, partying at private suburban homes, dancing at the local discos. I had fun. It was as if Africa was wooing me, and I was beginning to succumb.

• • •

July passed and August was drawing to a close and still Jim and I had not reached an agreement allowing us to go home. Mr. Clarke had made what we felt was a fair offer, giving Jim visitation rights upon our return to the United States of one full weekend (six p.m. Friday to six p.m. Sunday) and two partial weekends (six p.m. Friday to six p.m. Saturday one weekend and six p.m. Saturday to six p.m. Sunday another) per month, plus alternate holidays. Still, Jim stalled.

Then one day on one of our walks into town Whitney and I visited the office, where Mr. Clarke met me with: "I have bad news for you, Bonnie—" He told me Jim had inexplicably broken negotiations altogether and I should therefore be prepared to remain in Rhodesia indefinitely.

"What's the matter?" Mr. Clarke said. "You don't look at all surprised or disappointed."

"I'm getting used to the feeling of not knowing whether I'm coming or going," I said. "And besides, I like living here."

When Whitney and I returned to our flat that afternoon I told Noah and Joseph, who were working in the garden, that Whitney and I would be staying at the flat longer than I'd anticipated—at least another month. Their faces filled with genuine gladness and they clapped their hands. "Oh, that is *good,* madam!" Joseph said. Noah, smiling, looked at me shyly and nodded.

The following day I paid another month's rent and started to take steps toward finding a job. I applied for permanent residence and work permits, studied the newspaper's employment section, and investigated the nearby nursery school with Whitney. If I had to stay indefinitely, I thought, I'd be ready.

Then suddenly, without warning, Jim agreed to the proposals. The agreement was signed. On Friday afternoon, August 29, when Whitney and I went to the office, Mr. Clarke told me Jim and his parents had left Rhodesia that morning. They'd left, as far as I knew, without saying good-bye to Whitney, assuming, of course, that Whitney and I would follow soon after. But at that moment, I confess, I'd have sooner followed the devil to hell.

• • •

Returning with the Clarkes from a day at their friends' farm, approaching the sparkling skyline of Salisbury from the east on Jameson Avenue at sunset, something inside me shouted in a whisper: *NO, YOU MUSTN'T LEAVE! NOT NOW, NOT YET!*

Who would have understood Africa's hold on me? She seemed to rock me in her arms and croon, *You are special to me.* It was as if I were a puzzle piece that finally fit on the board,

158

or a slow record being played, at last, at the right speed. Although I was an alien in this country, nine thousand miles away from my own, I felt very much at home.

This feeling would not, perhaps, have been sufficient to keep me from following Jim to America. But Whitney at that time was not well enough to travel. She had contracted a cold that settled in her ears, and the doctor said that the trip, especially the pressurized aircraft cabin during the long flight, might exacerbate the problem. Each week when I brought her to his office the doctor prescribed a new medication, but nothing seemed to cure her racking cough or clear her nose and ears. The doctor said she might eventually require surgery, "a common operation for children in this country," to remove her tonsils and adenoids. He said we had to "wait and see."

This possibility forced me to consider another important factor: money. Medical and hospital costs were far lower in Rhodesia than they would have been back home. Also, child care was much cheaper there, as was food and housing. As a single woman supporting herself and her child, I felt that I was obviously better off where my money went farthest.

In a way I thought my staying there might even work out well for Jim. I fantasized that if he returned in due course, without his parents, free of his mother's choke-hold for the first time in his life, he might choose to marry his fiancée after all, have more children, live a more normal life, while at the same time seeing Whitney regularly. I searched my motives carefully and genuinely believed that revenge was not among them. I was not trying to do to Jim what he had done to me. I simply needed more time and a peaceful place in which to live happily with Whitney.

As it was, Jim had broken his engagement and left with his parents for America, and my remaining behind with Whitney represented the first deliberate legal transgression I could ever remember committing. Yet I felt I *had* to take the risk.

When I told Mr. Clarke I'd definitely decided not to return to America for a while, we had words. "You are a very stubborn girl, Bonnie," he said.

"Mr. Clarke," I said, "if I wasn't so stubborn, I would never have come to this country in the first place—I wouldn't be sitting in this chair talking to you right now!"

He seemed shocked by my impudence. "I think you're headed for trouble," he said sternly.

"Perhaps I am," I said, "but I have to take a chance. . . . Besides, that man will give me trouble wherever I am."

If Whitney had appeared to miss Jim, if she'd pined for him, cried to see him, even asked for him, I would have set aside all other considerations and returned to the States at once. But, as I wrote to George on September 8, "Not once has she even mentioned his name! It's as though he's just completely faded out of the picture and she's relieved to be rid of the strain. . . . She's just beginning to act like a normal child now. I allow her to run, although she sometimes falls; I encourage her to play outside, although she sometimes gets filthy dirty; I allow her to soak up the sunshine, although she sometimes gets a little burn. I truly believe she's enjoying her new-found freedom—to be herself and act like a little child instead of a museum piece. She's been terribly happy since he's been gone and seems to get happier every day. We have a lovely time together. . . ."

One evening in early September I invited Jim's ex-fiancée to join Whitney and me for dinner at our Fife Avenue flat. When she arrived she was timid at first, understandably wary. Her pretty hands played nervously in her lap. She spoke to Whitney longingly and lovingly, as one of the women Whitney had also called Mommy.

After we put Whitney to bed, I tried to console her.

"You're very lucky," I said.

"Oh, I don't know . . ." She spoke softly, her head was bowed.

"You know his mother would never have allowed your marriage to work—"

"She is very possessive, isn't she."

"And what if you'd had children—?"

"Yes, perhaps you're right."

160

"You are a lovely person. You'll meet someone else. You'll be happy—"

She looked at me and smiled. "Thank you," she said. She seemed to relax.

She stayed for three more hours, talking. She told me what life was like at Jim's home after my arrival in the country—how the grandmother openly and flagrantly indoctrinated Whitney against me. "She used to shake her finger in Whitney's face," Jim's fiancée said, "and scold her, saying: 'You are not allowed to kiss *that woman!*' 'You are not to listen to *that woman!*' 'You mustn't go swimming with that woman, or she will *drown* you!' . . ."

She said that during the trial, every evening in Jim's house, Jim, his parents, and Jerry discussed strategy and rehearsed their testimony to make sure the details coincided. She told me Jerry's wife had threatened to leave him if he agreed to go to Rhodesia and testify against me.

"Did she leave him?" I asked.

"Yes, I believe she did."

"You're lucky—you have no idea how lucky."

I wrote to George and told him I'd decided to stay. He replied that he would come to Salisbury on his vacation in October to see me, to meet Whitney, and to discuss our future plans.

I drafted a long letter to Jim explaining why I wasn't following him and showed the draft to Mr. Clarke for his approval. "Don't send it yet," he suggested. "Perhaps you'll change your mind when George gets here."

In mid-September I wrote to my mother:

I've decided to stay in Rhodesia for a little while to give myself time to think this whole thing out. Last Monday I started a job as a market researcher for commercial television, which will last until mid-October; while I work (about 8 a.m. to 4 p.m.), Whitney goes to the nursery school (crèche) diagonally across the street from where we live. It's large, clean, and well run. She has her own African nanny, named Ina, who cares for her all day. Since she's been only with adults for so much of her life with J., I think being with children all day now is the best thing for her. She seems to enjoy it very much,

161

too; she's acting like a real little girl now, jumping up and down, making noise, and getting into mischief. And the nursery school costs only £1.16 a week—approximately $4! . . .

I saw Mr. Clarke briefly yesterday and he said it wouldn't be a criminal offense if I stayed here, but it *would* be a civil one. After what J.'s ex-fiancée told me when she came to dinner here a few weeks ago, Mr. Clarke understands my reasons for keeping Whitney from those crazy people. Mr. Clarke is NOT encouraging me to stay. He's a very ethical man, and I think he thinks I'm being unethical; but at least he sees my point of view and realizes it's *my* life.

Whitney Lee is very happy and healthy now. I can't bear the thought of taking her back to those people so that they can continue to confuse and upset and threaten her. I just need more time to cement our relationship so that they can't destroy it again. Please understand, Mommy dear, as I'm sure you do. It's not my intention to shirk my responsibilities. I really want to do what's best, and I think it's best to stay here for a while longer now that he's gone. What a relief it is to have him at the other end of the world!

For all these years I've kept them in a large metal trunk I painted blue. All of the letters George and my mother had saved, each scrap of paper, every written word. I've kept them, I suppose, because I had a premonition that one day those words, brought together and linked end to end, might form a chain of understanding, a bridge of prayer beads.

The letters, with their dates and postmarks, prove it really happened. It wasn't a dream. And the diaries, with their cryptic notes and tiny writing, wrap up the time, pin it in place, and preserve it.

Here is a spiral notebook, smaller than my hand, with my name and address—22 Fife Avenue, Salisbury—on the inside, which accounts for the days in October 1969, when George came to Salisbury to see me:

Wednesday, the 15th: George arrived—"TAP flight No. 277, 2:05"; *16th:* "dinner at Sue's"; *18th:* "Lake McIlwain"; *19th:* "Clarkes' for day"; *20th:* "shopping; tennis at Sue's"; *21st:* "Whitney's Birthday Party in the Park," the menu: "sausages, chips, cook drinks, gingerbread men, birthday cake," and the invitation list: "Dennis and David Pichanick, David and Julie Rawstone, Leslie and Johnny McPhun, Karen and Hugh Andersen, Alan Clarke, Loren Black, Nicky deChassar."

George took photos at Whitney's party. Here is one: Six smiling mothers in sleeveless cotton dresses standing behind a row of towheaded children no taller than the mothers' waists. Little boys in safari suits with short pants; little girls in sundresses and sandals. We are standing on the grass in Salisbury Gardens, against a backdrop of flower beds and mimosa trees. Whitney, in front of me, her fine, fair hair lifted by a breeze, wears a blue gingham dress sent by my sister for her niece's fourth birthday, the first birthday I'd spent with Whitney since she was one year old.

October 22nd–24th: "Falls and Wankie." Whitney stayed at Sue's while George and I flew to Victoria Falls and the Wankie Game Reserve. I have moving pictures in my mind of our trip: the mist rising from the falls obscuring our view; the American tourists from Texas requesting the piano player at the hotel to play "Home on the Range" during dinner; the stately sable pointed out by our African guide from the game reserve's zebra-striped Volkswagen bus; the lioness resting in the open with her cub . . .

It might have been a kind of honeymoon had I accepted George's proposal. In the privacy of our thatched hut at Wankie, surrounded by the primordial sounds of nocturnal Africa, George asked me to marry him and return with him to America. He painted a cozy connubial picture: a comfortable suburban home not far from his family and mine; two cars, a dog, a cat, children—including, of course, Whitney.

"And Jim?" I said to George. "What about Jim?"

"I don't want anything to do with him," George said. "I'll adopt Whitney."

As night birds cried in the outlying bush and crickets droned in the distance, my heart heard Africa whisper, *Stay with me.* I saw the scene that George described as if it were the lion's cage at a zoo. Whitney and I were the animals inside; George, the kind zoo-keeper; and Jim the jeering public peering through the bars. Something inside me shouted, *No! I must stay here on the game reserve where I can rest in the open with my cub.*

"I'm sorry, George," I said, "but it won't work. There's no way we can prevent Jim from seeing Whitney—especially since he lives so close by—"

George was a sensible, rational man. He accepted my rejection well. "The way I see it, Bon," he said, "you have only three choices. Either you remarry as soon as possible, or you run away with Whitney, or you give her back to him—"

"Run away?"

"Go into hiding—go to Europe, Australia, anywhere; change your name, dye your hair—do anything that you have to do to keep him out of your life—"

"That's out of the question . . . I can't live like that . . . I'm not clever enough, I don't have the resources or the right connections. And why should I have to live like a fugitive? I've got to be *me,* and I've got to live openly."

"As long as you stay single and you stay here, you are a sitting duck. He's sure to come back—"

"I can't run away, George, and I can't return with you, and I won't give her up. I feel I must wait here a while, and see . . ."

Sunday, 26th: "Lunch at Andersens' (make salad)"; *27th:* "Geo. and I took Clarkes to dinner at the Cossack"; *28th:* "tennis at Sue's; dinner at Le Français"; *29th:* "shopping a.m.; lunch with Chris and Anne; dinner with Sue and Alwyn, Annie and John McPhun; took George to airport (very sad)."

When George left I cried for days. Not because I thought we might have gotten married and lived happily ever after, but because his leaving was so *final.*

• • •

When my market research job ended in October, I looked in the newspaper for work in publishing. Some months previously I had seen an advertisement in the paper which read: "Aptitude Testing and Career Counselling—phone Dr. Brian Norton— 55511." For the equivalent of twenty-five dollars I took a series of motivational analysis tests to determine my vocational preferences, and after my results had been compiled, Dr. Norton, a middle-aged psychologist, told me, "To score in the ninety-ninth percentile in the literary category means you are not only *motivated* to write, you feel a strong *compulsion* to write. In other words, you *must* write." Clutching this piece of paper as if it were a cable from God, I left Dr. Norton's office determined to become a writer some day and to take the first, tentative steps toward that end in the small, slow, unintimidating city of Salisbury.

But so far I had found nothing. So I took a temporary job selling Rhodesian cookbooks door to door in the city. Wearing Rhodesian-made cotton sundresses and Rhodesian-made sandals, I walked several miles every day, carrying a wicker basket heavy with cookbooks, into each office building, inquiring at every book, magazine, and newspaper publisher about vacancies. All through October, which is called suicide month in Rhodesia because it is the hottest month of the year, with temperatures in the nineties, I carried my basket through streets lined with towering jacaranda trees and their panicles of pale purple, bell-like flowers. In November, when the rainy season began, the purple bells fell along the wet sidewalks, mirroring the glamor of the trees.

In a country that sees no rain at all for almost eight months of the year, the dark rain clouds, which approach like gypsy caravans in the sky, are more than welcomed. Nearly every day during the rainy season, which lasts from November to March, the caravans rolled in and the rains filled the air with wild performances. I listened to them tap-dance on the corrugated metal roof of our flat, felt them pound the earth like a drum, watched them shake the trees like tambourines and then move on. Nowhere before had I seen such rain or felt as enveloped by it.

To keep Whitney from getting wet when I took her to the crèche, I carried her piggyback and covered us both with a large, clear plastic sheet. The African mothers who saw us cross the street stopped beneath their black umbrellas and stared— I assumed because they'd never seen a white woman carry her child their way.

After the rainy season began, Margaret and the caretakers at our flat drank their tea in the kitchen, where I would sometimes be preparing a meal.

166

"Madam," Margaret said to me one day, "do you have a boyfriend?"

"No," I said, surprised by her question.

"Noah doesn't have a girl friend. Would you like to be his girl friend?" She laughed her earthy laugh.

I turned from the stove and looked at Noah. His usually gentle and cherubic face was stiff with embarrassment and fear. His mouth fell open and he shook his head. Not knowing what to say, I left the kitchen.

I knew this was the sort of incident I shouldn't share with my Rhodesian friends. They would have given me another lecture on the importance of not fraternizing with the African servants. "It's not fair to them," my friends would say. "It gives them the wrong ideas."

. . .

For weeks Whitney's hearing had been getting worse. If I spoke to her when her back was turned or called her name from another room, she didn't hear me. After many weekly visits to a general practitioner, we saw an ear-nose-and-throat specialist, who confirmed the fact that her tonsils and adenoids had to be removed, and who agreed that it had been best for us not to travel back to America.

As far as I knew, Whitney had never stayed in a hospital before; so from the little experience I'd had with hospitals, I tried to prepare her for her upcoming operation. I told her she was going to spend a few days in a "special place," which was "large and clean and white as a cloud," where "lots of nice people in bright, white clothes worked hard to make sick people well again," and when she came out—"like magic"—her ears would be *all* better. . . .

She was delighted. The day I took her in, she skipped happily down the hospital corridor telling the nurses whom she passed, "I'm not going to have earaches any more!"

The children's ward was a spacious, sunny room on the hospital's ground floor, with rows of small white beds along the walls. Colorful, larger-than-life drawings of Disney characters had been painted on the walls so that it looked as if Donald Duck, Pluto, Mickey Mouse, and friends were playing tag around the room. "Look, honey!" I said to Whitney. "What fun!"

When it was time for me to go, Whitney nuzzled her head in my neck and said, "Mommy, you *are* coming back, aren't you?"

"Oh, yes," I said, as cheerfully as I could, trying not to frighten her with tears. "I'll be back first thing in the morning."

"All right," she said softly, "I'll see you tomorrow." She didn't cry.

After Whitney came home from the hospital, my friend Annie McPhun, who was a nurse, took care of her during the weeks of her convalescence, while I continued to sell cookbooks and look for a permanent position in publishing. An unexpected part-time job came my way when I entered the office of an advertising executive and television quiz program emcee, hoping to sell a cookbook to him to give his wife for Christmas. "The hostess we had for our quiz show just announced she's moving to Bulawayo next week, and I need another attractive girl right away. How would you like to be on TV?" It involved only one morning every other week—two shows were taped at one time—and paid only fifteen dollars each time, but I couldn't resist taking it—if only for the fun of telling my mother I was going to be a "TV personality." At that salary Whitney and I couldn't have survived, so of course I continued to look for a permanent job. And one afternoon in late November, in the offices of the *Rhodesian Farmer* magazine, I found it. When I told the magazine's receptionist why I'd come, her eyes widened strangely. "Wait here one moment, please," she said, and hurried to an office down the hall.

"Hey, Dud," I heard her say in an excited whisper as I studied the framed magazine front covers hanging in the hallway, "do you know that blond American bird on TV whom you said you fancy? Well, she's *here* looking for a job!"

I heard a man's voice say, "Tell her she's hired."

"But, *Dud,*" the young woman protested, "we don't have any openings!"

"We do now. She's your new assistant."

He was a large man in his late forties with sandy-colored hair thinning at the temples, and a large, pleasant, ruddy face. His features reminded me of my father. As I spoke he looked at me pensively, right forefinger pressed against his lips. "How would you like to be a sub-editor?" he said. My face must have registered my thought: *What is that?* "Oh," he said, "I think they're called copy-editors in the States. A sub-editor, or copy-editor, prepares the editorial copy—news and feature articles—for the printer. That means correcting our staff writers' stories for spelling, punctuation, and grammar; rewriting press releases; coming up with headlines; marking the copy as to type face and column width; proofreading galleys; and so on. Whatever you don't know, I'll teach you."

"How soon could I begin?" I asked, stifling the strong urge to rush around his desk and kiss him.

"Well, this position isn't available at the moment—I'll have to do some juggling of staff—but in the meantime, if you don't mind assisting the receptionist for a few weeks until we get ourselves sorted out, you can begin on December first. That's a Monday, I believe."

All the way home I practically danced. My wicker basket wasn't heavy anymore.

At the magazine's annual staff party I met the rest of my colleagues—June Selkirk, the secretary; Robin Hood ("my real name," he said) and Peter Turnbull-Kemp, staff writers; Beverley Owen, the advertising media manager; and Ady Bloch—"Hi! I'm the layout artist," Ady declared, as she promptly laid herself out flat on the floor.

Ady had come to the party with an artist friend, whom she introduced me to as Melvyn Northwood. When she excused herself to return to the buffet, Mel asked me to dance.

He danced stiffly, woodenly, and held me nervously. "I usually don't like to dance," he said. I nodded, and we both laughed. *What a lovely smile,* I thought, *and such kind eyes. You have the type of face I could look at forever. But your body is too thin! I'd like to feed you . . .*

Mel was from England, but had been in Johannesburg for five years before coming to Salisbury five months ago to take a better job as the art director of an advertising agency. He shared a flat with another single artist named Tony, who was also at the party as a guest of Ady.

I told Mel I was an American, that I was divorced and had a four-year-old daughter named Whitney.

"I like children," Mel said, as I stared at the deep dimple in his chin and realized he reminded me of Charlton Heston. "They're my favorite people."

•   •   •

In the days and weeks following Whitney's operation, there was a change in her attitude toward me. The trust that had been building, brick by brick, in the previous months seemed at times to topple to the ground. The anger and sullenness she'd exhibited immediately after I won custody returned in unpredictable waves of rebellion. She began to mention Jim: "My daddy is going to shoot you!" she'd shout at me, which I interpreted to mean: My daddy never left me in the hospital; he never made me have an operation; he's going to punish you for doing this to me! Would other four-year-olds who'd lived more normal lives feel similarly angry after an operation, I wondered? I didn't know.

There were Christmas lights strung throughout the city, and the churches chimed Christmas carols on the hour; but without the cold and snow of home, it didn't seem like Christmas. Whitney and I spent Christmas day with our friends the McPhuns, whose children opened their gifts loudly and enthusiastically. But none of the gifts I could afford to buy her seemed to impress Whitney.

170

• • •

In all the time that he'd been gone I hadn't heard from Jim. He knew my address, but he never wrote to me. And he never sent any child support for Whitney. There were times when I even thought he no longer cared.

But then it began: A barrage of letters and cables to everyone but me. Jim wrote two letters to Mr. Clarke and one to Mrs. Staub, the district social welfare officer, demanding a detailed report as to "Whitney's present care and condition, her living facilities and religious training," as well as the name of my employer. On December 9, Mrs. Staub replied to Jim's letter, informing him of Whitney's operation, telling him we were still at the same address, and assuring him that "Whitney is receiving good care and appears to have established a good relationship with her mother."

Finally, on December 31, 1969, Jim sent a telegram to a man he knew in Salisbury, requesting him to contact the authorities mentioned, in order to force my return. The telegram read:

FATHER RELEASED HOSPITAL TWO WEEKS AGO SEVERE MALNUTRITION LOSS OF WILL TO LIVE MOTHER TONIGHT OVERDOSE PILLS O'CONNOR ATTENDING PHYSICIAN IN TIME KEEP CONFIDENTIAL MAKE CONTRACT AGREEMENT PART OF JUDGEMENT FORCE RETURN BEST INTEREST OF BABY PARENTS LITERALLY DYING SELF UNABLE TO WORK REACH BURKE, BEADLE, CLARKE, COOK, IMMIGRATION URGENT RESPONSE RETURN AMERICA IMMEDIATELY STAUB PROBATION REACHED NOT PARAMOUNT INTEREST OF BABY US GOVERNMENT COOPERATING RHODESIAN GOVERNMENT REFUSAL TO COOPERATE WASHINGTON SITUATION CRITICAL JIM.

When I told Mr. Clarke I'd accepted a full-time, permanent position in publishing and I'd decided to stay in Rhodesia, he warned me: "There's going to be trouble, Bonnie. Just wait and see."

In January I was promoted to the position of editorial assistant, responsible for sending the editorial pages, roughly one-third of the magazine, to the printer, according to a strict schedule of morning and afternoon deadlines. For the first time in my life I knew how it felt to love my work—and be good at it. In addition, through Mel's advertising agency, I began to get free-lance modeling jobs, which helped to supplement my salary.

Mel phoned regularly to ask me out, and although I often had to refuse, I admired his patience and tenacity; he kept phoning. When we went out on our second date, I asked him why he'd sold his Land Rover and bought a Chevrolet. "To make you feel more at home when you go out with me," he said.

When Mel learned that Whitney and I didn't have a television set at our flat, he rented one and brought it to us so that we could all watch my Monday evening quiz programs together. Monday evening, then, became our standing date: Mel came to dinner, the three of us watched TV, he helped me tuck Whitney in and tell her bedtime stories, and then he'd stay until it was time for me to go to bed.

If he'd smoked a pipe and worn bedroom slippers, he couldn't have looked more at home than he did with us in our living room. Before long he'd chosen a favorite chair, which Whitney called "Mel's chair," and he'd found a place in both of our hearts.

"Will you marry me?" he said one evening.

"Pardon?"

"I said, will you marry me?"

"Are you joking, Mel?"

"No, I'm serious. I've never said it before. Never in all twenty-seven years of my life—"

"Shhh, you'll wake up Whitney."

"Well?"

172

"Sometimes I think marriage is a cage constructed by men to keep women in—"

"You had a bad experience the first time 'round. It doesn't have to be that way."

"I don't know, Mel. I'll have to think about it."

. . .

On Monday, February 16, 1970, I learned from Mr. Clarke that Jim was on his way back to Rhodesia. Frightened of what he might do upon his return, I asked Noah and Joseph to watch for his arrival, and I invited Mel to join Whitney and me for dinner every night.

Three days later, when I returned home from work with Whitney at five, Joseph came to my door. "Madam," he said, "the picannin madam's father was here today. He was in a car with another boss [white man] driving slowly, slowly up and down the street. I wrote the number of the car plate—" Joseph handed me a small piece of a brown paper bag with RSE-1582 written on it.

"And, madam," Joseph continued, motioning for me to follow him toward our front window, "do you see those Africans across the way?" He pointed to two African men standing together, as if in conversation, on the opposite street corner. "They were following you. Now they are keeping watch. You must not stay here tonight, madam," he whispered so that Whitney wouldn't hear. "It is not safe."

Trying to remain calm, I took Whitney's hand and told her we were going to a neighbor's for tea.

"But what about Melvyn?" she protested.

"He will join us later," I said.

While Joseph watched the detectives on the front corner, Whitney and I left our flat by the back door and walked quickly to my neighbor Edith's flat, a few doors away. As Whitney played with Edith's daughter in another room, Edith and I discussed what I should do. She felt I should phone the police. I decided to do nothing until I talked with Mel.

Mel usually came to dinner at seven, but that night he was late. I slipped back to the flat to leave a note on the back door.

"Gone to Edith's," the note read, "please meet us there." But in my nervousness I'd forgotten that Mel didn't know Edith or where she lived. At nine I saw Mel's car and rushed out to meet him.

"You're spending the night at my place," he said when I told him what had happened. "You'll be safe there."

Whitney slept on the daybed in Mel's living room, and he and I shared his single bed. From his bedroom window I could see the stars shimmering like sunlight on a deep blue river. "Please hold me, Melvy," I begged before he fell asleep. "I'm scared."

"Don't you worry," he said, patting me sleepily, "everything will be all right."

Once again Jim and I spoke through interpreters, our attorneys. My lawyer told his: No more detectives. His lawyer told mine: We're going to court again. Jim and I never spoke to each other.

Jim resumed his former visitation schedule, taking Whitney three afternoons a week and overnight on weekends, and once again Whitney returned from these visits emotionally distraught and torn. As I wrote to George, "J. is back here and is being more ruthless than ever. All the good I'd done in the six months I had with her alone here has been totally destroyed. She says she wants to live with him and not with me. She cries for him constantly, has nightmares, etc., and it's heartbreaking."

Although the detectives were supposed to have been called off, they still haunted me. One morning as I walked to work, I realized an African man was walking close behind me. I walked faster; so did he. I stopped to take a pebble from my shoe; he stopped too. I turned quickly and crossed the street; he followed me. I felt naked, exposed, vulnerable: *What does this man want with me?* The Africans I'd met in Salisbury were gentle, polite, peace-loving people; I'd never felt afraid. Yet this man, I knew, was after me. *What was he going to do?* I took a circuitous route to work, scanning the city streets for signs of a police car. I walked faster, and still he kept up. I looked quickly over my shoulder and caught a glimpse of his sneer. My heart was pounding crazily. I started to cry. Then I saw a police car and waved for the driver to stop. The officer asked to see the man's I.D. He was, in fact, a detective, hired by Jim.

Soon after, Joseph told me he'd been approached by more of Jim's detectives and asked to spy on me. They offered to pay him well to tell them what I did, where I went, how I lived, whom I saw, whether I had male visitors. Joseph said he'd refused their offer. I thanked him for telling me and paid him for his loyalty.

One of the major points of Jim's new case, I soon learned, was to prove I was an unfit mother because of my "immorality": I had a boyfriend; I had spent the night with him at least once (the detectives had followed us to Mel's flat the night of Jim's return); hence, Whitney was being corrupted by my "illicit" life.

"What is this about a boyfriend?" Mr. Clarke said after Jim's new allegations arrived.

"I do have a boyfriend," I told him.

"Have you in fact slept with him?"

"Yes," I said, with neither shame nor guilt.

"I'm washing my hands of your case, Bonnie. I'll let one of our junior partners handle it. I can't help you anymore."

Fine, I thought defiantly. *You can keep your antiquated morality, Mr. Clarke. I bought it once, and where did it get me? Marital sex with Jim was worse than rape. You may not understand this, Mr. Clarke, but I'll never be raped again.*

Once again I had to reply to Jim's accusations point by point. I worked at this in the evenings after Whitney was asleep and on the weekend when she was away. It took some time. Jim's papers were 130 pages thick.

Mel was tender and supportive throughout. "My marriage proposal is still open," he said. I looked up from Jim's allegations, soothed by Mel's sweet smile. *Yes, I could admire your face for the rest of my life,* I thought. "When this is all over, I'll accept," I said.

With Jim's return, Whitney became more confused and difficult than ever. At times she tried to taunt me with statements such as, "My daddy and I have SECRETS about going to America, and I'm not allowed to tell *you!*"

"No, you mustn't tell me," I said, "otherwise it wouldn't be a secret anymore."

"Oh," she said, and walked away, defused.

But usually I didn't know what to say to her reports of Jim's indoctrination. When she stood in the kitchen with her hands on her little hips and shouted at me as I worked at the sink— "My daddy says I'm not allowed to love you! He says I must not listen to you!"—what could I say? I wanted to say, *Whitney, your daddy is wicked and cruel to say such things. I am your mother. You are half me. If he teaches you to hate me, he's making you hate part of yourself. You should be free to get to know me and form your own opinions over time. But we need more time! He ripped two years out of our lives; now we need time to sew the pieces back together.* Instead, I looked at her, speechless, wondering how one reasons with a four-and-a-half-year-old, especially one who's been instructed not to listen, specifically, to you. I did what my mother would have done: I pretended I hadn't heard her. "You'd better wash your hands now, honey," I said. "Dinner's almost ready."

When she returned to the kitchen to show me her freshly washed hands, her tone had softened. "My daddy says you are horrible," she said, as I removed the chicken from the oven. "But he tells liers, Mommy. You're not horrible."

• • •

In spite of the impending custody suit, which hung from my shoulders like a heavy cape of dread, and Jim's frequent, wrenching visitations with Whitney, I felt thankful for the blessings in my life and quietly happy.

My job was a joy that made me look forward to each new day. When Ady, the layout artist, left the magazine, Dudley gave me her job in addition to my own. He praised my work, which made me feel proud, and doubled my salary to two hundred dollars a month, which meant Whitney and I could afford to move.

176

I found a nice-size, furnished one-bedroom apartment in a nearby block of flats for fifty-one dollars a month, and I asked Margaret whether she would like to work for me as a cleaning girl there.

"Oh, yes, madam!" she said, as pleased by her promotion as I'd been by mine.

"Weekday mornings—is that all right?" I said. "And perhaps I can find someone who needs a girl in the afternoons. How much should I pay you, Margaret?"

"I don't know, madam. But most cleaning girls are paid seven dollars per month—"

"Then I will pay you ten."

Our lives settled into a comfortable routine. Margaret arrived each morning at a quarter to eight, while Whitney was finishing her breakfast at the small table in her room and I was hurrying to get ready for work. I'd hear the knock at our front door and open it:

"Good morning, Margaret."

"Good morning, madam!" She'd laugh.

"Margaret, why are you always so happy in the morning?"

"I don't know, madam." She'd walk past Whitney's bedroom door toward the kitchen, still laughing. "Good morning, piccanin-madam-Whittenny!" she'd sing.

Before long, Margaret ran our household as if she were my wife. She would tell me what to wear: "That miniskirt is too mini, madam. When you bend over, I can see your bum. You must change it. Here, wear this one." And she would tell me what to pick up at the store on my way home from work:

"Hello, madam?" she phoned me one day as I was rushing to meet my three o'clock deadline for the printer. "This is Margaret. Do you have a pencil and paper?"

"Margaret, you wouldn't ask that if you ever saw my desk. I'm being buried in paper—"

"Good," she said, "take this down. We need: soap powder ... sugar ... tea ... Have you got that, madam? ... Good.

177

Now don't forget . . ." For the first time in my life, I could imagine what it was like to be a henpecked husband.

And when I would grow impatient with Whitney in the morning: "Please, honey, don't play with your eggs—*eat* them . . . We're going to be late . . . I mustn't be late for work again, honey . . . *Please* don't dawdle . . . ," Margaret would reprove me with, "But madam, she is only a *child.*" Margaret's words slapped my face with truth. *She is right,* I'd say to myself; *sometimes I forget.*

Although Whitney was only four and a half, she seemed older than that to me. Her new friend, Gigi Lincoln, who lived in the house next door to our block of flats, was ten; and from the way they talked and played together, there seemed to be no age difference between them.

Gigi was a happy, carefree child, the youngest of three girls in her family, who liked to pretend when she was with Whitney and me that Whitney was her little sister and I her mommy. Wherever we went she'd hold my other hand and call me Mummy loudly enough for others to hear, and then she'd stifle giggles.

One day as I was preparing dinner in the kitchen of our new flat and the girls were playing in Whitney's room, I overheard Gigi say to Whitney: "You have a wonderful mum."

"I *DO?*" Whitney said.

"Yes, you do. You're very lucky."

"I *AM?*"

As I peeled the potatoes I thanked God for Gigi's love for me and prayed that some of it might rub off on Whitney.

Whitney never played more happily than she did with Gigi. Because of her, or at least when she was with her, Whitney seemed truly happy. Happiness was Gigi's hallmark; she was always happy, and her happiness rippled like circles on the surface of a pond. She made up skits, songs, and dances and taught them to Whitney; she mimicked television commercials ("RRRRixi Taxi-six-oh-six-six-six . . .") and entertainers (Maurice Chevalier: "Thank *HEAV-EN* for lit-tle girls—"); she talked and giggled ceaselessly. I never denied Whitney time to spend with Gigi. I knew she was happier with Gigi than with me.

178

On the afternoons when Whitney wasn't visiting Jim, Gigi would come to our flat to play and sometimes stay for dinner. I would feed the girls at six, and when Mel arrived at seven the two would rush to the door to greet him, hanging on his neck, flattering him with their enthusiastic affection. As I stood by the hallway to the kitchen watching this scene, it reminded me of the way my sisters and I used to greet my father when we were very young. "Daddy's home! Daddy's *home!*" we'd squeal as he scooped us up in his arms.

"Put me *down!*" Mel would say to the girls in feigned protest. "You don't know where I've *been!*" And then he'd turn to me with a little kiss: "Hello, love. What's for dinner then?"

"*Men!*" I pouted in mock anger, while the girls giggled. "I won't tell you what we're having until I get a big hug." He'd reach out both arms and hold me stiffly. "Melvy," I teased him, "I love you very much, but you hug like a tree."

Mel and I made hand puppets for Whitney and Gigi. I formed the heads out of aluminum foil with a hole in the center for an index finger, then covered the heads with layers of papier-mâché. When they dried, Mel painted clownlike faces on each and I made arms and bodies out of fabric, hands of felt, hair of yarn. Together the two girls created their own plays and performed them in our living room for the neighborhood children and me.

It was like a happy, make-believe family: Mel and I playing the parents of both Whitney and Gigi. On weekends the four of us went everywhere together, and our outings were always filled with good food, swimming, sunshine, and laughter.

If, as we drove along in Mel's car, Whitney became rebellious and angry with me, Mel and Gigi quickly made a game of it, which never failed to break Whitney's dark mood. When Whitney shouted at me, "My daddy's going to shoot you with his gun!" Gigi added teasingly, "And my daddy's a lion tamer and he's going to hit Bonnie with his whip!" and Mel chimed in, "Yeah, and *my* daddy's a police chief and he's going to lock her up and throw away the key!" I pretended to cry, and then we all laughed and went on to another game.

Or when Whitney said, "My daddy's going to buy me my own white horse when he takes me back to America with him,"

Gigi began a new game to help heal with humor Whitney's confusion: "And I'm going to eat green cheese when I land on the moon," she said excitedly. "And I'm going to ride a kangaroo when I get to Australia!" Mel said. "And I'm going to wear glass slippers to the queen's ball," I said, and the game went on until our imaginations went dry. It was the closest I'd ever come to having my own happy family.

On the evenings when Jim returned Whitney to our flat after a visitation, Mel waited with me. He stood beside me at the open door protectively and spoke to Jim politely as I reached to bring Whitney in.

"How did you ever come to marry *him?*" Mel said candidly the first time he saw Jim.

"I don't know," I said. "I really don't know."

On my twenty-fifth birthday in mid-May, I counted my blessings—my much-loved job, our new homey flat, Margaret's household help, Mel's stabilizing love and presence, Gigi's joy and friendship, Whitney's growing sense of security and happiness, our many friends, our good health . . . In spite of the hardships, in almost every respect, my life was richer than it had ever been. It was only the imminent custody suit which caused my stomach to form a tight fist that pounded my spine, made me jump at any sudden noise, and made my hands tremble as they repeatedly reached for the nearest packet of cigarettes.

• • •

In late July, when Jim and I went to court a second time, the ironies of my life were summed up in one issue of the morning newspaper: FATHER CLAIMS CUSTODY OF DAUGHTER, the front-page headline read; several pages in, my smiling made-up model-face could be seen advertising Mayfair coffee; and in the TV section at the back, there was a listing of my newest weekly quiz show, "The Anagram Game." I observed myself in the media as if I were someone else. *That's not,* I said to myself, *the real me.*

Desperate for ammunition, Jim used all of this against me. He accused me of having three simultaneous careers—my magazine job, modeling, and television—"in preference to motherhood." He told the court I traveled in a fast, "swinging" crowd, "the RTV [Rhodesia Television] crowd"; that I was leading an "immoral" life; and that Whitney had "gone downhill" in the time he'd been gone. He testified he'd questioned Whitney as to my relationship with Mel, and then he played a long tape of his questions and her answers in court. When my advocate asked Jim whether he thought it helped a little girl to ask her such questions, Jim piously replied, "I am entitled to know these things."

I sat in the same sun-filled courtroom, watching for telltale expressions on the face of the same elderly judge, observing the movements and tactics of the same white-wigged, black-robed advocates as the year before. The only difference between that case and this was the color of Jim's cannons and where they were aimed.

"Now, Babe, tell Daddy," Jim's voice on the tape intoned, "does Mommy sleep with Mel?"

"Yes." Whitney's voice is soft and sleepy.

Whitney, do you know what he means by 'sleep'? Describe for him what you've seen: Naps, fully clothed, on a Sunday afternoon while you are napping. Or Mommy resting her head on Mel's lap or shoulder while you sit beside him watching TV. Or the time Mel had that terrible ear infection and was in such pain and I made him stay in my bed while I sat in the chair nearby reading through the night and watching the clock to put drops in his ear every hour. Yes, you are right, we do "sleep" together, Whitney, in the sense your daddy means. Some day you'll understand how good it feels to be a woman and to love a man. But you could never have seen that kind of "sleeping," Whitney, because it's only taken place when you've spent the night with Jim—

"And have you ever seen Mel with his clothes off?"

"Yes," Whitney's voice says, in the same tone.

Whitney, Whitney, what do you mean? Do you mean in his bathing suit? Yes, you've seen him in nothing but a bathing suit, but never naked, Whitney; you know that. Mel is so shy, so modest, so British—

"Where was this tape recorder placed when you questioned your daughter?" my advocate asked Jim when the tape had ended.

"Under the bed," he said.

"Under the bed that you and your daughter share?"

"Yes," Jim said.

"You asked her all of these questions at night, before you both went to sleep?"

"Yes."

"Thank you. You may step down."

The morning I was sworn in, the courtroom was filled with spectators, mostly elderly women. They watched me the way my grandmother had watched her favorite afternoon soap operas: hungrily. Some of them even brought snacks—thin tea sandwiches, jelly-topped scones, cheese biscuits—to nibble surreptitiously to sustain them through the day.

After I swore to tell the truth, Mr. Osborn, Jim's advocate, began questioning me:

Q. Now, Mrs. Jason, does a mother-daughter relationship exist between you and Whitney at present?

A. Yes, I believe it does.

Q. It does?

A. Yes.

Q. So there is no longer any need for you to build up a mother-daughter relationship with Whitney?

A. No, I disagree. I think that a lot of damage has been done to the fragile mother-daughter relationship which Whitney and I had built up and are still building up, and I think it will take a lot of time to have a proper mother-daughter relationship, as other mothers do with their children.

Q. Is your statement then that a mother-daughter relationship does exist, that you made a moment ago, is that incorrect?

A. No. There is a mother-daughter relationship. But I think that the child is very confused. She does not know who she lives with and who she visits. She has been pumped for information, as is obvious from the tape recording.

Q. Let us get down to a little more specific things. Would you say a characteristic of a mother-daughter relationship is affection and love on the part of the child for the mother?

A. Yes, of course.

Q. Would you say Whitney loves you?

A. Yes, I am sure she does.

Q. So that aspect of the mother-daughter relationship has been consolidated?

A. Consolidated, no. Love is a growing thing. I think this is beginning now and it will get better as the years go on.

Q. Is obedience on the part of the daughter to the mother an aspect of a mother-daughter relationship?

A. I think that children are sometimes obedient, sometimes disobedient. But she obeys me, yes.

Q. Now what about a feeling of security on the part of the daughter because of the accessibility of the mother? Is that what you call part of the mother-daughter relationship?

A. I have already said so, yes.

Q. Are there any further characteristics you can think of which identify the relationship between the child and mother as a proper mother-daughter relationship?

A. Yes, of course. I could spend a lot of time in this room explaining what I think about a mother-daughter relationship, but I do not want to waste the Court's time.

Q. I invite you to do so, if you think it is relevant.

A. I think one need only observe a child with a mother to understand a mother-daughter relationship. It is difficult to explain. She knows that I am her mother; she knows that I love her. We do things together. . . . We play together. She helps me cook. She watches me as I put on my makeup. We get dressed together. We do each other's hair. There is a lot involved in a mother-daughter relationship . . . the list is endless.

Q. You say you think you know when such a relationship exists?

A. It exists now, but it is very fragile.

Q. Pardon?

A. It is fragile.

Q. What is lacking?

A. Time.

Q. No, no. What is lacking in the relationship?

A. Time.

Q. That is not something in the relationship, Mrs. Jason?

A. We need more time to build up the relationship. It is fragile.

MR. JUSTICE MACAULAY—Fragile in what respect?

A. We are still getting to know each other, my lord.

MR. OSBORN—Just tell us—you seem to be going back again—is there anything on the part of the child which leads you to believe that this mother-daughter relationship does not exist now between yourself and Whitney?

A. I have answered your question. A mother-daughter relationship does exist on the part of myself and my daughter.

Q. Is it complete?

A. It will take a lot more time to be as complete as a mother-daughter relationship with another mother and another child of the same age.

Q. Just tell me once more, can you tell us any respect in which you feel it should be more complete?

A. Yes, we need more time together without strain.

Q. Is that all you can say?

A. I could say a lot of things, but that is the most concise thing I can say.

Q. Now do you suggest that a mother-daughter relationship did not exist between yourself and Whitney when Mr. Jason had this child with him in the company of his parents, prior to the judgment of his lordship, Mr. Justice Macaulay, last year?

A. No, my lord. I would not say that was a mother-daughter relationship at all. We were strangers to each other.

Q. So when Mr. Jason had the child your case is a mother-daughter relationship did not exist?

A. No, it did not have an opportunity to. I was brand-new to her, brand-new.

. . .

Q. [But] a situation did exist when Mr. Jason had the child where the child visited you and was happy and contented in your company?

A. Yes, but it was a very abnormal relationship.

Q. In what way?

184

A. I had been separated from my child for two years unnecessarily. I came back into her life. She did not know who I was. She came to visit me and lived with her father and grandparents. This is a very strange relationship for a child, I think.

Q. And despite that strange relationship your daughter was happy and contented in your company?

A. Yes, that is relative though, isn't it?

. . .

Q. Now, I would like just to ask you about a few points relating to your return to the United States. . . . Firstly, in the previous proceedings you told the Court, and it was so found, that you would not leave the child, no matter what the result of the case. Do you remember that?

A. I am sure I said words to that effect, yes.

Q. Well, it was so found and it is written in the judgment. Now is it still your attitude that it is desirable that you should remain in contact with that child?

A. My lord, it is my prayer that this is the last time this whole matter comes to court.

Q. Well?

A. May I speak, please?

Q. Certainly.

A. I hope that my lord makes a decision which he feels would be best for the child, and I would be happy with whatever that decision is.

Q. That is not quite the point.

A. I think it is.

Q. The point I was making is a simple one: Is it still your attitude that it is desirable that you remain in contact with the child?

A. Yes. I feel as her mother there is no reason why she should not be with me.

Q. If Mr. Jason is awarded custody of the child and returns to New Jersey with the child, would you also return to New Jersey to be close to that child?

A. I am not sure. I have given this a lot of thought. I think that if my lord decides that the child is better with her father, then my personal belief is that the child should be with one or the other, but this strain, this pulling, cannot go on, for the sake of the child, and if my lord feels she should be with her father, I think I would leave it at that.

Q. Do you not subscribe to the view that you should both be with the child, Mr. Jason to allow the child to have the benefit of seeing you?

A. I think Mr. Jason has made it very clear to this Court he does not think me worthy: He would only allow me a couple of hours; I would have to be supervised; I could not bring her in contact with my family; I could not take her on a trip, for instance, if I had a boyfriend. With all of these stipulations . . . I think there would be even more friction, more trouble, more strain on the child than there is now. I don't think it is fair to her.

Q. Let us assume access was properly regulated by the Court in the way his lordship thinks is correct, and you were given access to the child on a proper basis in New Jersey, would you not want to go back and see the child?

A. Theoretically, yes, but I am afraid after long experience with this problem that it just does not work that way.

Q. Do I understand your case that if Mr. Jason gets custody of this child you wish to exclude yourself from the life of the child?

A. At first I think I would, and then I would give it more thought and decide at that stage what to do.

Q. You say that as one of the parties who ought to have the child. This is really your premise, isn't it?

A. Yes, one or the other should stop the fighting.

. . .

Q. What motivated you to stay in Rhodesia when you decided not to honour the agreement to return to the United States? You say in your affidavit: "I deny that my failure to return to New Jersey was part of a scheme to prevent applicant having access. I was aware that he would probably come back to Rhodesia if I did not return to the States, but as mentioned above, I felt that I needed those few months alone with Whitney to build up a mother-daughter relationship with her." Now those few months, as I read that, refer

186

to the period you would have alone with Whitney before Mr. Jason came back?

A. Yes.

Q. You thought that within a few months after Whitney's illness you could build up that mother-daughter relationship, correct?

A. I could strengthen it, yes.

Q. Now was that period not long enough?

A. As I said to you before, Mr. Osborn, I need more time even now. You cannot sit down and say, "Today I think the mother-daughter relationship is complete." She is only a child and it will grow with time.

Q. How long do you think at this stage a satisfactory mother-daughter relationship will take to build?

A. I have no idea.

Q. Mrs. Jason, you know Mr. Berrian [George] in the United States?

A. Yes.

Q. What is the position between yourself and Mr. Berrian at present?

A. We are very close friends and we correspond.

Q. Do you intend to marry Mr. Berrian?

A. I doubt it.

Q. Do you intend to marry anybody?

A. I would like very much to marry as soon as this problem with Mr. Jason is cleared up. It is terribly aggravating. It disturbs my life. I cannot live normally because of it.

Q. Have you anybody in mind you wish to marry?

A. I have been asked.

Q. Have you accepted?

A. My plans for the future have of necessity to be undecided. A lot depends on the outcome of this trial, a lot depends on whether there is peace after this trial.

Q. There is no firm contract with anybody on marriage at present?

A. I am not engaged to be married at the moment.

Q. That is quite right. So your position now with the person who has asked you to marry him is precisely the same as it was with Mr. Berrian last year?

A. Yes, of necessity my plans have to be indefinite, undecided.

Q. The position is, nothing materialised with Mr. Berrian last year in relation to marriage, and it is quite possible nothing will materialise on this occasion?

A. I assure you I will remarry one day, as soon as there is peace with this problem.

Q. Who will you remarry?

A. I have no idea. It might be Mr. Northwood [Mel].

Q. So it might be Mr. Northwood and it might not be Mr. Northwood you marry?

A. I don't know what the future holds.

. . .

Q. I would like you to just address your mind to the situation during the course of [last year's] trial. During the course of this trial I think you told his lordship that if you were granted custody of the child by the court you wished to return to the United States and it was your intention to do so?

A. Yes, I did intend to return to the United States. I was flexible. You know, the United States is my country; I wanted to take my daughter back home. That is all. . . . I had no intention of coming to Rhodesia permanently when I left. Circumstances kept me here.

Q. I would like now to return to the agreement which you made after this victory of yours in the previous court proceedings, the agreement you signed in August of 1969. Your proposals were almost word for word incorporated in this agreement? You got your way in this agreement?

A. It is not a question of getting one's way; no, I am sorry, and I don't like it to be referred to as my victory. I regained custody of my daughter. She is my daughter. I had custody in America. I got custody here.

Q. All right. Now, Mrs. Jason, at some time after Mr. Jason left you took this decision not to go to the United States. You have told us this already, haven't you?

A. Yes.

Q. This was contrary to what you had stated your intention to be, both through your attorneys and in the agreement?

A. Yes, the child's illness was the reason why I stayed.

188

Q. And later you made an election because you had got a job?

A. Yes, several months later.

Q. Now, of course, you realised that the effect of this would be to deprive Mr. Jason of access to the child, correct?

A. My lord, I realised that he would be separated from Whitney for a period of time. His fiancée said Mr. Jason had been to a doctor, who said he must pull himself together—the doctor recommended a break with the child in order that he could get on his feet and I thought at the time it would also mean Mr. Jason could concentrate entirely on his law practice, instead of worrying about the child or being diverted in any way. I sincerely wanted him to have the opportunity to pull himself together.

Q. You thought he needed it, did you?

A. Of course, everyone did.

Q. Now, Mrs. Jason, did you take the view when you decided not to return to the United States that it was no longer important, despite what his lordship had said in his judgment, that the contact of the child should be maintained with the father and grandparents?

A. I believed sincerely that Mr. Jason would soon return to Rhodesia, so I didn't think the break would be so long.

Q. Mrs. Jason, did you think that Mr. Jason, after having gone back to the United States for the purpose of re-establishing a home in the United States, would immediately come back to Rhodesia?

A. Yes.

Q. Did you think it a desirable thing for you to wait here to invite a High Court case?

A. No. I realised, my lord, wherever I go there is going to be litigation with Mr. Jason. We don't communicate on a personal basis; we have to do it through lawyers, unfortunately. I did not plan on litigation. I don't like litigation.

Q. You realised then that the judgment contemplated access to the child by Mr. Jason and that your decision would deprive him of what the Court said he was entitled to?

A. Yes, my lord. May I explain?

MR. JUSTICE MACAULAY—Yes?

A. After your decision last year and while I had custody and while Whitney went to visit her father regularly, she came back in a very emotionally disturbed state. She would vomit; she would scream; and I realised that the decision, to be torn like this, was not a good one. After Mr. Jason left, as I have said before, I had to stay. The child never vomited, never screamed hysterically. There was such peace. She never asked about her grandparents, she did not ask about her father, until, I think, after she got out of hospital; and she was benefiting by this lack of conflict.

Q. Yes, I understand you.

. . .

MR. OSBORN—Do you lavish affection on the child?

A. I am affectionate towards Whitney.

Q. Would you describe your attitude towards her as lavishing affection on her?

A. No.

Q. Would you describe Mr. Jason's attitude as lavishing affection on her?

A. I would not use the word "lavish." I would say sometimes he overdoes it; he smothers her.

Q. Lavishing of affection, Mrs. Jason, is according to you then a little more than you would do?

A. I didn't say it was more than I would do.

Q. Do I understand you to say you do or do not lavish affection on Whitney?

A. I lavish love on Whitney.

Q. Not affection?

A. Not demonstrative, overpowering affection.

Q. Do you lavish affection on her?

A. That is a relative thing. I lavish love on her. I don't know how else to say it.

MR. JUSTICE MACAULAY—The witness has made it clear. She says she is not demonstrative in a sense, but she has an affection for the child; she loves her child.

MR. OSBORN—Now do you attend church in Salisbury?

A. No.

Q. Not at all? You no longer attend church?

190

A. I have not attended church since I came here.

. . .

Q. You don't give Whitney an opportunity of going to church with you?

A. We don't go to church together, but she does receive religious instruction at the crèche.

Q. Even though you don't go yourself, do you think there is no need for the child to attend Sunday school on Sundays?

A. She attends with her father every other Sunday, and I don't want to cause any more confusion to the child than she already has by perhaps taking her to a different church, where perhaps they might say something a little different to what she learns in her father's church. I would rather leave it to him at the moment.

Q. Before Mr. Jason came here, he was not here to take her to Sunday school, was he?

A. No. I didn't have a way of getting her there either.

Q. Do I gather from what you say that in the period 1st September 1969 to 19th February 1970 you did not make any arrangements for Whitney to attend Sunday school? Yes or No?

A. No.

Q. Why?

A. There were several reasons. One, I didn't have a car and it would be a bit far for her to walk. It is not far for me to walk, but it would have been for her. Another reason is that Mr. Jason had made such an issue of this religious fanaticism [in the previous year's proceedings] that I find I shy away from getting anywhere near anything that he could call religious fanaticism.

Q. Do you object to the present type of religious instruction which Whitney is obtaining in the Sunday school?

A. I don't know what she is being taught at Sunday school.

Q. You haven't inquired?

A. I know she goes to Sunday school. I don't know what she is being taught at Sunday school.

Q. You have no objection to it?

A. No.

191

Q. You don't think it isn't necessary?
A. I think religious instruction to an extent is necessary. She is receiving that. I am happy.

. . .

Q. I would like to ask you something about Mr. Melvyn Northwood. How long have you known him?
A. Since approximately November/December 1969.
Q. And how long have you been seeing him on a fairly frequent basis?
A. Since approximately January 1970.
Q. Since that time have you been seeing him every day, approximately?
A. Approximately.
Q. In the presence of the child Whitney?
A. Yes.
Q. Where have you been seeing Mr. Northwood?
A. He comes to my flat after work, he comes for dinner most nights.
Q. Most nights he comes to dinner?
A. Yes.
Q. Have you been away with him for weekends?
A. No.
Q. Have you ever been to his flat?
A. I have visited his flat on a few occasions.

. . .

Q. Now, on the occasions that you visited Mr. Northwood's flat . . . would Whitney have been with you?
A. Yes, she was with me all the time, unless she visited her father, which started in late February.

. . .

Q. Now, Mrs. Jason, I would like you to cast your mind back to the events of Thursday, the 19th of February, this year, which is the day on which Mr. Jason arrived in Rhodesia. . . .
A. Yes . . .
Q. Do you recollect your movements on that night?
A. Yes, I do.
Q. You had spent the night at Mr. Northwood's flat?
A. Yes.

. . .

Q. What was the accommodation which Mel had available?

A. He had two rooms, comprised of two bedrooms since there were just two bachelors living there—two beds, kitchen, bathroom, balcony.

Q. Lounge?

A. Well, the lounge was used as a bedroom for the other chap.

Q. Now, you know, of course, Mrs. Jason, that your child has said in these proceedings—or it has been testified to in these proceedings—that your child has seen you sleeping with Mr. Northwood. Is this true or untrue?

A. I have heard the tape recording in which Mr. Jason has asked my daughter: "Have you seen your mummy sleeping with Mel?" or words to that effect, and she has said, "Yes." That is all I have heard her say.

Q. Please answer the question.

A. I did answer your question.

Q. Is what the child said true or untrue?

A. I do sleep—or I have slept—with Mr. Northwood on occasion, but she has never seen this.

. . .

Q. And you have also heard Mr. Jason testify that the child has made reports to Mr. Jason about fairly intimate parts of Mr. Northwood's anatomy, haven't you?

A. Yes, I heard that disgusting remark.

Q. Would there be an opportunity for the child to see that?

A. Never, never ever.

Q. Are you sure?

A. Yes, I am more than positive.

. . .

MR. ANDERSEN [my advocate]—Mrs. Jason, you said that you had been asked to marry a person. Who was that person who asked you to marry him?

A. Mr. Berrian has asked me, and Mr. Northwood has also asked me.

Q. Mr. Berrian was in this country, I think you said, last year?

A. Yes, in October.

Q. And he left the country?

A. Yes.

Q. Was there a discussion between the two of you as to your future together then, whether you should marry or not?

A. Yes, we discussed it at that time, yes.

Q. And was any conclusion reached?

A. We decided that I would stay in Rhodesia for the time being and he would stay in America.

Q. Did the influence of Mr. Jason have anything to do with your relationship with Mr. Berrian?

A. Yes, very much so.

Q. What has it had to do with that relationship?

A. Well, my lord, Mr. Berrian is a very idealistic person, and he has never been married before and he expects the best in his marriage when he does get married, and I have been married before, unfortunately I made a mistake, and I wouldn't want any trouble with Mr. Jason to disturb a second marriage, especially with Mr. Berrian. He doesn't want to be bothered by Mr. Jason, and therefore, since I can't guarantee that he won't be, I felt it best that we don't get married for fear of this annoyance.

Q. Annoyance from Mr. Jason?

A. From the litigation and from courts and affidavits, and all that goes with it.

Q. After you made the decision you have referred to, you then later met Mr. Northwood?

A. Yes.

Q. And you grew to know him?

A. Yes.

Q. You say that he asked you to marry him. What was your feeling towards him?

A. I loved him, I do love him now.

Q. Have you made any decision as to whether you will or will not marry him?

A. Not a definite decision, no. The offer is still open, but I am anxious to see how this problem works itself out.

Q. Has Mr. Jason's influence disrupted your life at all in that regard?

A. Very much so. I wouldn't want a second marriage to be bothered by problems of the first.

Q. Now, you have been questioned, it has been suggested that you currently have three careers. Is that an accurate way of describing it?

A. No, not at all.

Q. Can your television appearances be called a career?

A. No, it is just one hour out of every week.

Q. And can your modeling be termed a career?

A. No, not by any means.

Q. Your real career is the one in journalism, your job?

A. Yes, that is my position.

Q. Do you enjoy that job?

A. I like it very much, I enjoy it very much.

Q. How does it compare with the secretarial jobs you have held previously, in America for example?

A. I find journalism much more creative, much more fulfilling, much more satisfying. It demands more intelligence and initiative.

Q. Do you think that this career helps at all in your development as a person?

A. Oh, yes, very much so.

Q. And what about the secretarial career in comparison?

A. As a secretary I felt like a machine.

Q. Now, you said, Mrs. Jason, in answer to some of my learned friend's questions, something to the effect that if Mr. Jason were to have custody of the child, you have seriously considered excluding yourself from her for the time being at least?

A. Yes.

Q. I would like you to elaborate on that. Why would you do so? Why does it occur to you that that might be necessary?

A. Well, my lord, I have very good reason to believe that she would be perhaps questioned, there would be things said about me if she lived with her father and her grandparents that would put her in the middle again. I don't want her to be torn any more than she has been. I don't want her to suffer. She should be with one or the other. I would love to see her, and perhaps in time I would, but knowing that she would have to go back to their home, where she would be grilled, "What did you do? What did she say? She's this and that"—I wouldn't want her to be subjected to that again.

Q. Mrs. Jason, what is your feeling towards the child?

A. I love my child, of course.

Q. What would your feeling be if you excluded yourself from her, did not see her?

A. My lord, I was without my daughter for two years, and as a mother it leaves a very empty feeling inside. I mean, you know in your mind that you are a mother, but you are not performing as one. It is very upsetting. (*At this stage witness becomes tearful and distressed.*)

Q. I take it then that it would not be a matter of desire that you would stop seeing her if Mr. Jason had her?

A. No, I would never ever voluntarily give her up.

Many of my Rhodesian friends took time from their jobs to come to court to testify in my behalf; the last to take the stand was Mel.

As I wrote to my mother:

Mel has been wonderful throughout this whole ordeal, and he's really proven his love for Whitney and me. He was so nervous and worried about testifying in court that he could hardly eat the whole week. But when he stood up there in the witness box on the last day of the trial, I felt so proud of him—so handsome and polite and honest.

We both admitted to being intimate (the judge would surely have seen through a lie), but both of us stressed that Whitney had *never* been aware of anything. Fortunately, Mel is very good-natured and doesn't seem to care what narrow-minded people might think. We're certainly not ashamed of our relationship.

The day after Mel testified, the front-page headlines read: ARTIST GIVES EVIDENCE IN CUSTODY CASE, and the article took up several columns. I cried the whole day, to think that Mel, sweetheart that he is, should suffer this humiliation because of me. He only laughed and said, "I've finally been recognized as an artist!"

I wasn't in court when the judgment was given. I was at work busily meeting deadlines when my lawyer phoned and told me the news: Jim had lost. The judge said a separation from her father would be in Whitney's interest. The judgment went on:

Whitney needs an undisturbed environment in which the maternal link can properly develop, and circumstances have not allowed this to occur. . . . It seems that [her father's] love for her tends to be of a possessive character and this certainly has dangers for the future of the child. All this and much that I have not mentioned casts a grave doubt on [his] suitability for the role of custodian parent and his fitness to bring the child up as a healthy-minded, balanced and integrated personality . . .

It has become clear in these proceedings that it is desirable that the occasions of access should be substantially reduced and that a moratorium from further dispute should now obtain in which the child will be free of the unsettling effects of the conflict between the parties which has dogged it since its infancy. In my view, the respondent should not see the child for more than one reasonable period a year for the next few years.

Jim's application to the court—to take custody of Whitney away from me—was denied; his visitations were to be confined to one four-week Rhodesian school holiday a year, in Rhodesia, during which time he would be required to surrender his passport to the registrar of the court prior to such period, and to let me know where he and Whitney would be; he would not be allowed to see her *at all* until August of the following year; and although I would have to stay in Rhodesia until I got permission from the court to leave, I could take Whitney away any time for holidays in South Africa or other African countries.

That same day, in a front-page story headlined JASON LOSES BID FOR CUSTODY OF DAUGHTER, *The Rhodesia Herald* reported on another aspect of the judgment:

. . . During his judgement of more than 2,000 words, which followed last week's five-day hearing, Mr. Justice Macaulay said . . . there was "one point of substance" which had caused him "some anxious thought." This was the conduct of Mrs. Jason in allowing intimacy to occur in her flat. . . .

"Had the child been a little older, I would have regarded her conduct as outweighing the need to retain the maternal link." The judge also said one had to bear in mind that an illicit relationship had not in itself been regarded as sufficient ground for depriving a divorced mother of the custody of her young children where other considerations pointed to her being better able to take care of such children.

Mrs. Jason was free of marital obligations and she was entitled to lead her private life. She was not, however, entitled to do so in a manner which jeopardized the child's moral upbringing. But her conduct, said the judge, had not been promiscuous. It had arisen from a genuine attachment to Mr. Northwood, who had proposed marriage and whom she might accept once her problems over the child's future could be resolved.

What the child needed, said the judge, was freedom from continual conflict and an undisturbed environment in which the maternal link could properly develop. . . .

. . .

While Jim made plans for an appeal, Mel and I quietly made plans for our wedding.

It would be a civil ceremony, held in the early evening in the Pichanicks' living room at Joymount, and a cocktail party for fifty or so guests would follow. Mel designed what was to be my wedding band and took the design to the best jeweler in Salisbury to be wrought in yellow gold. I made a simple, yellow satin floor-length wedding dress for myself and a matching minidress in the same fabric for Whitney. I planned to carry my favorite flowers, daisies.

We were happy. Without the stress of her frequent visits with Jim, Whitney became visibly relaxed, sometimes even joyful with me. Once, when she came in from playing with Gigi and greeted me buoyantly with, "Hello, my beautiful mommy!" I fleetingly felt the struggle was over, the torn pieces were sewn.

. . .

The appeal, which took place in October, was conducted in another courtroom, in which three wigged and robed judges presided. Jim's advocate renewed the fight for Jim's better claim to Whitney's custody, filling the small room with venomous statements about my "misconduct," "immorality," "illicit relationship," "Northwood affair."

Mel sat beside me, handsome and erect in his dark business suit, holding my hand. And with every one of Osborn's blows I squeezed Mel's hand harder, as if I were in labor.

Jim sat smugly on the other side of the room alone, listening to Osborn's pleas the way a playwright might enjoy hearing his words enacted. I wanted to run to the front of the room and scream, *What is morality?! Is stealing a child and poisoning her mind moral? Is loving a man who is gentle and kind, who would never hurt anyone or anything, immoral? What is moral, Mr. Osborn? Taking money to fight for a monster who is determined to take his child away from her mother? Tell me about morality, Mr. Osborn. I don't know what it is anymore.* But I didn't get up or say a word. I sat silently, stiffly, beside Mel, squeezing his hand.

●　●　●

Tuesday night
October 13, 1970

Dearest Mom,

. . . Judgment on J.'s appeal was given this afternoon at 2:15 by the Chief Justice of Rhodesia, Sir Hugh Beadle. . . . Thank God, the judges saw through J.'s filth, and he lost again and will have to pay everything ($). . . .

I nearly cried when the judge stressed how cruel it was that J. took a 16-month-old baby away from her mother for two whole years, etc., etc. He said that any man who would do a thing like that is merely obsessed with getting custody of the child and has no regard for the child's welfare. He also said that it was terribly wrong for J. to question Whitney on whether or not I slept with Mel and then to make a tape recording of it for the court. The three judges agreed with everything that the High Court judge decided, and they didn't change a thing from the last judgment.

I think perhaps J. will leave Rhodesia now and return to his parents and his practice. But of course he'll be back here again next year to have Whitney for his once-a-year, four-week visit. . . .

Mel has been wonderful. Whitney, of course, hasn't been aware of what's been happening. She's perfectly happy without J., and she never asks for him. . . .

I love you dearly,
Bon

Time. I had told the court Whitney and I needed more time in which to strengthen our fragile mother-daughter relationship. And the judges had concurred. They granted us a "moratorium from further dispute," a period in which Whitney would be free from her parents' "continual conflict," a time of peace.

Between the time Jim left Rhodesia in October 1970, after losing his appeal, and the time prescribed for his next visitation the following year, lay ten months—roughly forty-five weeks or three hundred days—of potential calm, a sanctioned separation from Jim. *What would I, or could I,* I wondered, *accomplish in that time?*

In the first ten months of Whitney's life, before I returned to office work, we were together continually (except for the time she spent with Jim). At that time her body was almost an extension of mine and mine of hers. I knew her life better than I knew mine. We were connected. I breathed her exhalations. But she was just an infant then. Time and evil circumstances changed all that.

While she was missing and I cried for the baby who "needed me," she was growing into a little girl who didn't know she needed me at all. And after I reappeared in her life, I unwittingly became the source of her life's major upheavals. The damage that had been done to our relationship in the years since her infancy was incalculable. And the repairs we'd effected since our reunion seemed, at times, negligible.

I looked at her. She was tall for five years old, healthy and well built. She had beautifully shaped legs; an even honey-colored tan; and long tapered fingers like Jim's mother's. Her fine, straight fair hair fell softly around her face. She had Jim's face, but my chin.

She was an aggressive child, strong-willed, and independent—far more so than I had been at five, or ten, or even twenty. *Good,* I thought, when I'd overhear her asking others the same questions she'd just asked me, to get a consensus before she'd accept my answers, *she won't make the same mistakes I made. She'll never be so naive.* I had been a quiet, timid child. Whitney was openly hostile at times, often angry toward me.

I looked for myself in her, but couldn't see me. I searched for common ground, but seldom found any. *Do other mothers feel this way?* I continued to wonder. *Do all children, as they grow up, grow away? Become people their parents hardly recognize as their own? Would Whitney have behaved this way toward me even if she hadn't been taken by Jim and subsequently poisoned against me? Was it that I didn't love her enough? That I had the wrong touch? That I wasn't a good mother after all?*

I had cherished my motherhood when she was a baby. I knew without a doubt then that as a mother I was good. And when she was missing, one of the deepest aches came from not being able to function as a mother, do what I felt best at, what I loved most to do. It was as if I were a dancer with a fractured spine, a violinist with a severed arm, a painter gone blind. But now that we'd been together for over a year, I couldn't help feeling at times that as a mother I'd become a failure. "No more children for me," I wrote to my mother one day in desperation. "Isn't motherhood a thankless task?"

Perhaps that's why I loved my job so much then. I could say to the page of type, confidently: *Go here. Move there. Insert. Transpose. Delete. Flush left. Bold face.* And the words obeyed. At my desk, confronting a language I loved, working with it, ordering and shaping it, learning from it, I was a general in charge of a small army of words, and as such I felt I was succeeding.

But the five-year-old Whitney I lived with now was far more than a word or a page of type. She was a private diary, in secret script, with large sections permanently locked away, at least from me. *Please let me read you,* I wanted to beg. *Please open up to me.*

On weekday afternoons when I walked to the crèche to pick up Whitney after work, I watched with a pang of envy as the other children ran to greet their mothers with hugs and kisses. Whitney usually walked toward me reluctantly, sullenly, scuffing the toes of her shoes along the way. Sometimes she wouldn't even allow me to take her hand as we crossed the street; I had to hold her wrist.

"Hi!" I'd greet her at the crèche's front gate. "Did you have a nice day?"

"Yes," she'd say flatly.

"What did you do today?"

"Play."

"What did you play?"

"Games."

"What did you have for lunch?"

"Meat and veg."

"Anything else?"

"Pudding."

We continued to take baths together every evening, and her bedtime ritual included our favorite stories and poems about the adventures of Christopher Robin and Winnie-the-Pooh. But there was still a barrier between us that I couldn't break through. Although I sat close beside her on her bed, when I tried to hold her while I read, she pulled away. Sometimes her head would fall against my shoulder, but then I'd discover it was only because she'd gone to sleep.

What can I do to make her love me? I wondered. *How can I wash the residual poison from her mind?* The only answer I could find was to be myself and to try to provide an environment in which she was free to be herself, a loving environment, blessed with promised peace.

• • •

I woke at six on weekday mornings, went to my kitchen, made a pot of tea, and brought it back to bed with me—the daybed in our living room—to read the just-delivered morning paper. This was my quiet time, a favorite time, alone with my thoughts and my sweet, milky tea and the news of the faraway outside world and the slow-moving sounds of Salisbury at sunrise. Then, at six-thirty, when I woke Whitney with a glass of freshly squeezed orange juice, the pace of the day quickened.

This morning could stand for all the others: I opened the draperies in Whitney's room to let in the clear morning light and began to sing, *"Soooo, let the sun shine in, face it with a grin. Smilers never lose and frowners never win! So—* Do you like that song? It used to be my favorite in fourth grade. I sang it *all* the time and must have driven everybody *mad.* Would you like to hear more?"

Whitney, sitting up in bed only half awake, sipped her juice and nodded politely.

"Sooooo, open up your heart and let the sun shine in! . . . Ta da! Now, what would you like for breakfast? And what shall we wear today? . . ." Questions and admonitions filled the morning hour we had together. "When you finish your cinnamon toast, please come to the bathroom so I can brush your teeth and comb your hair. . . . Why are you staring out of the window, darling? Haven't you heard anything I've said? Please finish your breakfast now. We must leave soon. . . ."

When Margaret arrived one morning, she was not her usual cheerful self. She seemed weighted down, tired, old.

"What's wrong, Margaret?" I said. "You don't look at all well—"

"Oh, madam," Margaret sobbed. "It is my firstiborn. She has run away. I received a letter from my sister. My sister said

204

my firstiborn has run away from the mission school. And she is pregnant, madam!"

"How old is she, Margaret?"

"She is sixteen years old, madam. And she is not married."

"What can you do?"

"I cannot go back to my village now, madam. It is too far away, too long a journey. My sister is there. She will look—" Margaret's voice broke with a sob. She wiped her eyes with a clean white hanky, lowered her head and shook it slowly from side to side. "Childrens are too much troubles," Margaret said, wringing the white hanky in her thick black hands, "too much troubles."

• • •

One day as we walked home from the crèche Whitney was particularly pensive. I asked her what was wrong.

"Are you going to get married?" she asked me soberly.

"Some day I'll get married again," I said.

"When?"

"Oh, when I'm a big girl," I teased.

She looked up at me seriously. "Who will you marry when you get married again? Melvyn?"

"Mel and I are planning to get married—"

"No," she said sternly, "you can't marry Melvyn. He's *mine!*"

"All right," I laughed. "He's yours.

• • •

Mel drank. It wasn't a problem, but it was important to him. He liked to go to his favorite pub after work and have a beer or two, relax, talk with his friends, or just be quiet, lost in his thoughts. Unlike my father, who became belligerent when he drank, Mel became more affable and outgoing. The beer refreshed him, revived him, and helped him overcome his natural reticence and shyness.

So every weekday evening, while I cooked dinner in my little kitchen and Whitney played with Gigi, Mel was at the pub drinking beer; and when he arrived at dinnertime, he was always in a good mood.

"Why don't you join me?" Mel said one day. "I'd like to have you there with me."

"I can't Melvy," I said. "I don't like to drink—"

"Just one beer?"

"No, I can't. I have the children—"

"Whitney and Gigi could come too—"

"No," I said, "I just can't." Somehow I couldn't tell him how much I hated bars or pubs—and how much his daily visits to one troubled me.

• • •

I knew when I saw it down the road—as soon as I saw the colored lights that made it different from all the other buildings and houses we had passed—I knew what would happen next. The wheels of the car would veer off their course and roll toward the lights—the lights that belonged on a Christmas tree but this was July—and onto the gravel lot that crunched under the weight of my father's big old car.

I knew we might never get to the lake. My big brother's fishing pole would remain in the skinny cardboard box behind us. Our bathing suits and towels would stay dry and folded in my mother's beach bag. And all the food my mother had prepared for our cookout in the woods would be baked by the sun in the trunk of the car before the end of the day.

But I didn't say anything when the car turned from the road, onto the gravel, and stopped in front of the place with the Christmas lights. It had happened before; and I knew nothing could stop it now.

"Just a quick one," my father said to the steering wheel, "and then we'll be on our way."

These places are all alike, I thought. *Small, white buildings, outlined with single strands of red-and-blue-and-green-and-yellow Christmas tree lights, and owned by men with short names. Bill's Bar and Grill. Tom's Tavern. Pete's Place.* My father called them all gin mills, but I didn't know why. I knew about cotton gins and gin

206

rummy and lumber mills and windmills. *But what does "gin mill" mean? And what is a gin?*

When the front door closed behind us, it sealed out the summer day. There was no sunshine inside, no daylight, no air. Only the bluish-gray cast that shone from the television above the bar, and the stale fumes of old beer and burning cigarettes.

My father sat at the long wooden bar, near workmen in summer undershirts and dungarees drinking tall glasses of beer and watching baseball on television.

"Sit over there," my mother said to us, pointing to a table in the corner of the dark and airless room, "and be good kids, and the man will bring you some Cokes."

I followed my brother through the darkness to the table. He pulled a chair out for himself and slumped his thin body into it. He folded his arms in front of his chest and hung his head forward, staring at the stripes on his T-shirt.

The bartender came toward us carrying a round metal tray. With sweeping strokes he wiped the table, put down cork coasters, and placed a glass of Coke on each.

"Sir," my brother said, straightening himself in his chair, "would you please open the curtain up there? We'd like to read."

"Sure thing," the bartender said, as he reached to push aside the dark curtain covering the small window, the only window in the room. "Anything else?"

"No, thanks."

"Like something to eat? Some potato chips? Pretzels?"

"No, thanks," my brother said. "We're gonna have lunch soon. At the lake." He took a comic book out of his back pocket and began to read about Robinson Crusoe.

I had a sip of my Coke. Then I counted the ice cubes in my glass . . . then the stripes on my brother's shirt . . . and the black and white squares on the floor . . . and the bottles behind the bar . . .

All of the people in the baseball stadium stood to sing to the flag.

> THE BOMBS BURSTING IN AIR . . .
> THAT OUR FLAG WAS STILL THERE . . .

Why aren't they standing here? I wondered. *Isn't everybody supposed to stand?*

O'ER THE LA-AND OF THE FREEEEeeeee
AND THE HOME OF THE BRAAAAAAVE

HI, EVERYBODY, THIS IS MEL ALLEN,
COMING TO YOU FROM YANKEE STADIUM
ON THIS BEAUTIFUL SATURDAY AFTERNOON—

Above the sound of the television announcer, I heard my father call my name, and I ran to the bar to obey.

"Ready for 'nother soda?"

"No, thanks."

"Why not?"

"I'm not thirsty anymore. I've had enough."

"Oh, you have, have you? Y'hungry? Want something t'eat?"

"No, thanks."

"Well, what do you want, then?"

I crossed my fingers behind my back. "Nothing."

"That's easy enough! Hey, bartender, bring this old lady here a glass of nothin'!"

The man on the stool beside my father reached out for me, but I backed away.

"Say, whatsa matter, don't ya like me? Come'ere, sweety, I'm not gonna bite."

I looked down at my sneakers. One of them, and then the other, moved closer to the man. He held out his hand and laid it heavily on my head. I closed my eyes and saw a huge spider crawling over my hair.

"Where'd ya get yer lovely hair, sweety? From yer mommy over here?"

I wished that the sun would come into the room and shine through my eyeglasses and burn his face. Once, outside in the woods, my brother had taken my glasses and held them close to a dry leaf; the point of a sunbeam went through the glasses and burned a hole in the leaf. I wanted to burn his face.

"What'sa matter, sweety, cat got yer tongue?"

"She's just shy," my mother said. "Talk to the man, honey. He asked you a question."

I turned to the man. "*GOD* gave me my hair."

"God, huh? Ha, that's good! And where's God, sweety?"

"Out *there*," I said, pointing to the window across the room.

"Smart kid ya got here, fella," the man said to my father.

"Na, she's just a dumb blonde like all the rest."

AND IT'S A HIGH FLY TO LEFT CENTER!
MANTLE'S RACING OVER—
HE'S UNDER IT—
HE'S GOT IT!—FOR THE THIRD OUT!
AT THE END OF FIVE, IT'S—

I watched as a fly walked slowly and carefully around the rim of my glass of Coke, balancing itself like a tightrope walker in the circus. I had never been to the circus, but I'd seen one on television once. The wild animals sat on high stools like the stools at the bar, and they growled at the sound of the whip.

The fly made a full circle around the glass and flew to the window above my head. *I wish I could fly, too,* I thought. *You're lucky, fly.*

From my seat at the table I watched the square of daylight in the window—the trees and sunshine and clouds and light-blue sky—all beyond my reach.

I imagined I was at the bottom of a well . . . I had set out on foot for the lake by myself . . . it was many miles through thick woods . . . along the way, I slipped and fell into an abandoned well, fifty feet deep and four feet wide . . . for hours I called for help but no one heard me, no one came to my rescue . . . finally, I sat quietly, exhausted and thirsty . . . I was so thirsty I had to drink the water in the well, which was as brown as Coke . . . there were huge spiders and rats and lizards in the well; they crawled in my hair, but I tried not to be afraid . . . I kept looking up at the clear blue sky and clean white clouds through the opening way above my head . . .

The bartender brought a dish of potato chips to the table and more glasses of Coke. I wondered why we were allowed to drink so many Cokes at these places but never any at home, because "it's bad for your teeth." Or why we could eat potato chips here but never at home, because "they're not good for you."

I watched my father order two more beers and I thought about my bathing suit, folded neatly in my mother's beach bag, ready for the next Saturday when my father would say at the breakfast table, "Hey, kids, what'd'ya say we go to the lake today?"

• • •

"Melvy, do you love me?"

"Hmmmm?"

"I said, do you love me?"

"Pardon?"

"Do you love me?"

"Sorry, love, I didn't hear you."

"You heard me. Why can't you say it?"

"Why do I have to say it?"

"Because I'd like to hear it once in a while."

"I come here for dinner every night—I see you every day. Doesn't that tell you anything?"

"Yes, it tells me you like my cooking."

• • •

Mel and I approached the jeweler's shop as nervously as thieves. We walked in and stood at the glass counter without looking at each other. "Are you as terrified as I am?" I whispered to Mel when the jeweler went to bring out our custom-made ring. "Quite," he said, drumming the counter top softly with his fingertips. I looked at him. Was it that his usually healthy, tanned complexion had suddenly faded to a pale, grayish green—or was he merely reflecting my complexion? "How does it fit?" the jeweler said. "Not quite right," I told him.

We left without the ring, in silence. "Melvy," I said finally,

210

"let's forget the whole thing. Let's go on as if we'd never mentioned the word marriage—and let's never mention it again. I love you, but I just can't go through with this. It's not you, it's—"

"I know," he said. "I understand." He, too, seemed relieved.

"I think I should start saving to go home. I haven't seen my family in over a year—" *Please say you'll come with me.*

"Yes, I think that's a good idea. Sometimes you seem homesick."

"I'll try to put away some money each month, and when I have enough I'll leave—" *Please say we'll go together; I couldn't bear to say good-bye—*

"Yes, you must do that."

• • •

During the months between Jim's return to Rhodesia in February 1970 and his departure that October, he paid thirty-nine Rhodesian dollars per month in child support (maintenance) for Whitney. This, plus the approximately twenty-five dollars I earned each month from freelance modeling and television appearances, and the twenty-five dollars Mel gave me every month toward groceries, helped to supplement the small beginner's salary I earned as editorial assistant at the *Rhodesian Farmer* magazine.

But after the second custody suit and the accompanying bad publicity, freelance modeling and television work was no longer offered to me. And after Jim returned to the United States, he stopped paying any maintenance for Whitney. At Mr. Clarke's suggestion, I wrote to Jim to request it of him.

"It is my intention to write to you periodically," my November 5 letter began, "to inform you of Whitney's welfare. This is the first of such letters. I trust it will reach you at the above address." I related Whitney's news: that she'd come down with chicken pox (she called them chicken pops) two days before her birthday but had since recovered completely; and then I asked to know "what provisions you are making for sending monthly maintenance cheques for Whitney." My letter was brief (four paragraphs), businesslike, and clear. Jim did not reply.

I wrote to him again, on November 27, and sent this letter registered mail. ". . . Just this morning," I told him, "Whitney said she wondered why you have not written to her at all. I told her that I had written to you but had not received a letter from you either. I told her perhaps you were very busy, and she said, 'Maybe he's busy counting out all of his money.' "

Once again, I tried to ask politely for child support: "I trust that in the coming month the spirit of Christmas will move you to send a maintenance cheque for November and December, in addition to a Christmas gift for Whitney. She hasn't asked for anything specific, but I'm sure you can think of something nice. . . . If you write to Whitney I'll read the letter to her and take down an answer—whatever she wants to say. And it won't be long before she'll be at school and learns to write her own letters. . . ." I received the signed return receipt proving Jim had gotten my letter, but there was no indication he had read its contents. He didn't write to Whitney or to me. He did not send money.

By the end of December I was growing desperate, and my letter of the twenty-ninth reflected my anger: "This is my third attempt to communicate with you. I have received no answers to nor acknowledgements of my previous two letters, so I trust this try will be more successful. . . . As you know, Whitney starts school this coming month. The cost of outfitting her with school uniforms, jerseys, blazers, shoes, and so on, will certainly far exceed my budget allowance. I should think that if you really cared about her welfare (regardless of where she lives), you would take these matters into consideration and would send the monthly maintenance cheques for her without fail."

I continued to wait for a reply.

• • •

My diary during this period became less a record of daily events than a record of monthly expenses. I opened accounts at a pharmacy, butcher, and grocer in Salisbury, as well as two major department stores. During the month I shopped solely on credit; and, when I received my monthly salary check, I paid all of my bills at once and had little or nothing left over:

Expenses:	Paid
Rent	$ 51
Braemar (crèche)	14
Margaret	12
PDS (grocer)	20
Supreme (butcher)	25
Medix (pharmacy)	10
City of Sby (electricity)	6
Ministry of Education (W's school)	3
Rhodesia Herald (home delivery)	3
Greaterman's (dept. store)	10
Barbour's (dept. store)	10
	$164
Income:	
Rhodesian Farmer (net salary)	$153

Without Mel's financial assistance of twenty-five dollars a month, I wouldn't have known what to do.

How did my mother do it? I often wondered during those months. *How did she support her four children when my father failed to do so?*

• • •

My father couldn't keep a job for long. Perhaps he tried. But there always seemed to come a time when he had had enough and had to either tell his boss what he truly thought of him or get drunk and run off to God-knows-where. When the company phoned our home to inquire as to his whereabouts, my mother, in all innocence, would reply, "But I thought he was on a business trip—?"

After he returned, penniless and jobless, from wherever he'd been, my father would lie on the living room sofa all day reading paperback books while my mother went to work to support the family.

He'd be there reading when I got home from school and would still be reading when my mother came home from her job and started supper. "That gee-dee-ess-oh-bee!" my mother would softly hiss between clenched teeth as I helped her peel the carrots and potatoes for stew. "All he's good for is reading books. Who ever fed his family by reading?!"

For a while my father tried to sell real estate for a friend who had an office up the road. He told me once that he hated selling—"Just don't have the knack," he confessed—but he liked the fact that he could sit alone in the real estate office reading while he waited for prospective buyers to walk in. He worked on a commission-only basis, which meant he wasn't paid for reading.

Two or three times in the course of several years he sold a house, and we celebrated the event for days. In between, all of his dreams and fantasies—a new car, new coats for the kids, the family's first vacation somewhere, whatever—included the phrase, "NEXT BIG DEAL—" The phrase became a joke among my sisters and me, meaning, "It's nice to think about, but it will never happen."

"Next big deal," he once said, "I'll give each of you kids a hundred dollars to do whatever you want with. How'dya like that?" We nodded knowingly. But one day this fantasy did come true, and he kept his word. I spent my hundred on two weeks at a church-sponsored summer camp in the Adirondack Mountains. I was fifteen at the time and would have sold my soul to get away from home.

When I was eleven and my youngest sister had just started school, my mother went to work full-time. She started as a typist at an aeronautical firm an hour's drive from our home, earning less than seventy-five dollars a week, and gradually worked her way up to be the private secretary to the vice-president of the company. My mother was efficiency incarnate.

I can still see her standing outside in the cold at seven-thirty in the morning waiting for her ride, looking so alone and thin.

214

From my bedroom window I would watch her stand there shivering, until the car pulled over and she quickly got in and they drove away.

I woke my younger sisters the way my mother woke me, by rubbing their backs gently and whispering, "It's time to get up—rise and shine!—breakfast is on the table—"

It was all there ready for us: a pitcher of orange juice, an assortment of cold cereals, fresh fruit, toast and jam and butter, milk and sugar, bowls and plates, placemats and napkins. Nothing was ever missing. Except her presence, and her voice telling us, "Eat all gone," and "Don't forget your lunches."

Before she left for work she also made our lunches and lined them up on the edge of the kitchen counter in a row. Each bag contained a thick sandwich filled with egg or tuna salad or sliced meat, an apple or pear, celery and carrot sticks, a hard-boiled egg and a small saltshaker, some cookies, and milk money (four pennies) wrapped in foil.

Almost every day when I opened my lunch at school one of my friends would remark that I had a better lunch than she or he had. *And their mothers don't even work,* I thought; *some of them even have maids.* I used to eat my lunch slowly, almost haughtily.

My mother did it all, stoically: working to support the family while my father dreamed aloud about the "next big deal"; cooking, cleaning, laundering, marketing; raising four children while my father either drank or read to flee responsibility.

How did she do it? I repeatedly asked myself in Rhodesia when I had such trouble supporting only Whitney and myself, with no help at all from Jim. Even from a distance of many years and thousands of miles I could see my mother clearly, waiting outside in the cold for her ride, and I thought: *Somehow she did it. And so will I.*

• • •

On the last Thursday in November 1970 we celebrated Thanksgiving. It was Mel's first Thanksgiving dinner, and Whitney's first with me, and they both indulged me. I spent days planning and preparing. I bought a fat, fresh, ten-pound turkey for $5.15 and left instructions for Margaret to put it in

215

the oven for me while I was at work. The night before, I made an apple pie. Then I left the turkey giblets, with onions, carrots, celery, and seasoning, to simmer slowly while I slept. All I had to do when I got home from work was make the gravy and vegetables.

"Thanksgiving is a *special* dinner," I announced when the three of us sat down to eat.

Whitney, who seldom accepted what I said without corroborating evidence, asked the inevitable, *"Why?"*

Mel, who was carving the turkey with a draftsman's care and precision, added, "Doesn't look very much different from your usual efforts, love. I mean," he added, taking as much care with his words as he was with the carving knife, "it's up to your usual standard of excellence—"

"In *America*," I began, as if I were a kindergarten teacher, "Thanksgiving is a holiday in which families gather together for a traditional feast commemorating the Pilgrims' first Thanksgiving in 1621. The Pilgrims," I explained to Whitney, "were the first settlers in America. They were brave people who came from far away to start a new life in a new land. Their first year in America was very hard and some of them didn't survive. But those who did made a feast of their first harvest, and they called it Thanksgiving because they were thankful to God for bringing them through." Whitney chewed her food and looked at me dubiously. "The Pilgrims had roast turkey and cranberries and corn and pumpkin and succotash—"

"Suck a what?" Mel said.

"Succotash is an Indian word for lima beans mixed with corn. So in America we—"

"My daddy is in America," Whitney corrected me. "We are in Rhodesia."

"Yes, honey," I said, dispensing with my lecture. *This is not America, and we are not a family, and I am failing* . . . "Please eat all of your turkey now. Meat is good for you."

• • •

For several weeks after Jim's departure, Whitney never mentioned him. Then one day she announced she had "visited" me

216

"long enough." "When," she asked, "am I going to my daddy's?"

"Your daddy is coming back next year to take you on a special holiday," I told her.

"Good," she said. "How many days is 'next year'? He has my tennis dress, and I want it."

"Next time I write to him I'll ask him to send it," I said.

• • •

We spent Christmas 1970 at our flat. On Christmas Eve while Whitney slept, Mel and I decorated the tree he bought for us; and in the morning, early, when Mel returned, we opened our gifts together. Mel brought with him my gift for Whitney—a Siamese kitten (that I'd bought for six dollars) whom we named Samson—as well as his gift to her—a scooter (which she called her scrooter). There were other things, too. With a check for twenty-five dollars from my mother and one for ten dollars from one of my sisters, I'd bought Whitney a new dress, some books and paints, puzzles and toys. And there was a large package from Jim, delivered to our flat a few days before by one of his Rhodesian friends (we still hadn't heard directly from Jim), containing a beautiful tall walking doll with a pretty pink dress and pink ribbons in her long shining hair, who held another doll, a baby doll, in her arms.

"Oh, she's *lovely!*" I said when Whitney opened the box and stood the doll up—it was as tall as Whitney was, sitting on the floor—"I would have loved a dolly like that when I was a little girl!" It was true. The doll was breathtaking. "Very expensive," Mel said to me softly so that Whitney wouldn't hear. I looked at the box—"Made in Italy"—searching in the crevices and through the wrapping for a card or a note or a check from Jim. I found nothing. *If only he had sent some money, too,* I thought. *Whitney doesn't even play with dolls.*

With the new flash attachment I gave him for Christmas, Mel took photos of Whitney opening her gifts. When I wrote to Jim on December 29, I offered to send him copies. "If you should like prints of those pictures [of Whitney opening Jim's package], just write to me—including a cheque for Whitney's main-

217

tenance for November, December, and January—and I will send the photos to you." He did not respond.

At a large New Year's Eve party on a farm outside of town, I met a young, attractive businesswoman who owned and operated one of the few modeling agencies in Salisbury.

"I've seen your ads," she said to me as we were being introduced.

"Oh?" I said, flattered by her interest and impressed by her self-confident good looks.

"Yes. And I think you need to take my course. Badly."

"I'm afraid I can't afford it," I said, deflated.

"My dear," she said, "you can't afford not to. You can pay me later. I'll see that you get jobs."

Needing the supplementary income, I accepted her advice and her offer. I brought Whitney with me to the classes, and she sat beside me and listened attentively to the lectures on skin and hair care, makeup, dress sense, camera movement, exercise. During one of the exercises, when the class inched around the room sitting on the floor with our legs outstretched, Whitney sat cross-legged on a table watching the strange procession. As I passed her on my rounds and waved to her, she giggled.

One of the first ads I did for this agency was a group shot of three models—the owner's daughter, Sharon, who was exactly Whitney's age, born the same day and year; another model; and me—wearing hand-knitted woolen stoles, suitable for chilly evenings in Rhodesia's mild winter. But it was midsummer at the time we did the ad, hot outside, even hotter under the studio's strong lights, hotter still beneath the woolen stoles.

Sharon fidgeted and whined. "This is *prickly,*" she complained, pulling at her stole and doing a wiggly dance of discomfort. "Stop it," her mother warned her a few times, but Sharon only continued to dance and whine. The owner, Bea, who was divorced like me and supporting her daughter on her own, lost her patience. She walked toward us and slapped Sharon's face. "Didn't I tell you to stop it?!" she shouted. The child began to cry, whimpering, "I'm sorry, Mummy."

Bea bent over, put out her arms, and Sharon wrapped her

arms around Bea's neck and her legs around Bea's waist. "I know it's hot," Bea said to her daughter softly, blowing gently on her neck. "But you are a model now. You are a *professional.* You are doing a *job.* The sooner you stand still and smile, the sooner we can take this bloody photograph and go home for a swim. Do you understand me?" Sharon nodded and kissed her mother spontaneously. "Yes, Mummy."

"All right then, let's get back to work," Bea said as she put Sharon down and smoothed her daughter's hair.

All of a sudden, I wanted to cry. *Why?! Why?! What's wrong with me? Why can't I get through to Whitney like that? I've never shouted at her, never slapped or spanked her. Yet she's never held me the way Sharon held Bea. She's never even kissed me—* I smiled for the camera, my made-up, model smile. But all the while I was choking back tears, tears of confusion, disappointment, and envy.

· · ·

"Whitney started kindergarten on Tuesday of this week," I wrote to my mother on January 21, 1971. "She looks so cute in her uniform. When I took her on the first day she was quite happy, but I got a bit choked up. The mother of a school-aged child—wow. . . ."

What I *didn't* write to my mother was that, in order to be able to send Whitney to school, I had to buy her school uniform and supplies at Barbour's department store on credit. The total bill—for two green plaid jumpers, one cardigan, one pair of Wellingtons (rubber boots), one pair of Clark's shoes, a briefcase, and a gray felt hat—came to only $28.33; but I couldn't afford to pay it. I sent Jim a breakdown of Whitney's school items, with the Barbour's receipts attached, and begged him to pay this bill at least. "And if you doubt the cheque would go to the proper destination if you sent it to *me,*" I wrote, "then send it direct to Barbour's. . . ." Jim never paid the Barbour's bill, and I continued to wait for his first letter.

· · ·

After Whitney started school, I would take her to meet her bus at seven every morning and return to the flat to read the paper and drink tea. When Margaret arrived, we had time to chat before I left for work.

Once we discussed the political situation in the country. We were standing in my kitchen—she washing the dinner dishes from the night before, and I pouring myself another cup of tea—and I asked her what the Africans really thought of the white people.

"We need them, madam," she said. "Where would the African be without the European? There would be no jobs. No shops. No schools for the childrens. No hospitals. Yes, we need them, madam."

But most of the time we talked about children. Or men.

Margaret told me about her new boyfriend, Edwin, with whom she was living in the African township of Highfields.

"He is a good man, madam. He is very good to me. He is a clerk at Barclays Bank. And he does not drink."

On his days off Edwin came to the flat to help Margaret with her ironing. One day when I came home for lunch I met him. He was standing at the ironing board, tall and handsome, looking all out of place in his dark three-piece suit. He bowed stiffly and shook my hand. "Hello, madam," he said softly. "I am very happy to meet you."

"Oh, Margaret," I said to her the next morning, "Edwin is really nice! Imagine, coming here to help you with your ironing. I don't know any American men who would do that."

"*Really,* madam?" She giggled.

• • •

Jim finally wrote. It was an incoherent letter containing a convoluted excuse for not sending child support because he was returning to Rhodesia in August to take Whitney on a holiday. I replied in a rage, ". . . You say, 'I have no other solution unless you do not want me to see Whitney at all.' Well, it's not up to me to decide whether or not you see Whitney. That has already been decided. However, it *is* up to me to see that Whitney is adequately supported; and that is why I have written four letters since November, politely requesting you to send maintenance money for Whitney. . . . If in fact you can *only* afford the holiday, then your genuine concern for your child's daily needs, is, in my opinion, questionable." Our correspondence ended there.

• • •

Bea phoned me one day at work: "I have a mother-daughter job. Are you interested?"

"Bea, you know I'm always interested in earning a few extra dollars, but what about you and Sharon?"

"I think you and Whitney would be better. You look more alike—"

"We *do?* . . . Who is the ad for, Bea?"

"Barbour's. It's their fiftieth anniversary. A big ad campaign. They're looking for rich-looking models to represent their posh store—"

"Oh, if they only knew—I can't even afford to pay their account!"

In mid-March Whitney and I did the ad. I modeled a hand-embroidered organdy dress for Barbour's worth five times more than my monthly rent. I tried to look rich.

The young photographer, fresh from London, was nervous about the shot. "All right now, this is going to be a tight close-up. . . . Mum, put your arm around your little girl—"

I did as he said; Whitney squirmed uncomfortably. "Please be still, darling," I whispered, "this won't take long."

"—tilt your head down a bit, love, would you? Now look up ever so slightly—" He hit his forehead with his palm. "Bags, bags, bags! Did anyone ever tell you you have bags under your eyes, Mum? I can't get rid of the flippin' shadows!"

Whitney grew increasingly restless. She didn't like having my arm around her. "Pretty soon," I said, talking like a ventriloquist through my model-smile. "Just hang on a bit longer."

"—lick your lips . . . that's it. . . . Don't stare! Close your eyes and open them when I say so . . ."

The session lasted less than two hours, and together Whitney and I earned twelve dollars.

The following Saturday I took Whitney shopping so she could buy what she wanted with her half of the money. I also took her to the hairdresser as a treat to have her hair trimmed, instead of my doing it for her. "You're a model now," I told her proudly. "You have to have your hair done *professionally.*"

I read as the hairdresser worked on Whitney's hair. I'd asked him to trim it; but while I wasn't watching, he cut too much. Suddenly Whitney started to scream at me, "I'm going to tell my daddy on you! I'm going to tell my daddy and he's going to shoot you with his gun!"

Everyone in the salon turned and looked in our direction. Women took their curlered heads out from under hair driers. All scissors stopped. Whitney continued shouting as I paid the bill. "My daddy is going to burn your house down!" she screamed, with tears streaming down her angry face. Stunned by her outburst, unsure of what to say or do, I quickly took her arm and steered her out the door.

"What *is* it?" I said as we walked home. "What's gotten into you?"

"I'm going to tell my daddy!" she shouted. "I'm going to tell!"

"Tell him what, Whitney? Are you angry that your hair is too short?" She nodded angrily. "It's a pretty hairdo, honey. It's called a pixi. And when it grows in it will be even prettier because it will be thicker. You have very thin hair, and every once in a while we have to trim it so that—"

She wasn't listening. Her face was tight, hateful, frightening. "I'm going to tell my daddy on you!" she screamed all the way home.

After we got home, I set the top of Whitney's hair, and when it dried it looked longer, softer, more feminine. She seemed placated. But when Mel arrived, he took one look at Whitney's short hair and asked me to join him in the kitchen for a "private chat."

"What did you *do?*" he whispered. "Why did you let them cut it so short?"

"I was reading," I stammered. "It was so quick. I—" I start-

222

ed to cry. "I can't seem to do anything right! I'm a complete failure! If I had the money I'd get out of here on the next plane. I don't know where I'd go, but I'd go somewhere—*alone!*"

Mel hugged me. "There, there. I'm sorry, love. Looks like you've had a bad day."

• • •

Whitney was free to play outdoors with Gigi until the sun set at six. She knew that the sunset was her signal to come home for dinner. But one evening she didn't come home.

I phoned Gigi's house, thinking she was surely there, but Gigi's sister Jean told me Gigi was at her ballet lesson, and Whitney had not been by. I called Whitney's name from our balcony, but there was no response. I paced the flat frantically, afraid to leave it to look for her, lest she arrive while I was out and wonder why the door was locked and no one was home.

At six-thirty I phoned Gigi's house again and asked Jean to check each room. No Whitney. My mind climbed treacherous peaks and peered down. *Has someone taken her? Has she run away?*

When I was about Whitney's age, I'd tried to run away from home. I walked out into the woods one summer evening and planned never to return.

I walked for about a mile, or so it seemed, until I got to the big rope swing that hung from an oak tree in the clearing. I decided to stop there and swing for a little while before I continued my journey.

The swing was old, worn by weather and years of use, and it creaked with every move. The long ropes that tied it to the tree carried the wooden seat and me far up into the dark summer sky. As I pumped my legs as hard as I could, pointing them straight forward on the way up and bending them in tight on the way down, the swing took me higher and higher until I was above the treetops, almost touching the moon with my toes. There had been times before when I had been afraid to go so high, but not that night. That night I wanted to fly away.

That afternoon, when my father was working in the backyard, he'd called to me, "Get me a monkey wrench!" Quickly, without asking questions, I ran into the house and down the cellar stairs to the workbench, where I nervously tried to imagine what a monkey wrench could be. Knowing he'd get angry if I took too long, I picked up one of the many tools and quickly brought it out to him. "That's not a monkey wrench!" he yelled. "Don't you even know what a monkey wrench is, you stupid good-for-nothing kid?!" I shook my head. "Get out of my sight," he said, and as I ran from him, I decided to run away.

He won't miss me, I said to myself, as I pumped even harder on the swing.

Just then I heard my brother's voice in the distance, calling my name. *If they want me, they'll have to come and get me,* I thought. As his voice came closer, I pumped harder. At the height of a swing, surveying the treetops, I listened as the sound of my name filled the woods, and I smiled.

It didn't take long for my brother to find me. *Perhaps he tried to run away, too, when he was my age and only got this far,* I thought. "C'mon home," he said, as he gently pulled me from the swing and led me through the woods, across the field, and down to the dirt road where he had parked his car. It had been Grandpop's car until he died the spring before. It was a beetle-fat, black Oldsmobile, which we called the Old-Mobile. Inside, it smelled like paint and reminded me of Pop.

I never tried to run away again. I never had to. Because from that night on I lived in a home of my own creation, full of love and happy children. My own children. Although I returned with my brother that summer night, for the remaining years I lived at home I was never really there.

At seven o'clock Whitney walked in.

"Where have you been?" I said. "I've been worried."

She looked me in the eye and said, "I've been at Gigi's."

"But I phoned Gigi's and Jean said you weren't there."

She put her hands on her hips and said defiantly, "I *was!*"

Suddenly I saw in her eyes, her face, her stance, not Whitney but Jim. I saw him look at me before we were married and lie,

224

"I am a Christian, too; I believe the same things you do"; I saw his affidavits, hundreds of legal pages, blackened with lies; I saw him on the witness stand, looking so pious and sincere, yet uttering nothing but twisted facts and blatant lies. All of the rage I felt toward him rushed through my bloodstream, red and hot, burning every cell of my body.

"I know you weren't at Gigi's!" I shouted. "Where were you?"

"I was at Gigi's!"

My friend Sue had often told me that what Whitney needed was "a good hiding," but I'd replied, "No, I can't spank her; it's not her fault she's a difficult child."

I took Whitney by the arm, turned her around, and smacked her buttocks. "Don't lie to me!" I shouted. "Liars are the worst people in the world!"

Stunned that I had actually struck her, Whitney glared at me vengefully. She looked around the room, saw that the doors to her balcony were opened, and screamed as loudly as she could.

The temperature of my anger soared out of control. "Never spank your children with the same hand you use to hold a tennis racket," Sue counseled her friends. So I opened my left hand flat and brought it down again on Whitney's buttocks. She screamed even louder.

"Tell me the truth, or I'll spank you again," I shouted.

"No!"

Throughout my childhood my mother struck me only once, because I'd refused to wear a certain pair of shoes.

"They're ugly!" I told her.

"They're the only school shoes you have," my mother said.

"I *hate* white bucks! They're *boys'* shoes, and they're *ugly!*"

"YOU WILL WEAR THEM!" she yelled as she picked up one of the shoes and hit me with it. And then she hit me again and again and again. I knew even then that something had snapped inside of her, that her suddenly uncontrollable anger was much larger than me or my shoes.

As she pounded me with the white bucks, I called to her, "No, Mommy, no!" hoping my voice would be heard in the distant place where her mind had gone.

"No, Mommy, no!" Whitney was screaming as I pounded

her buttocks repeatedly with the flat of my left hand. Her voice reached the place where my mind had gone, and I started to cry.

"I'm sorry," I said, realizing I'd really been hitting Jim. "Sorry." The force of my blows, even with my left hand, had been so hard my watch had come apart. "I'm so sorry," I said, sitting limply on her bed in tears, meaning "sorry for everything"—sorry I had lost control, sorry she had been the rope with which her parents had played tug-of-war, sorry I had ever met her father, sorry I'd been born.

Whitney stood in the center of the room, head bowed, sniffling.

"Honey, don't ever tell lies," I said softly, defeated. "You must always, always tell the truth. Now please tell me where you were tonight. You weren't at Gigi's, were you?"

"No," she said. "I was talking with someone."

"Who?"

"A lady."

"Where?"

"In the flats."

"Here, in our block of flats?"

"Yes."

"Why did you tell me you were at Gigi's?"

"I don't know."

"Were you afraid I would be cross if I knew where you'd been?"

"I don't know."

"What were you talking with the lady about?"

"My daddy."

"You could have told me that. You can tell me anything, as long as it's the truth. Will you promise me you won't tell any more lies?"

She nodded.

Still sitting on her bed, I held out my arms; she walked toward me slowly, and, for the first time, she reached out and hugged me.

•　•　•

"Glad to see you made it in today," my boss said with feigned sarcasm whenever I arrived late for work. I was, in fact, usually late, after getting Whitney off to school, but I knew Dudley didn't mind. "I don't care what you do, as long as you meet your deadlines," he told his staff. And I prided myself on never having missed a deadline.

When I sat down at my old wooden desk—its surface littered with unedited articles, layout sheets, black-and-white photographs, rulers, reference books, stapler, cigarettes, ashtray, rubber cement, and pencils—my mind was fully focused on my work. Every day I exchanged Shona greetings ("*Mon-gwan-nanee,* madam!" *Mon-gwan-nanee,* Luke") with the printer's messenger and endured the brotherly teasing of the journalists I worked with, one of whom dubbed me "The Hatchet Woman."

"You make everything sound like 'the-cat-sat-on-the-mat'!" he complained one day.

"Dudley says, 'Short and simple,' Robin. I'm just doing my job."

When my copy-editing deadlines were met and my hands were busy pasting up the editorial pages, I'd chat with my colleagues. One day one of them did my horoscope for me.

"Because of the adverse position of Saturn in your chart, you have had to endure, over the past five or six years, the worst patch of your life," Mike said.

"You can say that again," I laughed.

"After June of this year," he continued, "when Saturn leaves Taurus and moves into Gemini, it should all be smooth sailing for you. Your life's biggest trials and tribulations will be over."

"That's certainly good news!" I said, weakening in my resolve not to take astrology at all seriously. "What does my chart say about marriage and career?"

"Looks like you'll be going overseas next year, where you'll land a super job in journalism."

"And marriage? Will I ever have the nerve to try it again?"

"Not until you're well past thirty."

———

Every Saturday morning, to Mel's dismay, I cleaned my flat.

"You have Margaret here every morning of the week," he said, "and yet you go over everything again on Saturday. What's *wrong* with you, woman?"

"I won't have Margaret forever," I said, dusting the dustless bookcase. "I don't want to get out of practice."

"You Yanks are all mad," Mel said good-naturedly, shaking his head.

On Saturday afternoons Mel, Whitney, Gigi, and I went to Lake McIlwaine, where Mel and his friend Robin kept the outboard-motorboat they shared. While Gigi and Whitney stayed at the yacht club, of which Gigi's father was commodore—playing on the trampoline and swings and swimming in the shallow cement pool under Gigi's mother's and older sisters' supervision—Mel and I went waterskiing or fishing for a few hours. (Whitney was afraid of the boat; she refused ever to come into it with me. I felt at the time it was because Jim's mother had instilled the idea that I was going to drown her.)

Afterward, the four of us would often drive slowly through the game reserve that bordered the lake, observing the baboons, ostriches, giraffes, zebra, impala, and other indigenous animals in their natural environment casually observing us, their uninvited guests. Seeing the game became commonplace for us, like watching squirrels in city parks scamper up trees.

Sundays were spent with friends at their homes in the suburbs, swimming in their pools, playing tennis on their private courts. One friend frequently held open-house parties on Sunday afternoons to which all of his friends were invited. Everyone who came—couples with children, singles with dates, older people, young people—brought an offering of food or drink and spent the day enjoying good exercise, good food, good friendship, good fun—including Whitney and Gigi.

It was on these Sundays in particular that I saw evidence of Whitney's changing attitude. She played nicely with the other children, spoke politely to adults, seemed proud to be with me. Sometimes she even came up to wherever I was sitting or standing and put her arm around me. Once again my hopes rose. Time, it seemed, was eroding the barrier between us. *The months of promised peace,* I thought, *are working miracles after all.*

One night before I tucked her in, after I'd read her a story, sitting close beside her on her bed, I asked Whitney gingerly, "If you had a choice, honey, who would you rather live with, your daddy or me?"

"My daddy," she said softly, without anger or hostility. She patted my leg. "But you can come and visit, Mommy."

What should I do? I wondered. *Who can I go to for counsel? Who would be impartial, professional, wise?* I had many loving friends who listened and cared, but they knew no better than I did what I should do. I had no money for psychologists' fees. I could think of only one person who was sufficiently wise: the judge. *Yes,* I thought, *I'll speak with the judge who heard both cases. He will know what's best. He will help me.*

One afternoon at work I picked up the phone nervously and called the judge's home.

"I'm sorry, my dear," his wife said sweetly, "but the judge can't speak with you. It's not—"

"Not ethical?" I said. "But the case will never go to court again—"

"I'm sorry, dear. I wish we could help you." I pictured her— petite, white-haired like her husband, stately. She sounded sincere, genuinely sorry.

"I'm sorry, too," I said. "I'm sorry to have bothered you."

• • •

I'd given Whitney the Siamese kitten thinking it might be good for her to have a small, dependent creature to care for. Sammy, I told her, was her "baby"; but she preferred to leave his care and feeding to me.

Sam became the comic of the family. He rode on Margaret's back, she told me, when she was on her hands and knees scrubbing floors; he sat on the edge of the tub and toyed with the water while Whitney and I bathed; he played ball with Mel on the floor. When I cooked or sewed he sat near me on the counter top or table watching my every move, as if his job in life were quality control. He grew large and loud and adventuresome. And one day he ran away.

"Sammy! Sammy!" Mel walked through our neighborhood

calling the cat's name. He walked along the sidewalks, between each building, past the servants' *kaias* that lined the service road, calling, "Sammy!" and inquiring of everyone he met whether they'd seen a large, sealpoint Siamese cat wearing a red tartan collar.

After canvassing the neighborhood on foot, Mel and Whitney took his car and drove slowly around town calling, "Sammy! Sammy!"

"No sign of him," Mel reported upon his return, holding Whitney's hand.

"Maybe somebody took him for keeps," Whitney said.

"No, I think he just decided to take a holiday but forgot to let us know where he was going or when he'd be back," I told her.

"Maybe he went to America," Whitney said.

Mel sat in his favorite chair, silent and morose. Of the three of us, he was the most despondent about our loss.

Every day after work, instead of going to the pub, Mel searched for Sam, calling his name, and returned to our flat dejected. Then one evening about a week later, while we were having dinner, we heard Sam's shrill Siamese cry coming from the courtyard below. When we brought him up, he strutted through our living room like a proud conquistador.

"See," I said to Whitney, "I told you he'd come home—and it looks as if wherever he went he had a very good time!"

Whitney brought a workbook home from school, labeled "Draw and Write." On one page she'd written MOTHER and drawn a stick figure with a blacked-in face and eleven fingers on one hand. On the next page was FATHER; his face was large and smiling, his hair was yellow, his body green like a plant; he had no hands or feet.

Her first report card read:

Conduct: Good. Very immature at first, but has steadily gained in self-confidence. A polite little girl and cooperates readily.

Progress: Whitney has settled down well and is beginning to have

230

a most interested approach to all her activities. Am pleased with her efforts and progress.

Reading: Steadily improving.

Comprehension: Lacks confidence in this—will improve with reading maturity but she tries and makes an attempt.

Writing: Very good hand control—shows a steady development.

Arithmetic: Not quick, but she perseveres.

But I noticed something strange when Whitney wrote at home. She wrote backward, right to left: cat, T-A-C; dog, G-O-D; Tom, M-O-T, so that the word when finished read correctly. "Here, honey, try it this way," I said, but she shook her head. I told myself I must discuss this with her teacher the first chance I had.

• • •

As the time drew near for Whitney to spend her school holiday with Jim, I grew increasingly nervous and apprehensive. Whitney became more and more excited. One day she said to me, "Mommy, why aren't you happy that I'm going on holiday with my dad?"

"I'll be happy, darling," I said, "when you come home and tell me you've had a nice time."

"I'll have a nice time, Mommy," she said.

On Friday, the thirteenth of August, Mel and I left our offices at noon to pick up Whitney from school. "See you in September!" her teacher called, as the class scampered out, clutching their school bags with one hand and their school hats with the other.

I gave Whitney a bath and dressed her in her favorite light-blue dress, white knee socks, and her best shoes, which Mel had freshly polished. I brushed her baby-fine blond hair and sprayed it lightly to keep it in place, then I dabbed Joy, my favorite perfume, behind her ears. "You look *beautiful*," I told her, and Mel concurred. Suddenly she seemed as shy and demure as a young bride dressing for her wedding.

I packed a small suitcase with her best clothes, which Margaret had freshly laundered and folded. And there was room for her dolls, Dale and Dawn, and their clothes, too.

"You're all set," I said, trying to be cheerful. "When you come home, you must tell me about all the things you saw and did on your holiday. I can't wait to hear all about it."

"I will, Mommy," she said.

When Jim arrived promptly at two, Whitney's first words to him were, "Dad, do you know I go to big school now?"

Jim gave me an itinerary of their trip, which included Lake Kariba and the Victoria Falls. He babbled a few garbled words to Whitney and said nothing to Mel or me.

Mel and I held each other close as we stood on the balcony and watched as Whitney skipped out of the building holding her father's hand. We waved to her as they drove away in Jim's friend's silver Jaguar, but she didn't see us.

"Melvy, I'm so worried," I said as I held him even tighter.

"You need a holiday, love," Mel said. "Why don't we go away for a few days?"

The following Wednesday evening Mel and I and our friends Jacquie and Malcolm Stuart and Melanie and Martyn Hurst drove for five hours to the Chimanimani Mountains on the country's southeastern border, where we stayed at a cottage originally built by pioneers and now owned by one of Malcolm's colleagues at the University of Rhodesia. It was twenty-four miles away from the closest town and high up in beautiful green pine forests. There were no signs of civilization anywhere—no other people, no phones, no newspapers, nothing except pure beauty, mountain air, mountain springs, wild flowers, the smell of pines, the sounds of rushing streams and singing birds. Marty, Malcolm, and Mel behaved like ten-year-old boys—building dams in the streams, chopping trees, and shooting at wild birds (and missing). Melanie, Jacquie, and I took a six-mile walk in our shorts and summer tops; when we found a huge waterfall, knowing no one was around, we took off all

232

our clothes and sunbathed by the water. The sun, the water, and the air give us enormous appetites, and we ate ravenously when evening came. We had brought our own food with us, and we had an African cook-boy to prepare our meals.

"Melvy, what's that up there?" I said, pointing to the ceiling of our room in the cottage.

"Where?"

"There, against the wall. It looks like a long black string, but it's moving."

"You're imagining things, love. Go back to sleep."

"Melvy, please come into my bed with me. Why are we in separate beds?"

"Because I'd like to get some sleep tonight."

"You're no fun at all. . . . Look! It just moved again! I can see it by the moonlight."

"What?"

"The string! Please take a look at it. Light a candle or something."

"That's no string, my dear," Mel said after inspecting it, "that's a rat's tail."

"*A RAT?* You mean there's a *live* rat up there? Right above us?! Mel, please may I get in with you? I don't want to sleep alone."

"No, love. Just be a good girl now and stay where you are. The rat won't do any harm."

As I lay awake listening to Mel's breathing, I stared out of the window near my bed to avoid looking at the moving tail. I watched the full moon roll slowly over the sky. I saw Saturn shining yellow-bright, outstanding among the myriad of silver twinkling stars, and I remembered my colleague Mike telling me that Saturn is "the most powerful, evil, and malignant" of all the planets. *Good riddance, Saturn,* I thought.

Suddenly, I felt a chill, as if Fear had ripped the blankets from my bed in an effort to lie down beside me. I rose quickly, quietly, without waking Mel, dressed and went outside to sit alone and wait for the sun to rise and comfort me.

I'd never seen the sun rise in Africa, although I'd watched

it set at least a hundred times. It sets in a dramatic show, like that of an old magician who knows his act cold: plucking colors from the day in a dazzling display—bougainvillea red, jacaranda mauve, flame-lily orange—and pulling them in vivid ribbons through the sky into the inverted hat of the horizon. Then—POOF!—lights out—the show is over, and a huge, royal-blue, star-studded curtain covers the stage. Secretly, you applaud. You ask the child inside of you, *Where did the colors go?* And a small voice within responds, *It's magic.*

The sun, I saw, as I sat on a large flat rock near our cottage, hugging my knees against the dawn's chill, doesn't rise that way. It rises like an old magician, an aging actor, the morning after: wheezing and coughing up clouds of soft pink, pale lavender, and yellow-orange. You feel embarrassed to see the sun this way—without his teeth. The sunset-spell is broken. Yet you watch in disbelief as the sun fumbles with his makeup, dons his gold costume, and stumbles, yawning and groping his way, onto the stage of a new day.

· · ·

That Monday morning, even without having to take Whitney to school, I was late for work as usual. "Sorry, Dud," I said, "but I just *had* to wash my hair. If Africa had more paved roads, I wouldn't have gotten so filthy."

"Typical spoiled American."

"No such thing as a typical American, Dud."

"There's a message on your desk. Your lawyer phoned. Says it's urgent."

As I listened to my lawyer's voice, my heart and mind went numb. It was like a trans-Atlantic call, broken by static in my mind. I picked up broken pieces: Jim had kidnapped Whitney. (My brain inserted "again.") Had stolen a boat at Lake Kariba. Crossed into Zambia on the weekend. Was apprehended. Taken to Lusaka. Put in jail. Whitney was there. Being cared for by the Prisoners' Aid Society.

At first I thought: *He was caught. He didn't get away with it this time. They'll send back Whitney. The court will change its order: He'll never be able to see her again.* I asked my lawyer to confirm this for me. He said: "No; don't be so hasty; we're contacting the American consul in Lusaka; don't say or do anything until you hear further from me." Like a patient in an emergency ward, I was not in control of my life or my destiny; I was at other people's mercy.

The next day news of the kidnapping was front-page headlines: FATHER IN GAOL AFTER LAKE DRAMA. When Margaret arrived, I was sitting on my bed, numb. She picked the paper from the floor where I had left it and approached me slowly. She spoke tenderly: "All of the mothers in Highfields are crying for you, madam," she said.

On the front page of Wednesday's paper, a Lusaka journalist quoted Jim: " 'I shall never take my daughter back to Rhodesia. . . . I've lost $1 million fighting this case. But now I've got Whitney with me and she's going to stay with me. . . . I planned the whole thing very carefully. . . . Rhodesia does not exist under international law, so I have done nothing wrong.' " The long news story ended with: "As far as Mr. Jason is concerned, the battle for custody of his daughter is now over. 'Look,' he said, pointing to his daughter, 'you can see how happy she is with me.' "

That afternoon, my lawyer called me: The American consulate in Zambia would not help me. No one would return Whitney to me. If I wanted her back, I'd have to go there myself and do as I'd done when I came to Rhodesia, take the matter to court for a judge to decide who should have custody. My lawyer advised against this: "Zambia is very hostile towards Rhodesia; they're not cooperating with us now, Bonnie, how do you think it will be for you—as a woman—on your own up there? No; it would be too dangerous, extremely costly, and perhaps futile. But it's up to you." I told him I needed time to think. Could I see him in his office after work?

• • •

Jim knew I had no money. He knew from my multiple requests for child support that my finances were strained. Even if I'd felt it safe or wise to chase after him into Zambia, I would not have had enough money for as much as a one-way plane ticket. And there wasn't enough time to borrow from friends or family as much money as I would have needed for more litigation in another foreign land.

Jim must have known the American embassy in Lusaka would refuse to do anything to help me. Their attitude was the same as that of the U.S. consulate in Salisbury when I arrived in Rhodesia expecting to retrieve my baby and return to the States within days. It was a hands-off attitude, a we-can't-take-sides-in-this-family-matter attitude, a we-don't-want-to-get-involved attitude.

He knew how dangerous it would have been for me, a young white woman with "Rhodesia" stamped in her passport, to travel on her own to Zambia, a country at that time hostile to Rhodesia. He knew I would be strongly advised not to go, especially alone.

Jim had heard my testimony. He'd heard me say repeatedly in court the previous year that it was my deep conviction that the fighting should cease, that Whitney should be with one or the other of us and not split between two.

And I knew that even if I did go to Zambia, start a new case, and win it, there would be no guarantee that Jim wouldn't kidnap Whitney a third time, take her to yet another state or country, and start all over again. I knew, and Jim knew, too, that I couldn't and wouldn't let that happen.

August 26, 1971

Dear Mom,

. . . My phone hasn't stopped ringing since Monday. . . . People are sending me flowers (which makes me cry) and saying such sweet, consoling things, that I've had a swimming, thudding headache for days.

Mom, there's nothing anyone can do now, so you mustn't get upset. . . .

If there is any decision for me to make, it is that I'm ending the fight. Mom, I sincerely believe it best that I start a new life, forget the name Jason, and forget the past six years altogether. It seems very hard and cold, but I have no alternative. I have no more strength; and if I continued fighting, he'd break me. . .

236

Throughout the week, African mothers who worked in the neighborhood came to my door, knocking softly. When I opened it, each would bow her head, pressing her hands together in a prayerful gesture, and repeat, "Sorry, madam; sorry, madam," and walk away.

On the front page of the Wednesday, September 1, issue of *The Rhodesia Herald* there was a short item reporting that Jim and Whitney had left Zambia and were believed back in the United States. Ironically, on page 5 of the same paper there was a three-quarter-page advertisement for Barbour's: "Exclusive in Rhodesia for 50 years," the ad copy read, above an eight-by-ten black-and-white portrait of Whitney and me. It was the mother-daughter ad we'd posed for in March. It was a beautiful photograph, the nicest one I'd ever seen of us together. And we did indeed, as Bea had said, look alike.

W hen I was four and my world reached as far as the wild blackberry bushes at the other end of the woods, I had a friend named Ruthie. Ruthie lived in the white farmhouse across the county road, and every day when she came home from school I would carefully cross the road by myself to visit her. She was my first friend.

Ruthie was two years older than I, tall, and thin. She had a thin, delicate face, thin arms and hands, thin spindly legs. She looked as if she seldom ate. The only thing large about her body was her hair, which stood out from her head in feather-soft ringlets, surrounding her face like a honey-colored halo. She cried every time her mother tried to comb through it.

Ruthie was born when her parents were already old and her sister and brothers fully grown. She was more than special to her parents; her mother said she was "sent from heaven." Indeed, Ruthie was an angel.

"Be a good girl like Ruthie," my mother used to say to me, and I tried. I watched Ruthie, I listened to her, I learned from her, I idolized her. On warm days we would sit on the wide wooden porch in front of her house, and she would read to me with a voice so soft it seemed to be coming from far away. Or she would show me how to sew: we made cloth clothes for our

238

paper dolls. Or she would sing to me or teach me what she had learned in Catholic school that day.

"If you want to pray to God, you go like this," she said, tightly folding her thin fingers together until bony knuckles showed through her transparent skin. "Or you can go like this," she said, pressing her hands flat with her fingers pointing to the sky. "God will listen to you either way." I looked up at Ruthie's God. He was a large white cloud with big ears.

"When people do bad things," she told me, "God punishes them by causing an accident. People think it's an accident, but it's really God doing it on purpose. If you fall down and hurt your knee, God is saying you did something wrong, and you have to say you're sorry. If you say you're sorry, God will forgive you and make your knee all better." *Ruthie knows God,* I thought; *she knows everything.*

A year later, Ruthie became ill. One day my mother told me Ruthie had been taken to the hospital in an ambulance. Ruthie wrote to me, funny letters, in big, clear printing, which my mother read to me. She wrote that she would soon be home again—the doctors and nurses were taking good care of her—and we would soon be sitting on her front porch together.

Ruthie didn't come home. I overheard my mother say Ruthie had "loo-key-mee-ah," and when I asked what that meant, she said Ruthie was very very sick.

Ruthie died.

"What does *died* mean, Mommy?" I said. I had never known anyone who had died.

"God has taken Ruthie to his home," my mother said. I had heard my mother use the word God before, but never in this way. Never as though God were a person who had a place to live.

"Why did God take Ruthie?"

My mother explained that God loved Ruthie very much because she was such a good girl, and he hated to see her so sick. So he took her to heaven to be with him. "Ruthie's very happy now," my mother said. "She'll never be sick again."

I pictured God's home as a palace, immense and golden as the sun, protected by pretty, winged angels like the ones on our

Christmas tree, and filled with healthy, happy, special people. I saw Ruthie there, laughing and singing, and I thought: *Lucky Ruthie, lucky Ruthie.*

Ruthie's mother never recovered. Her husband and her older children tried their best to keep her in the house, but every so often she would get out. I watched from across the county road, hiding behind a tree. It was a horrible sight—to see the old woman in her worn-out bathrobe; her long, thick, curly white hair looking as if it hadn't been combed since Ruthie died; wandering around the yard, waving her arms, screaming, wailing, and shouting at God.

· · ·

The first time Jim took Whitney, he took a part of me as well. I felt hollow, as if my heart, stomach, and lungs had been removed, and I was forced to go on living without them. No, more than these, my guts and womb also. Like an empty shell, a pin-pricked egg with the insides blown out, I felt fragile, delicate, afraid I could too easily fall and break. I leaned on God.

But now, the second time, I felt different. Instead of empty, I felt filled—engorged—with a cold, acrid rage. *What was wrong with me that I could have allowed this to happen? Why did I not heed the signs?* I hated myself for not having learned; for being passive, helpless, a fool; for letting this man rape not my heart and body but my soul—again.

When my capacity for self-loathing became sated, I turned the blame on God. In my secret bitterness and angry confusion I decided to go my own way, make my own rules, live as I pleased, learn about life, be more aggressive and self-seeking, grow. I felt filled with selfish ambition, unfulfilled dreams, hostile power. Instead of fragile, I felt outraged, angry, wild.

During the first week, Gigi came to my flat when I got home from work to keep me company. We sat close together, sometimes saying nothing to each other for long stretches. Then, in a burst, unanswerable questions tumbled out of her: "Why did

240

he take her, Bonnie? . . . Why did he do it? . . . Where are they going? . . . What will happen to Whitney now? . . ." I'd never seen this happy, carefree child so serious and sad.

How could I explain what I, too, didn't understand? "I don't know," I said, sickened by the impotence of the statement. "All I know," I said, groping, "is that God allowed it to happen, and He will take care of her." *Don't ask me what kind of God would allow this to happen, Gigi. Please don't ask me—*

"Do you think she misses me?"

"I'm sure she misses you, darling," I said, thinking how cruel it was for the two little girls to be so senselessly separated. The bond they'd formed by their own choice and personal need had made them closer than sisters. "When I was Whitney's age," I said, "I lost a special friend, too, and I've never forgotten her." Then I told Gigi about Ruthie.

"But Whitney didn't die, Bonnie," Gigi said. "She's not in heaven. Where is she? Will I ever see her again?"

"I don't know, honey." *Please don't ask me.*

Margaret, in her womanly wisdom and sisterly love, said nothing more about our loss. After the first newspaper report, she never asked about Whitney, she never questioned me. Instead, she carried on as if nothing had changed in our household, although she was well aware that everything had. She tried to be as cheerful as ever, but when our eyes met—cold blue to deep brown—a thought, like a shout in a canyon, echoed across the space and time and differences between us and repeated: *Childrens are too much troubles . . . too much troubles. . . .*

I didn't touch a thing in Whitney's room—her toys, her clothes, her doll's baby carriage, her dollhouse, her scooter, remained in the same places as before she left. When I arrived home from work I just sat down with a good book and, as my father had done at home for years, read myself away.

———

Mel still came to dinner every evening at seven, but it wasn't the same. There were no little girls to greet him with adoring affection. There was no three-course meal ready and waiting. There was no longer any family feeling.

Mel sat in his favorite chair, as sullen and remote as when the cat had disappeared. But this time he knew he couldn't walk the streets calling Whitney's name; she was gone. I remembered how she used to sit on his lap in that chair, with her arm around his neck, and cheek against cheek they'd watch TV together. Sometimes, I confess, I was jealous that he showed her more affection than he did me and that she loved him more than she loved me. But at other times I was content to observe their love and to derive mine vicariously.

In my selfishness and anger I was blind to Mel's grief. I tried to cause arguments, accusing him of being cold, unfeeling, unsympathetic. He became an easy target, an outlet for my rage.

"You'd think she was *your* child, the way you are behaving!" I snapped at him over a hastily prepared supper of scrambled eggs and toast. "She's my daughter—mine! *MY* child was taken, and you can't even comfort me. Not even a pat on the hand—or a hug—or a sweet word—NOTHING! Why do you even bother coming over here? Is it just a habit? Or is it to make my life more miserable than it already is—?"

In all the time we'd been together—nearly two years—Mel and I had never had words. We never had long discussions, either; somehow we didn't need them. We accepted each other whole, we liked each other, we were friends. On most things we agreed; so our communication required only a kind of shorthand, sometimes little more than a smile across the room, a met glance, an almost imperceptible nod. We usually knew how the other felt or what the other was thinking; words were superfluous. Even our silences, I often thought as I worked at my sewing machine in the evening after supper while Mel sculpted in soapstone or read or watched TV, were like music. Until Whitney was taken, we were in harmony.

Mel paid no attention to my outburst; he refused to argue. He spoke softly, as if to himself or the eggs on his plate: "I feel as if she were my child. . . . I feel as if she were mine. . . ."

242

Everywhere I went, people stopped me on the street to ask for news of Whitney. And I knew, just as I'd known four years before when the people of my church, salt of the earth, had burned my open wounds with well-meaning inquiries, that I had to leave.

But I couldn't leave immediately; I had no money. So I booked to leave by ship the following April, by which time, I calculated, I would have enough saved. I saw no point in chasing after Jim; I wouldn't have known where to begin. My mother reported in a letter that he was no longer at his former address. Once again, he had disappeared.

"What I would like to do," I wrote to my mother, "is give Whitney some time with him now, and then when I get home I'll try to find her, talk with her, and see how she feels. If she doesn't like living with him and wants to come back with me, I'll do everything and anything to get her back. But on the other hand, if she still resents me and believes her father's horrible lies, I'll leave things as they are and keep in touch with her so she knows where I am if ever she changes her mind (and eventually she will)."

• • •

One lunch hour one of the secretaries in Mr. Clarke's office stopped me on the street. *Please don't ask, please*—my eyes begged.

"Did you hear about Joyce?" she said.

"Joyce? No," I said, relieved. And then I felt guilty for being so absorbed in my own life I hadn't taken time to keep in touch with old friends. I thought of Joyce and her husband, Louie, how generous and hospitable they'd been to me when I first arrived in the country; how I'd shared Joyce's office during the months before the first case went to court; how she'd had me to dinner at their flat several times and shown me slides of their world travels; how they'd taken me with them on weekend daytrips when Whitney was with Jim. I thought of Joyce and Louie together, still so devoted and in love, even after thirteen years of marriage. "No," I said. "How is she?"

"You didn't hear about the accident? Joyce is dead."

"Dead?!" *At thirty-three? Joyce? with the long, straight, light-brown hair pulled back in a ponytail that cascaded down the length of her back and swayed when she walked? who typed so fast, cooked so well, loved to travel, loved Rhodesia, loved Louie? who was so beautiful and bright and youthful and alive? Dead?*

I phoned Louie and invited him to dinner. He arrived when Mel was still at the pub. We sat and held each other, this large bearlike man and I, and he sobbed while I rocked him in my arms. Louie came to dinner regularly after that, and in so doing, he helped me to put aside, for a time, my own anger and self-pity.

One day in early October Margaret told me she was five months pregnant. I hadn't noticed; Margaret was a large woman who hid her pregnancy well.

"But I thought you had a loop put in, Margaret?"

"I did, madam. It is still there. It didn't work."

"Oh, my God, Margaret. I'm so sorry. I feel as if it's my fault—I recommended the loop to you."

"It's all right, madam," she said consolingly. "I want to have Edwin's baby. Edwin and I say if it is a girl, we will name her Bonnie after you. And if it is a boy, you may give him his name."

"A baby," I thought aloud, suddenly excited by the prospect, "we're going to have a new baby in the family."

Mel went to England for four weeks to spend the Christmas holidays with his family. I wrote long letters to him almost every day, and at first I waited patiently for a reply. I knew Mel disliked letter writing—it was I, in fact, who'd written to Mel's mother from time to time during the previous two years to let her know her son's news—but I begged him to respond nevertheless. "It's lonely here without you," I told him. "No

Whitney, no you, nobody to cook for . . . Someone's firing cannons through the fabric of my world! You could help mend some of those gaping holes by sending me a letter or two. . . ." But Mel didn't write. After three weeks I rashly concluded he no longer cared.

On New Year's Eve I went to a dance with friends. I met a man there who was new to Salisbury and therefore unaware of my publicity—a tall and handsome Dane with steel-blue eyes and graying hair. As we danced each dance together, moving in unison around the crowded floor, I felt graceful and light, young and carefree. My large hand felt small inside of his; I looked up at his strong, square chin.

"Dah-ling," he whispered in thickly accented English, "you are the most beau-tee-ful woman in this room. . . ."

"Dah-ling," he said as he held me close and kissed me while the rest of the room exploded in celebratory noise, *"Happy New Year."*

"Dah-ling," he said the following week in my flat, "do sit down and relax . . . here, put your feet up. . . . Shall I make you a nice drink? Vodka and tonic? Yes, fine. . . . No, don't worry about dinner now. We can fix it together later. . . . Here is your drink. There. Now tell me about your day. . . ."

"Dah-ling," he said later over the dinner he'd helped me to prepare. "Dah-ling," he repeated as he reached across the candlelit table to take my hand, "do you know how beau-tee-ful you are? I have met many beau-tee-ful women in my life. Most of them were tinsel and glitter. You are not like that. Your beauty is deep and complete and *real.* . . ."

"Dah-ling," he said that night in bed, "dah-ling. . . . dah-ling . . ."

When Mel returned from England on January 11, he asked me to marry him.

"I missed you the whole time I was away," he said. "I really appreciated how much you've come to mean to me. Everywhere I went, I thought, Bonnie would like this . . . too bad Bonnie isn't here with me—"

"You didn't write—"

"I was too busy, love. You know we only have one writer in the family and that's you—"

"You should have written. I—"

"Sorry, love, you're right. That was remiss of me. But believe me, I truly missed you. Every minute. I don't ever want to be separated again—"

"Melvy, I—"

"Why do you look so upset, my love?"

"I'm in love with someone else."

When Mel drew his arm back, I was sure it was to strike me. I didn't move, half wishing to be punished with one blow, half frozen in fear of him. Mel struck, instead, the nearest thing to me—a lamp—with such force it soared to the length of its cord, then plummeted to the floor and broke into tiny glass pieces. Without saying a word, he left my darkened living room. I knew he was going to his pub.

On January 17, 1972, Margaret's baby was born. She let me name him; so I named him what I would have named a son, if I had had one then: Gregory. Edwin phoned me at work to tell me.

"Please tell Margaret she should bring the baby to work with her," I told him. "There's no need for her to leave him with her sister."

He was a perfect baby, with small, delicate features. When Margaret arrived in the morning with Gregory strapped to her back, I would lift him off and carry him around the room, bouncing him in my arms, singing to him sometimes. It made Margaret laugh to see me holding her baby and talking to him as if he understood.

"You know, Margaret," I said to her one day, "I have a premonition that Gregory is going to grow up to be a great man, a leader of his country. I'm going to read about him in the newspapers in America. . . ."

Sometimes, on my way home from work, I would see Margaret in town talking with some women friends. She would introduce me to them as "Gregory's Granny," and her friends would giggle shyly.

I told my friend Sue, expecting her to laugh, too, but she didn't. "She considers you a member of her family," Sue said. "That's the highest compliment an African can pay a European."

• • •

My mother wrote to me of riots in Salisbury. "Hurry home," she wrote, "there's going to be trouble there."

Trouble? Riots? I hadn't read of any in the *Herald.* I asked Margaret what she knew.

"Do you mean the bus, madam? Somebody burned a bus."

My mother sent a clipping from her local paper dated January 20, 1972:

RHODESIAN RIOTS LEAVE TWO DEAD

SALISBURY, Rhodesia (UPI)—City workers guarded by armed police today cleared away the debris of rioting by Africans protesting the Anglo-Rhodesian agreement on independence. Two blacks have been killed in the violence, which began Sunday.

The first mob violence since Rhodesia unilaterally declared its independence from Britain in 1965 started in Gwelo, 172 miles south, and moved to Salisbury yesterday. In the capital—a city of wide, tree-lined boulevards—bands of stone-throwing rioters smashed store windows and set fire to cars.

Seven whites, including two nuns, were hospitalized.

Premier Ian Smith has made no public comment on the riots.

My mother's next letter contained more warnings and another clipping:

RHODESIAN VIOLENCE ERUPTS; FIVE KILLED

SALISBURY, Rhodesia—Police shot and killed at least five blacks today in the sixth day of antigovernment rioting over a recent political settlement between Britain and its former colony. . . .

At present, Rhodesia's five million blacks and 250,000 whites are ruled by the government of Ian Smith, which declared independence from British colonial control in 1965, largely on the issue of white supremacy. The settlement, reached two months ago, sets no timetable for one-man, one-vote representation which would give blacks control. . . .

Since Sunday, crowds here and in Umtali, Gwelo, Bulawayo, and Fort Victoria have chanted "No! No!" to the agreement. "We have been oppressed for six years. No longer. No settlement."

It had been so still there. Peace, like an heirloom patchwork quilt, snugly covered the slumbering country in smug security. For most of the whites, Rhodesia was a haven from the outside world, a clean and sunny sanctuary, with a high standard of living and a low crime rate. An enviable, tranquil place to live.

But now, more and more, the words "trouble," "danger," "war" entered into everyday conversation. Young men of draft age who had come to the country in the course of wider travels muttered among themselves to the effect that Rhodesia was a nice place to spend the night but they wouldn't want to fight and die there. Others, born in Rhodesia, dug in their heels and maintained they would stay to the end—whether that end came in the form of natural death or a terrorist's bullet. As more people woke to the sound of war's rumblings, tension filled the air like heavy rain. All at once, the three years I'd spent in Rhodesia seemed ominously placid in retrospect. It had been a period, quite literally, of stillness before a storm. But before that storm broke, I'd be gone.

• • •

Sven and I had no past—no court cases, no lost child, no publicity, no history. But we had no future, either: I was leaving Africa in April. We had no responsibilities or reasons to go home after work, so we played, like children, in Never-Never Land, but the pleasure was always ephemeral and the feeling in the pit of my heart, empty. Our affair was as heady as champagne—and just as unstable and unthirstquenching.

Alone at home, sitting on my bed with Karen Blixen's *Out of Africa* and a glass of vodka and tonic, I pined for Mel.

"I'm sorry," I said to him over lunch at our favorite Spanish café. "I'll never forgive myself."

"It's all right, love," he said. "I'm the one to blame. Never gave you enough of what you need—enough affection, I mean. Well, I learned my lesson, didn't I?"

"Oh, Melvy," I said, looking at the sad smile on his handsome face and gripping his strong artist's hands. *Why? Why?*

"Let's have none of that, now," he said, freezing the pools of tears in my eyes with one glance. "No scenes. Stiff upper lip, remember?"

"I'm not English. I have a good excuse."

"Oh, yes. I forgot," Mel teased. "Poor thing." We both laughed.

Two and a half years before, I'd heard Africa whisper, "Stay with me." Now, just as clearly, my heart heard, "There's nothing left for you here."

When I read what Karen Blixen wrote about leaving Africa, I copied her words in my journal: "As I stood and looked at them a fancy came back to me that had taken hold of me before: It was not I who was going away; I did not have it in my power to leave Africa; but it was the country that was slowly and gravely withdrawing from me, like the sea in ebb-tide . . ."

"I am leaving Africa in spite of myself," I told my journal. "I'm going, yet I can't quite explain why. I'm going, although part of me is reluctant to do so. But I know I must go."

———

Before I left Rhodesia my lawyers gave me all of their files on my cases (two feet thick), plus the transcript of the second case (900 pages), which had been required for the appeal. They gave them to me "in case I needed background for further litigation," but with them they also gave me free advice: "Don't bother with further litigation; you may win the battles, but you'll never win the war."

My office gave me a farewell party and a gold bracelet inscribed: "R.N.F.U. [Rhodesia National Farmers' Union], April 1972." When I said good-bye to my boss, Dudley, I couldn't control my emotions. I had loved this man, who resembled my father, as if he *were* a father to me; and as he wrapped his large arms around me, I grieved for the father I'd lost long before and the surrogate father I was now losing. I left my farewell party then and hurriedly walked home, choking back sobs. When I arrived at my flat I found a large bouquet with a note attached that read: "You are one of the world's lovely people. It's been one of my great experiences to know (and adore) you. Dudley."

When I said good-bye to Sven, he cried.

I gave Margaret most of my kitchen things—dishes, pots and pans, and silverware—as well as bed linens and towels. And I gave her Whitney's toys and bedtime-story books, because she had a five-year-old, too.

As Edwin carried these things out of my flat and into a car he'd borrowed from a friend, Margaret and I stood in the kitchen, hugging each other and weeping. She gave me a photograph of herself, apologizing for not being able to give me more. I told her she had given me enough already.

"Will you come back, madam?" Margaret said, sniffling.

"I don't know," I said. "Perhaps some day. I'd like to. I'll try."

"Please come back, madam."

"In the meantime, Margaret, I'll write to you," I said, although I didn't know her home address nor the spelling of her last name.

Mel drove me to the boat in Durban, South Africa—a two-day drive from Salisbury. At night we held each other close and talked softly in the dark.

"I'm afraid to go back home, Melvy," I whispered. "I don't want to go. Is it too late to change my mind and stay? We could get married, have a child, live a norm—"

"You must go," he said. "You know you'll never have any peace of mind unless you try to find Whitney."

"But how will I be able to find her? And what will happen when I do?"

"Take it one step at a time, love. First, get home, then see what you can do from there. You can't do anything more in Africa."

"Except forget."

"No one in Salisbury will let you do that. You're too well known."

"In America I am a cipher. Nobody knows or cares."

There was snow in the Drakensberg Mountains. Large, evanescent flakes. Snow in Africa.

An old black woman with a large wool blanket wrapped around her head and shoulders ran down the road beside Mel's car. She looked too old to run; but the snow-pocked wind was chasing her, so she ran for her life.

· · ·

It is hard to leave Africa once she has held you. I'd been her foster child for three years, and when it came time to go I had to leave her gently, slowly, by ship. If I had flown away, the break would have been too sharp, too painful.

I stood at the ship's railing and watched the landscape of Durban slowly shrink, then disappear. I watched Mel standing on the dock, and I waved to him until he became a speck on the receding horizon. *Don't leave me, Melvy!* my heart cried. *Please don't leave me!* But it was I who was leaving him.

Africa was letting go of me. For three years I'd felt newborn, sleeping in her strong arms, close to the steady thudding of her heart. She'd fed me fresh fruit from her gardens and bathed me in her sunlight, and made me feel more beautiful than I'd ever felt before. Now, I felt, Africa was tossing me out to sea, and I wasn't at all sure I could swim home.

When my father left there were no good-byes, no hugs or kisses, no promises to phone or write. No explanations. In fact, it was a long time before we realized he had gone for good. That is, before we understood he would not be coming back.

Often before he had left, but he always returned, sometimes in the middle of the night. Then the big old car would whirl up the driveway and crash into the back of the garage and wake us. And we'd listen, holding our breath, to the slam of the car door and the heavy approach of his footsteps.

He would enter the house, shouting my mother's name, along with profanities, in an effort to start a fight. And when he succeeded, I stood between them, holding him away from her with one outstretched arm against his chest and keeping my mother behind me with the other. I knew he wouldn't hit me, even in his condition. He only wanted to hurt her.

Once he pounded on the door of the bedroom my mother and I shared, until the door broke off its hinges and fell onto my bed. But sometimes he did nothing; he simply staggered upstairs to his own bed, the king-size bed in the master bedroom, where for the last two years he slept alone.

His final departure took place the week we went to court to testify against him. My sisters and I were taken out of school

253

for the day to go with my mother to the county courthouse. When we arrived, we waited outside the courtroom for my mother's lawyer to meet us.

My mother was nervous, and everything about her looked tired, more tired than ever before, as though she had not had a good night's sleep in all twenty-three years of her marriage and the effect had suddenly hit. Only her hands were fully awake, anxiously picking at her nail polish and playing with her thin silver wedding ring.

My mother had beautiful hands. Long, delicate fingers and carefully tapered nails. I had always admired them and wished that my hands would someday be like hers. But I had stopped growing by then, and my hands had remained square and thick, like my father's.

When my mother's lawyer arrived, he took her aside. He spoke to her in a whisper from the side of his mouth without looking at her face. My mother nodded and tried to smile.

"Girls," my mother said to my sisters and me, "Mr. Kroehler would like to talk with you."

As he came toward us, I saw that his black shoes needed polishing and his tie was badly stained. His hair, slicked down with oil, looked like a freshly ploughed field, showing every ridge where the comb had gone through.

"This won't take long," he said to us. "You'll be in and out before you know it. All you have to do is answer a few simple questions with a yes or a no. When your turn comes, just listen to the questions carefully and answer to the best of your knowledge. Speak up, so the judge can hear you, and don't be nervous—he doesn't bite."

My youngest sister, who was twelve, led the way into the courtroom taking slow, careful steps as though she were a bridesmaid in a wedding ceremony. She had a sense of the theatrical. When she was very young she used to wait until the whole family was absorbed in a favorite television program and then dance in front of the screen—exotic dances she created herself—until everyone applauded her performance. Then she would press her palms together in front of her cherubic face, curtsy for the audience about ten times, and scamper from her

254

stage. For her, the courtroom that day was pure drama; and she enjoyed her role.

My other sister, two years younger than I, marched behind the youngest defiantly. She made no secret of her feelings. When her turn came to answer the questions, she snapped her answers angrily.

My father sat alone on a bench in the fifth row. He sat slumped in the seat like a massive marionette with severed strings. He didn't look up.

I felt sick to my stomach. The small, wood-paneled room was airless and hot and I wished I could open the window. Instead, I stood beside my sisters and stared out at the parking lot below until my turn to answer questions came. Outside, the wind was shaking the trees and tossing the autumn leaves. Although it was only late September, it was already fall.

"Do you recall an incident that occurred last summer in which you had to phone the police?"

I answered the question with a yes that I hoped wouldn't reach the fifth row.

"Would you please tell the judge what happened that day?"

I didn't want to tell the judge anything. I was too embarrassed; and besides, he didn't seem to be interested in anything that was being said. I wondered why they made us come here in the first place, why we were forced to take sides.

"My father came home," I said.

"Did he appear to you to be intoxicated?"

"Yes," I said.

"And what did he do?"

"He started fighting with my mother."

"Did he strike her?"

"Yes."

"And you called the police."

"Yes."

"Will you please tell the court why?"

"Because he knocked her down and started kicking her and I couldn't make him stop."

My father looked up at me in disbelief. I knew he didn't remember. He never seemed to remember afterward.

I wanted to cry but I couldn't. I wanted to explain, but I knew they wouldn't let me. *He was not always like that,* I wanted to say. *He is not himself when he drinks. He didn't mean to do it. He has a problem—doesn't anybody realize it? Isn't it a sickness? Can't somebody help him?!* I wanted to scream, to run from the courtroom alone, down the wide marble staircase, into the parking lot and the free-falling leaves.

"Thank you," the lawyer said to me. "You may step down." And I went back to join my sisters.

When it was all over, my father left the room by himself, holding his coat and staring at his shoes.

In the car on our way home my sisters cheered my mother's victory.

"Did you see his lawyer?" my youngest sister said. "He looked just like Jimminy Cricket!" They both laughed.

I sat with my mother in the front seat and silently vowed I would never enter another courtroom again. I told myself this was *their* problem; some day I would have a family of my own, like the families at my church—peaceful, loving, and happy.

When we stopped for a red light, my mother quietly rolled down the car window and threw her silver wedding band into the gutter.

Things became different at home. One day soon after we'd been to court my mother called my sisters and me into the living room. "Girls," she said, "I have something to tell you. The bedrooms are upstairs and the kitchen is in there." She pointed straight ahead, as if we hadn't lived in the house all our lives. "Sleep when you're tired and eat when you're hungry. I'm not a housewife anymore."

We told her we understood. After all, she'd worked, she said and we already knew, "like a slave" for twenty-three years and "never got any thanks for it." Besides, we were old enough to take care of ourselves.

My mother became a pretty bird let loose from a rusted cage. She had her hair done every week; she took a new interest in

256

fashion. Her beautiful hands no longer smelled of onions or ammonia.

At forty-five she was still slim and attractive. When she and my sisters and I went out together shopping, holding hands and giggling as we usually did, we looked like four sisters. People often said so, and my mother loved to hear it.

Sometimes she would look at me and say with a sigh, "Oh, if I only had *your* face—!" And I would look at her expectantly, wishing she would finish the sentence so that I would know what to do with it.

Our home became a girls' dormitory with no curfews and no communal dining room. Our stockings hung boldly along the bathroom shower rod like flags of femininity. Our clothes became community property. "Where's my blue cardigan?"— "It's not *your* blue cardigan, it's *my* blue cardigan, and I left it in my locker at school!" . . . "Who broke the zipper on my gray pleated skirt? I just *made* that skirt and never even got a chance to *wear* it!" . . . Arguments over clothes sounded like phonograph records played too fast: high-pitched and whining. I secretly longed for the sound of a deep voice in the house. More and more I dreamed of having my own family some day. I would have five sons, I decided, and they would never argue over clothes.

None of us knew where my father had gone, and of course we didn't inquire. To mention his name at all was a form of treason. My mother seldom spoke of him, and when she did it was hatefully, between clenched teeth. "That gee-dee-ess-oh-bee," she would say, "doesn't pay a dime in child support—"

My sisters and I never used the word "daddy," even among ourselves. It was as if we no longer had a father, as if he had died and been denied a burial. We knew that if we spoke of him with any concern and my mother overheard, she would feel betrayed.

The year after my parents' divorce, I went away to school, secretarial school, on a full scholarship. With the money I had saved to go to college, I rented a small apartment, which I shared with two other girls, on the third floor of a large old home not far from the school. I took a part-time job at a department store on weekends to pay for my clothes and groceries. I found a church nearby where the minister was warm and fatherly, the people were friendly, and I felt at home. I was elected president of my class and editor of the class paper. Everything was going well. Until one day in mid-fall.

One rainy afternoon when school was over for the day, my roommate Kathy and I decided to take the bus home, instead of walking, as usual.

"Kath, did you see that man?" I asked.

"What man?"

"The man standing by the entrance to the Y?"

"No. What did he look like?"

"He looked like me," I said, mostly to myself.

"That's funny," Kathy said, not knowing what I meant.

It was his face but not his body. *That man was thin. It couldn't be him.* But he had seen me, too, through the rain-streaked window of the bus, which wound through parts of town where Kathy and I seldom walked; and in the time it took for the bus to pass, we had recognized each other. *No. It couldn't be him. What would he be doing here? It was my imagination.* I erased the passing image from my mind.

The next day the man was waiting for me by the front gate of the school when I got out of class. At first I didn't see him standing by the pretty little foreign cars that belonged to the rich girls who commuted from home, but I heard him call my name. *Yes. It's his voice. It's his way of waving.* I went to the gate to meet him, leaving my classmates behind.

"Hiya, honey," he said.

The word "daddy" stuck in my throat. I started to cry. Standing beside the pretty little foreign cars, I broke into sobs I couldn't control.

"Don't cry, honey," he said. "I don't want to see you crying." He took out his handkerchief and patted my eyes. "Can we go somewhere to talk?—Can I walk you home?"

All I could do was nod my head. As if I were afraid my mother would hear, words wouldn't leave my mouth. My father

258

took my books in his left hand and put his right arm around my shoulder, and we walked to my home on the other side of town together.

My efforts to control my crying gave me a headache that blocked all other senses. Then the pressure of the headache caused my nose to bleed. By the time we reached the house, my father's handkerchief, which I held up to my face, was heavy, dripping, with blood.

My landlady rushed from the front door to meet us. Her frightened eyes and tight, contorted mouth asked silently, *Accident? Has there been an accident?*

"I'm fine," I told her. "Just a nosebleed. . . . Mrs. West, this is my father."

Relieved, but still bewildered, she offered her hand. "How do you do," she said. "Perhaps," she turned to me, "you and your father would like to sit here in the study, dear?" Mrs. West did not allow men upstairs.

I sat beside my father on the love seat by the bay window. The study, like all the other rooms in Mrs. West's large old house, was warm and homey.

"Here, honey, tilt your head back so the bleeding will stop," my father said. "Try to relax. Take deep breaths."

I nodded and tried to breathe deeply, but the air seemed to catch in my throat. It came up in short chugging gasps that shook my whole body.

"Some reunion," I said, trying to laugh. I kept my head back and counted the beams along the ceiling.

My father brushed his hand across my forehead to take the hair out of my eyes. Then he took my hand and stroked it. "Remember the nosebleeds you used to get when you were a kid?"

I shook my head.

"Terrible. Had to take you to the doctor once. Damn thing wouldn't stop."

"Oh," I said, embarrassed by the subject and my inability to stop the flow of blood. *Why blood? Why now? Why did we have to speak of it, look at it, be bound by it? When would the bleeding stop?*

"How did you know where I was, Daddy?" The word finally came out.

"Your brother told me," he said. "I stay in touch with your brother."

"How is he?" I said, still staring at the ceiling. "He never writes anymore."

"Fine. Doin' fine. Likes his job. Loves the weather down in Florida."

"That's nice." I nodded. A rivulet of blood rolled down my chin.

"So, tell me. How's it feel to be a Katie Gibbs girl?"

"I'll let you know next year when I graduate."

"Good school. Fine reputation. How did you come to choose it?"

"It was a compromise. I wanted to go to college, but Mommy wanted me to get a secretarial job like hers right out of high school. So I compromised by applying to a secretarial school. Gibbs gave me a scholarship."

"Well. . . . I'm proud of you, honey."

I couldn't remember ever hearing him tell me that. Just when I thought I'd exhausted my sea of tears, a new wave came in and knocked me, tumbling, to the beach.

"Maybe I should go now," he said, standing up. "I don't want to upset you any more than I have—"

"Where do you live, Daddy?" *Don't disappear again,* I wanted to say.

"Oh, I'm staying at the Y. Just temporarily. Till I find the right job. I'm actively looking. . . . Say, honey, when can I see you again? Can you spare some time for your ol' father?"

"Gibbs is a very strict school," I said. "We get four hours of homework every night, and I work on Friday evenings and all day Saturday. . . . What about Sunday? Would you like to go to church with me?"

To my surprise, he agreed.

He arrived at the house promptly at a quarter to eleven wearing the same gray suit and khaki-colored raincoat he had worn three days before. His clothes were cut for a thinner man than he had been, yet they hung loosely on him now, as though he were a punctured balloon, steadily losing air.

260

"You've lost a lot of weight," I said, as we started off for church.

"Yeah, how about that," he said, pulling at the front of his raincoat. "Fifty-five pounds. Not bad. Been trying to lose weight for years."

"Have you been on a diet?" As soon as I asked the question I regretted I had.

"No, not really. Just cut down on eating, that's all. And I've been walking a helluva lot. Good exercise, walking." As if he had read my thoughts, he added, "I sold the car."

It was hard to keep from crying during the church service, while the man who for years had teased me about my church-going sat stiffly at my side, earnestly listening to the sermon. When we stood to sing he seemed to know all the words to the hymns. His voice was deep and strong. We harmonized.

"Nice church," he said on the way home. "I always liked Presbyterian churches."

The sidewalk was covered with drying autumn leaves. I kicked them with my foot as we walked. I liked the sound.

"Y'know, honey, I've been doin' a lot of thinking. . . . Life is like the seasons. It's autumn for me now. Like the song goes, 'I'm in the autumn of my life. . . .' Soon it will be winter—"

"No, Daddy," I said. *Why "No"?* I asked myself. *No, it will not be winter for you soon? No, I don't want to hear any more?* I wanted to tell him that I thought he should have been a poet or a professor instead of a businessman; he thought too much to be a businessman. But this was no time for should-have-beens. All I could say was no.

He walked somberly, with his head bowed. Where was the big comedian? The sarcastic, searing wit? Where was the mammoth man whom we had feared for years? He studied the fallen leaves as he spoke. "Did I ever tell you you were my favorite?—Oh, I know it's not right for parents to pick favorites, but—"

He had never told me, but my mother had. She'd said when I was small he used to carry me everywhere on his shoulders, showing me off to his drinking friends. He'd say, "See my girl? This is my little girl!"

"No," I said, still kicking the leaves.

"I've made a mess of things," he said. "Like the song goes, 'You only hurt the ones you love—' "

When he left me at the front door of the house, I went inside, ran up the spiral staircase to the third-floor apartment, took off my clothes, and spent the rest of the day in bed.

My father and I went to church together each week for about a month, until he seemed to grow bored with the arrangement. Instead, he took to borrowing a car from a friend at the Y and trying to stop me on the street when I was walking with my friends.

He would pull the car up to the curb. "Hiya, honey," he'd say. "Wanna go for a ride?" I could tell from his voice and his eyes that he'd been drinking. *Yes,* I'd think, *he is the same man.*

"No, Daddy," I'd say. "I can't right now. I've got to get back to school; I'm on my lunch hour."

He'd drive away.

I never knew when the borrowed car would reappear or what condition he would be in.

The director of the school called me into her office one afternoon in late November. I had been to see her only once before since school began. I had felt so out of place in the beginning, among all the rich girls with their pretty clothes and perfect posture, that I'd gone to the director's office one day to say I felt that Katharine Gibbs wasn't the place for me. "Nonsense," she said. "You have every right to be here. Why, when the scholarship committee met last spring to decide who should receive our full scholarship this year, they chose you *unanimously.*" I pictured a group of prim spinsters sitting around an oval conference table, each holding up a card with my name on it in large letters. I decided I'd stay.

"I've called you here today, my dear, because I've heard some disturbing reports—" She leaned across her desk with a look of genuine concern. "Miss Ryker tells me that your schoolwork has been suffering lately. Can you tell me why?"

262

I suspected she already knew; she just wanted to hear it from me. I told her what had happened.

"My dear," the director said gently but firmly, leaning toward me across her desk, raising her eyebrows as she lowered her voice, "your personal, family problems are none of my business, but when they impinge upon your performance in school, then it *does* become my business. I'm sure I don't need to remind you that you, as a scholarship recipient, have a special responsibility to apply yourself to your studies. You must allow nothing to interfere with your schoolwork. Nothing."

One cold, clear afternoon in early winter, when Kathy and I were walking home from school, the borrowed car pulled up to the curb and stopped beside us. The driver rolled down the window. "How y'doin', honey?" I could see he had been drinking.

"Daddy," I said, bending close to the car, "I can't see you anymore."

"Oh, yeah?"

I knew he could have punched me then, the way he used to punch my mother. "The director of my school said—it's interfering with my schoolwork—I have a responsibility—I can't . . . fail—"

He laughed humorlessly and turned the ignition key. "Okay. Sure. Seeya, honey." He drove away.

I never saw the borrowed car again, nor my father in it. I assumed he left town, but I never checked at the Y to make sure. And it was a long time before I told my mother I had seen him.

She was young and, people told her, beautiful; single and free of responsibilities; traveling home to the other side of the world, alone. She told no one why she'd live in Africa or why she was leaving. And, mercifully, nobody asked.

Late in the evening of May 18, somewhere between Cape Town and the equator, everyone in the ship's smoke room surprised her by singing "Happy Birthday to You." It was 1972; she had turned twenty-seven.

"My husband would have loved you," the elderly English widow who sat beside her at dinner said with a wink. "He had an eye for the girls."

In England she stayed with Mel's parents in Hampshire (his father: "How could my son have let you go?") between trips to London and Europe. She took an inexpensive bus tour of Belgium, France, Germany, Luxembourg, and Holland, talking only to her notebook-companion, and leaving the tour group in every major city to wander off and explore the back streets by herself.

In London she stayed with friends from Rhodesia who shared a one-room flat in Twickenham. At night they lay in bed, staring at the street lights reflected on the ceiling, whispering like children in the dark, talking of Africa and how much they missed her unspoiled, primitive beauty.

264

Instead of sightseeing, she spent her days in London job hunting in an effort to remain. She tried modeling: "Sorry, love, but you're too thin"; journalism: "Sorry, but you're not exactly qualified—one needs to have apprenticed here"; secretarial work: "Do you have working papers?"; working papers: "Do you have proof of a job?" In July she reluctantly sailed home.

• • •

From the porthole in the ladies' room she watched as the island drew near. It was a misty picture painted penitentiary gray: gray river, gray skyscrapers, gray sky. She wanted to hide— *where?*—where no one would find her until after the ship set sail again. She wanted to be a stowaway, like her Scottish grandfather—only going in the opposite direction.

She lingered over breakfast and was one of the last to disembark. She saw her mother waving in the distance and thought: *It's been hundreds of years.*

The July air, which stung her eyes, was hot and gray, too thick to breathe. The noise of traffic and press of people frightened her, and she thought: *How can people live here?*

She returned to America with fifty dollars in her pocket and two metal shipping trunks containing all that she'd retained of her stay in Africa. One trunk held nothing but papers: volumes of court transcripts, a drawerful of legal files, diaries, photograph albums, books. The other held all of her clothes, souvenirs for her family, and the teddy bear she'd bought at Heathrow to bring to Whitney three years before.

She returned to serious issues and earnest movements: the Women's Movement ("Up with women's lib!" she'd teased with Mel; "Down with women's pants!" he'd responded); the climaxing antiwar movement ("What are you doing over there?" she'd written from Rhodesia to a friend fighting in Vietnam; "You tell me what you are doing over *there,* and I'll tell you what I'm doing *here,*" he replied); ecology ("What on earth are you saving all these bottles for?" she asked her sister;

"For the town's recycling program," her sister told her, but she still didn't understand); Watergate; *Future Shock.* It was all alien to her.

She lived with her mother for a while, in the red brick house where the little girls had hidden from their drunken father, in the same town where she and Whitney had shared their first apartment—a lifetime, it seemed, before. Then, as if to punish herself further, she moved to the town where she'd last seen her father driving away in the borrowed car; and she found a job in Newark, where the ugly scars of the race riots of five summers past still hadn't fully healed.

The magazine experience she'd gained in Rhodesia was sufficient for her to be hired to write and edit a bimonthly corporate publication.

"Can you *write?*" the director of marketing asked at her second interview.

"Yes, I believe so," she said, "but I don't have a degree."

"I wouldn't care if you had an M.B.A. from Harvard," he said. "We're looking for someone who knows how to write and write clearly."

The cat sat on the mat. "Oh, yes," she said, "I can certainly do that."

She re-enrolled in college, taking courses toward a B.A. degree at night. She played tennis after work and on weekends, hitting the ball with all her might, pretending she was hitting Jim. She played with men—strangers she met at the courts— and delighted in beating them.

• • •

"Where are you from?" people asked her. "You have an accent."

"Accent?"

"Yeah. It's sort of British."

"I lived overseas."

"Oh, yeah? Where?"

"Africa."

"Why *Africa?*"

"I always wanted to go there."

"Wow. Where did you live?"

"Rhodesia."

"Gee, what made you choose *Rhodesia?*"

"I went there on business, liked it, and stayed."

"You actually *liked* Rhodesia?

"I loved it."

"Of *course,* with *your* coloring you *would!*" And the look in their eyes added: "*Racist.*"

She saw the doelike African women standing at her door looking at her pityingly, pressing their palms together prayerfully, and repeating, *Sorry, madam, sorry, madam* . . . And Margaret: *All of the mothers in Highfields are crying for you, madam.*

Nobody understands! she wept, forgetting that nobody knew. She kept her past a secret, in an effort to forget and begin her life anew.

She worked hard. (Her secretary: "You're a very aggressive woman." And she: "Who? Me?") She studied hard. She played. When people asked her, "How'y'doin?" she smiled broadly, her professional, model-smile, and replied, "Fine. *Fine.*" But at night before she went to bed she confided to her diary, "If only I could die . . ."

God took Ruthie to His home, honey, because He hated to see her so sick. Ruthie is happy now. She'll never be sick again . . .

Lucky Ruthie, lucky Ruthie . . .

Somehow, in the daylight it was easier to forget. But regularly, rhythmically, with the going down of the sun, her heart uncontrollably bled.

Lying alone in her narrow bed, she cried for the baby girl she'd lost so long ago, for the child she never really regained and whom she might never see again; she cried for Whitney-Mel-and-Gigi, her little make-believe family; she cried for Mel, whom she still loved; she cried for Africa, the only place she'd ever felt at home. She cried because she saw no future and wanted desperately to die but knew she didn't have the nerve to do it herself. Each night, as she cried herself to sleep, she shouted at God to take her life. And then she dreamed.

・ ・ ・

Long, steep, winding driveway. Spanish villa, red-tile roof. Looks deserted. No, a gardener clipping hedge. Tiptoe past him while his back is turned. Climb the wall to the open window up above. See her sitting cross-legged on the carpet in a large, unfurnished room, eyes fixed on the television four feet from her face. She is three, perhaps four. All alone.

Softly, so as not to startle her (heart pounding, short of breath): "Hello, hello, it's me, honey. Do you remember me?" She turns and stares blankly. "I've come to play with you. Would you like to play?"

"No," she says flatly and turns back to the TV.

Sitting beside her on the floor: "Where's your daddy?"

"At work." Her voice is distant.

"Are you alone? Does he leave you all alone?"

"Yes."

"I brought a book to read to you. It's your favorite book about Winnie-the-Pooh."

She looks at me strangely.

"Do you remember this one—?"

The sound of a car approaching. The crunch of a car coming up the drive.

"I must go now, honey." Heart racing, body trembling, backing toward the window. "Would you like me to come back tomorrow?"

"No," she says without emotion.

Jim walks in the room. Huge, enraged. "GET OUT OR I'LL KILL YOU! GET OUT AND NEVER COME BACK!"

She stares at us as if we were on TV.

Stepping back and back and back as he approaches.

Falling backward from the open window.

・ ・ ・

Hope was an ephemeral fragrance she seldom smelled. What was there to hope for? To find Jim? To go to court again? To

268

see Whitney alone and ask her how she'd been? To forget, pretend it never happened? To end it all? Or begin again?

What should we do? What should we do? And her baby looked at her and softly cooed.

To the extent that she was able on her own, she tried at times to locate Jim. She made phone calls, checked records, asked friends. But every avenue she took came to a dead end. *And what if I were to find him,* she thought, *what then? Would he take Whitney and run away again?* She preferred to think her daughter might be happy now, settled somewhere in one place, one school, making lasting friends.

But the doubt of that, the fears and worries, churned inside her like chunks of broken glass. She could feel the glass, like sharp knives, cutting into her intestines. In time, she saw proof of this destruction in the toilet: every day there was blood. *Good,* she thought, telling no one, *at last I'm going to die.*

. . .

Listen. *I can't!* Concentrate. *Please*— Take notes: "April 4, 1975—United Nations Conference: Women in Business— Helvi Sipila: International Women's Year was proclaimed in order to draw attention to the problems faced by women in their daily lives—" *I can't! I can't!* You must. *But the pain!* ". . . The quality of life of the future generations depends largely on the health and well-being of their mothers . . ." *My stomach, my stomach hurts, it hurts*— You have a story to write. *Let me wrap my arms around myself and rock*— You must be strong. ". . . Since one-half of us are women, it is beyond argument that the greater opportunity for women to utilize their minds, their hands . . ." *It's like being bayoneted*— Don't stop now. Focus the camera on the podium. Is there enough light? *Please let me lie down and close my eyes—here—anywhere*— *Let me curl up on the floor*— ". . . requires increasing awareness among women of their need to play an important role . . ." *I must leave*— You must finish your work. *Please.*

"I'm sorry, but I won't be able to stay for the second half of the conference. I'm not feeling very well."

I can't walk. Hail a taxi. Please stop crying. *I must close my eyes and rock.* "Oh, Penn Station, please. Please hurry." Where's that piece of paper with the doctor's name and number? *Oh, the pain, it's like a knife*— Pay the driver. "Keep the change, sir." Find a phone booth.

"Hello, my friend recommended me to— His day off?—No, I've never been to him before, but— No, I'm sorry, it can't wait until tomorrow, I— Forgive me for shouting, but I think it's an emergency— I'm in such pain. Thank you, thank you. I'll be there within an hour. Yes, I'm calling long distance, from New York—"

Don't cry here, not on the train. Take deep breaths. Look outside. *But the pain! The pain!*

Find your car keys. Pay the attendant. "Going home, Joe. . . . No, I'm fine. . . . Just a stomachache or something. Bye—"

Hold the steering wheel like a life raft. *But I'd rather sink and drown!* No, you must hold on. *I can't!* I said, HOLD ON.

"The doctor said he'd be here shortly. In the meantime, I'd like to ask you a few questions— Madam, did you *hear* me? Could you please sit up and pull yourself together? It can't be *that* bad."

"Well, hello! I'm Dr. Braddoch. You must be my newest patient. What can we do for you?"

Be my daddy. Hold me, rock me, pat me. Make the hurt go away. Sit up straight and tell the doctor—

"Oh? We'll have to look at this. Please come with me. . . ."

"You're very ill. Why have you let this go so long?"

"I wanted to die."

"Now that's the silliest— Run out of Kleenex? Here, take this box—the silliest thing I've ever heard. You're young and beautiful. You have a whole life—"

"No. No, *NO!*"

"How can you say that? What's made you this unhappy? Tell me."

270

Tell him. *NO!* You must. *I can't!* He wants to help— *Nobody can.* It must come out. You must tell someone. Tell him. . . .

"That's an awful story. I'm sorry. . . . I can't help you get your daughter back, but I *can* help you get yourself back to health. I don't want you to die. I've just met you, and I think you're a lovely girl who should live a long and happy life. So. I'm going to make you better! Now, throw all those soggy tissues in this basket and gather up your things. I'm taking you to the hospital. Okay?"

Rising from the anesthetic, like a diver with the bends, she heard herself cry out, "Mommy! Mommy! Mommy!" as if she were a child of three instead of a woman of thirty. And her mother was there. Washing the vomit from her mouth, wiping the hair from her eyes. Her mother said, "Shhhh, honey, I'm here. It's all right. Everything will be all right. Mommy's here . . ."

When she'd entered the hospital on April 4, the weather was still wintery. The trees were bare. But by the time she was well enough to go home, the trees that lined the streets were filled with shiny new leaves, sweetly unfolding like babies' hands. Spring had never come to her so suddenly before. Everything looked vernal and new.

The doctor kept his promise: He made her better. He removed her ulcers and gave her a prescription for Valium to dull the deeper pain. The drug worked wonderfully for a while. It froze her turbulent emotions the way a windy lake freezes smooth in winter, and she skated on the icy surface in a semistupor.

She wrote to her diary: "Some day, some way, all that has happened may make sense, might fall into place. . . . In the meantime, I must do something to make my life worthwhile."

She marched to the beat of her heart's inner urging: *You must be strong. You must go on.* She resolved to rise above: If she couldn't find Whitney, she would make it easy for Whitney to find her.

She got a job in New York as the editor of a mass-circulation magazine. Her name was on the masthead for all 300,000 subscribers to read. Perhaps one of them, she thought, could someday be Whitney.

She transferred to Columbia University and entered its writing program. She moved to New York and shared a large apartment with a friend.

• • •

One Sunday morning in March 1977 the telephone rang.

"Hello, Bonnie?"

"Yes, who is this?"

"Your father."

Do I still have a father? "Daddy?"

"Yes, how are you?"

I'm numb. "I'm fine. How are you?"

"Fine. What are you doing?"

With my life? "This minute?"

"Well—yes, this minute."

"I was reading the *Times.* I just came in from jogging a few minutes ago."

"Jogging, eh? Are you fat?"

"No. In fact, I'm thin. . . . How did you get my number?" *And why has it taken so many years to call—?*

"From your brother. So, how are you? What are you doing with yourself?"

"I'm an editor, and I'm going to Columbia." *You see, I'm not stupid-and-good-for-nothing after all, Daddy. You were wrong about that.* "I made the Dean's List last semester." *I just had to prove to you—*

"I know."

"How do you know?"

"Well, I mean, I would expect it of you."

"What about you, Daddy? How are you? Are you well?"

"Oh, yeah. Are you? Well, you must be if you're a jogger. . . . Have you seen your brother lately?"

"No. We have a strange family; we don't keep in touch."

"Do you see your mother often?"

272

"Not often. She doesn't like the city, so she doesn't come in. But we talk frequently. She's taking good care of herself. Eats health food—" *Do you want to hear about your grandchildren, too? I'm sorry I can't give you a full report—*

"What is that I hear? There, there. You better stop that crying. I can't give you a handkerchief like the last time I saw you. Remember?"

"Yes." *I remember it. I remember the blood . . .* "Why did you call?"

"I thought maybe I could help you find your daughter."

"Find—? How?"

"Listen, does Macy's tell Gimbel's?"

"Yes, if they're related."

"Yeah, well. Now don't get your hopes up. I can't promise anything. Maybe nothing will come of it—"

"I know. That's all right. But, if you can do anything, I'd appreciate it."

"Well, I'll see what I can do—"

"But what can you do?"

"Just let me see what I can do. All right, honey?"

"All right."

"Now, don't cry. I don't want to upset you."

"No. I'm happy you called. I'm glad to know you're all right. I think about you a lot and wonder whether you're all right."

"Yeah, well. I'll see what I can do for you. But don't get your hopes up, okay? I'll say good-bye now, honey. This is long distance."

"Good-bye."

•   •   •

Find her? Where? In Rhodesia. Return at once. Work and school are secondary. See Jim from a distance, smiling. No, get closer: It's a sneer. He is standing tall and haughty. Whitney, clinging: "Daddy dear, my daddy dear."

"Darling," I say with outstretched arms, "it's me. I'm here. Your mommy's here." Slowly, coyly, she comes closer.

"STOP!" he tells her. "Don't go further. You are MINE. You stay right here."

"YOU CAN'T DO THIS!" I implore him. "I'm her mother. She needs me." I scream until I'm nearly breathless, shaking my fists, raking my hair.

He, the victor with his trophy, picks her up (she looks like me): "You've already served your purpose. Now get out of here."

She woke, trembling and exhausted.

•   •   •

Whenever the phone rang, her skates slipped on the smooth surface of her frozen emotions, she lost her footing and fell. *Is it—? Did he—? Will I—? What then—?* Before the third ring she picked herself up again: "Hello?"

"Hello-hello. It's me."

"Oh, hello."

"Told you I'd call."

"Yes, What—?"

"Well, I missed class last night and was wondering whether I could borrow your notes. You take terrific notes—"

Every day there were calls but none from him. Even with the Valium she could feel the ice getting thin. And then she recognized his voice; it was him. Drunk. Calling long distance to tell her she was good-for-nothing. Her roommate said, "Tell him not to call again." *But he doesn't know what he's saying.* "Thank you for calling." *I don't need to hear that anymore.* "Good-bye." The ice gave way, and she fell in.

Death is small, round, and black—the period completing an unfathomable sentence. Unlike a comma, or colon, or question mark, it says, "THE END." It is a resolution.

, And all she wanted was a resolution. Was Whitney well and happy? Then she'd rejoice. Was she dead? Then she'd mourn. *Did she need her? Then she'd be there.* If this, then that. But as long as she didn't know what "this" was, what could she do about "that"? Once again she asked the futile question "Why?" and tortured herself with the timeless one "How long?" And once again her answers narrowed to one sweet and succinct word: Death.

• • •

She dated a man briefly who suggested she seek professional help. "There's something very sad about your eyes," he told her one evening over dinner. "Perhaps you should speak with someone who can help you.

"I see a therapist three mornings a week," he said with more pride than confidentiality. "He's on Park Avenue. Costs me a fortune, but it's worth it. He is God."

"I believe in God, too," she said lightly, sipping her wine, "but I didn't know He lives on Park Avenue."

"He has a son," the New Yorker went on in earnest, "who's just started his own practice in your neighborhood. Let me see if I can arrange for you to see him at a reduced rate—"

"Wonderful," she said as she carefully sliced her blood-red chateaubriand. "Son of God."

• • •

She sat in a rocking chair in the small, book-lined study of his apartment. He sat in a rocking chair, too, diagonally across the room from her, about sixteen feet away. She could hear young children's voices in the next room.

"Your children?" she asked. *Tell me about yourself. Tell me about your children.*

He nodded impassively. He wore a navy blazer, khaki trousers, loafers. He sipped black coffee from a large mug, slowly.

She picked nervously at a chip in the arm of her rocker and studied him: *Young, maybe thirty; younger than I. Preppy. Handsome and well aware of it. Rich. Only child? Spoiled?*

"Have you read all of these?" she said, half joking, lightly stroking the spines of the books within reach of her right hand.

"Not *all*," he said impatiently, taking another draft of coffee. *Intense. Humorless. Either bored or hung over.*

She wanted to say: *I should tell you right away that I've never believed in psychotherapy. I think—ideally—people should listen to one another's troubles out of love. All we really want is to have someone who cares and listens. We shouldn't have to PAY someone to listen. That's like paying for sex—*

Instead, she said, "How long will this take?" and "How much will it cost?"

"Well, that depends," he said. "Sometimes these things take a while—"

"My problem, I think," she said, quickening the pace of her usually slow speech to save herself time and money, "is rather clear-cut. I have a daughter who is missing. I don't know where she is or how she is. I don't know how to find her or even whether I should. I don't know how to live with this problem. I can't talk about it because it upsets me and nobody understands anyway—not even my mother. I do talk to my mother, but what can she—or anybody—say? She says, 'Honey, you're not eating properly. Eat bananas—they're full of potassium—good for the nerves.' I don't know what to do—"

She dug what fingernails she had into the chip in the arm of her rocking chair and felt the softness of the wood. A choking feeling stuck in her throat. She blinked back tears. "I'm tired of constantly crying in private and pretending to be happy—or at least normal—in public. I'm *not* normal. Or *is it* normal to go through life wishing you were dead, having to take pills every day to relieve the pain of living? Does *everyone* have a private heartache that won't go away? I don't know; I've never had another life. All I know is I'm tired of the one I've been given. I feel as if I've lived and now I'm old and ready to die. I *want* to die. I think about suicide all the time. That's no way to live. *Is it?*"

She searched his face for a reaction but found none. She wasn't looking for sympathy; she loathed pity. She simply wanted some confirmation that her words had carried sixteen feet across the room. Were they too heavy to trust to air? Had they reached his ears? Should she speak louder? Her mother always told her she spoke too softly. But why was he sitting so far away?

"What is your first memory of your father?" he said.

The choking feeling in her throat subsided. Her eyes went dry. *"First—?"* she repeated, numbly. *He mustn't have heard me.* "I remember my father coming into the living room of the apartment we lived in until I was about two. It must have been 1946 or '47. He was carrying a large television set—our family's first TV. It was heavy, and he was swearing." *Perhaps this is only the memory of a dream—*

"And your mother?"

"I don't remember what she was doing at that—"

"No, what is your first memory of your mother?"

"I—" *Think. Search.* "I don't seem to have a first memory of my mother. She's just always been there. My mother has been a constant in my life. Perhaps the only one."

For nearly two months she saw him two mornings a week for fifty minutes. She told him about her childhood and her brief marriage to Jim; about Whitney's birth and infancy, their two-year separation and their life together in Africa. . . . She told him everything, in detail, withholding nothing. And as she spoke she watched him, despising his cool silence, his impassivity. She listened to his children playing in the next room and wanted to scream: *What if someone took them away from you? Would you understand then?*

For the most part, he said nothing. She would talk, as if to an empty rocking chair, exposing the old, unhealed wounds she'd so carefully kept bandaged for years, sometimes sobbing, sometimes choking back tears; and he would sit sipping his coffee, keeping one eye on the clock on his desk, sometimes stopping her in midsentence to tell her coolly, "Your time is up," and she would go to work with swollen eyes, feeling empty, lost, exhausted.

Say something! she wanted to shout. *Anything!* One morning he did tell her to stop taking Valium because it was probably making her more depressed. On another occasion, when he inquired about her sex life and learned she no longer had any desire or feeling, he said that of course WASP women tend to be frigid. And then another morning—her last—when she asked him for a Kleenex and he left the room and returned five expensive minutes later and handed her a dish towel with which to dry her eyes, she begged him to tell her what he thought her problem was, and he said, "You're a very emotional woman."

She sought help elsewhere. She went to a well-respected child psychologist, a gentle, warm woman with children of her own, who advised her not to disrupt Whitney's childhood any further. She said that Jim was probably a good father, providing for her needs—

"But doesn't she need a mother?"

"Perhaps she has one now," the doctor said. "Why don't you wait until she's older before you try to find her again?"

In her desperation she even visited a fortune-teller once. The gypsy woman took her hand and studied her palm: "People tend to be jealous of you," she said, "because they just see the outside and they think you have everything. But you don't have everything. You are missing something, and it makes you hurt on the inside—"

"My child is missing. My ex-husband took her nearly six years ago and disappeared—"

"Ahhh," the gypsy woman nodded. "Well, you know he is remarried, don't you? His new wife is very good to your daughter, and she is a happy child. You must not try to find her now—it would only hurt her. But you will see her again later in life, when she's grown."

• • •

She was granted a full scholarship at Columbia, so she quit her magazine job to complete her degree full time. She found a small apartment of her own near school and a part-time editorial position in publishing, which paid barely enough to cover rent and food, and she tailored her life-style to fit her new life as a student. Everything that could be cut from her budget was cut: entertainment, new clothes and shoes, cigarettes, Valium. In old clothes, without crutches, working and studying without sufficient sleep or play, she soon found herself crawling on her

278

hands and knees through a narrow, deep subaqueous tunnel with no light at the end.

It was in the midst of this depression, when her writing class was given the assignment "Why I Write," that she wrote:

... I want to live a normal life, but find I can't. Someone shot me in the back of the soul and made me a cripple from here, down. The dead legs of my heart dangle from the wheelchair, lifeless— See? I can no longer dance or make love. Only the hands of my heart can move. They move along the smooth paper, dragging a pencil, leaving a trail of jagged marks that spell: I AM STILL HERE.

I am not a writer. I am a nothing, a no one, a meaningless being, barely alive, who's been blown halfway to nowhere, and has nowhere to go. I only write to prove that I was there.

She loved Columbia the way she loved snow-capped mountains, star-flecked skies, crashing waves, and African sunsets: distantly and reverentially. She thrilled at the old buildings with their marble staircases worn down by countless students' shoes, the professors with their esoteric specialties and their messianic drive to share their knowledge, her earnest classmates discussing the protagonists of novels the way doctors might discuss their best cases. But in most of her classes, she felt ill-equipped and overawed, scrambling to keep up with the lectures, trying to take careful notes, straining to make sense of it all. Often, she felt as if she were an interloper, a gate-crasher at a highbrow cocktail party.

It was only in her writing classes that she felt she belonged. There, sitting in dimly lit classrooms at conference tables where they offered up their lives like sacraments on platters of white bond, she and her classmates were comrades, bound by the same neurotic need to write. And there she was a scientist performing experiments on herself, trying to find the true origin of her problem and the cure for her pain. Why had her life turned out this way? Where had she gone wrong? She probed and examined her past as if it were lying in a petri dish, and then she reported her findings in the form of short stories.

Through her microscope she saw the little girl who ran away from home but got only as far as the swing in the woods; her friend Ruthie who left her for a far better place; her friend Lindy who moved away; her brother reading comic books in a bar waiting for their father to finish his last beer and take them all to the promised lake; herself at seventeen the summer before her grandmother retired, the summer before her parents' twenty-three-year marriage was finally dissolved. . . . She wrote about her life as if it were fiction.

• • •

They say if you throw a stone on the pile at the top of Mount Batty you will return one day. At least that was what the girl told me who had lived in the town all her life. She told me to pick up a stone and throw it on the pile, and I did. But that was many years ago, and I haven't been back yet.

I had met her at the dock where I used to go every afternoon at two when everyone at the house was sleeping and I had too much energy to rest. I would walk the two miles to town and go to the dock to watch the fishermen repairing their lobster pots and the old men whittling sea gulls out of driftwood and the vacationers returning from a week's windjammer cruise and the others waiting to board.

I don't remember her name now, but I remember that we were the same age and about the same size; she had dark hair and sad eyes, and I knew just from looking at her face that we could be friends. She told me there were lots of wild blueberries on Mount Batty, which was not far away, and did I want to go berry picking with her one day?—and I said yes. So we did.

I got a small bucket from the cook at the house and went off one afternoon to meet my friend. We climbed the mountain in a great spiral, picking blueberries off the bushes as we went.

That was the day she made me throw the stone.

She told me she was the eldest child at home, and her dad was in the hospital most of the time—a special hospital for veterans of the war. He used to come home for the weekend every other week, but one day he took a ladder, climbed to the top of the roof, and set the house on fire. When he jumped off the roof he hurt his head. There was no other damage—the fire was soon put out—and her father was returned to the hospital. But he seldom came to visit after that.

She shrugged her shoulders when I told her how sorry I was to hear this, and as we continued berry picking I thought: *I'm not so alone.*

When I got back to the house that afternoon, the cook was pleased to see the bucket almost full. She said we could make blueberry muffins if I'd like to; so we did. And the next day she told me she put two of my muffins on the madam's breakfast tray, and the madam told the cook they were delicious.

The cook's name was Emmy. She was a seamstress by trade, but she came up to the Maine house that summer as a favor to her sister, Frieda, the parlor maid, because the old Maine cook had died the fall before. Emmy was a good cook; we all thought so. I can still see the salmon she prepared for a special Sunday brunch—a whole, cold poached salmon, swimming on a sterling silver tray, iced like a cake with the thick homemade mayonnaise Emmy made. It had eyes of olive rings and pimento strips for fins. She said it was easy to do—even I could do it. But I haven't tried to yet.

Sometimes when I had nothing to do, I would go down to the kitchen and watch Emmy cook. Doesn't it make you nervous to fix such fancy food? I once asked. What if something goes wrong? No, she said, I don't get nervous—I don't think about it—I just *do.*

One afternoon she called me from the hall: Pssssst—psssssst—I've got something for you! It was a half pound of lobster meat—to fatten me up, she said. And I took it back up to my room and ate it all. For several days I felt the lobster—claws and all—crawling up the sides of my stomach, trying to escape. I felt green, like the bottom of the sea. But I never told Emmy.

Emmy and her sister Frieda were big-boned German women, toweringly tall, who had lived through the war and still carried scars in their eyes. One evening I took a skirt that I was making to Emmy's room, and as she showed me how to make the pleats—bending her head over the gray wool, exposing the thick white part dividing her dyed-red hair—she told me she had lost three husbands during the war. Each time she had to run for her own life, running from the bombs, carrying everything she owned in one suitcase.

Frieda never married—Grandma said she was a spinster-lady—and she was a vegetarian, which Grandma also thought was strange. Frieda ate her meals alone in her room, running raw carrots and celery through a special machine that turned them into awful-tasting juice. They'd had another sister, Grandma said, who was found dead—hanging from a rope in the hall closet of their family's home. But don't let on I told you, Grandma said.

Each morning at six-thirty Grandma came into my room with a cup of fresh black coffee to wake me. Hot-black-coffee-on-an-empty-stomach-first-thing-in-the-morning is the best thing for regularity, she said. And she was right, of course. Grandma was an expert on regularity.

After breakfast we would begin our work. Starting with the guest bathroom across the hall, we polished, mopped, or dusted everything on the second floor. Or rather, *I* did, and Grandma showed me how it should be done: Close the drain—dry the sink—don't let water marks remain; dust each rung along the stairs—lift each plant—move each chair— Her instructions became a litany I sang to myself.

My room was the first door on the right at the top of the servants' stairs. Grandma said I should be honored that the madam said I could stay in this room for the summer—after all, it was a guest room in *their* part of the house—and important people had stayed in the room—members of the royal family, famous musicians, beautiful actresses— But that was years ago, when the madam was young, Grandma said.

The bed in my room (I called it my room, though I knew it wasn't mine) didn't look like a bed. At the foot and the head it rose up and curved like a tulip and ended in a scroll. It made

282

me feel like an ancient Egyptian princess—lying there surveying all the objects in the room, antiques and artifacts from
around the world, worth thousands of dollars each, I was sure.
I never touched them, except when I was cleaning with Grandma. It was as though I slept in a museum and everything in the
room were encased in glass.

What I liked best was the view of the bay from my window,
and the sound that the waves made when they hit the stony
shore below. The steady rhythm of the crashing waves kept me
awake all night the day I arrived—and rocked me to sleep each
night for the rest of the summer.

When the morning work was done I would go down to the
barnacle-covered shore and sit on a large flat rock and write letters to my mother and try to get some sun. (I tried to swim
there once, but the water made my legs numb.) Dearest Momma, I wrote, No, Grandma says, I am not to get an allowance.
She says my air fare up here and back is to be my summer's
pay. . . . I agree with her that this is a special vacation for me,
but it would be awfully nice to have a little spending money
when I go into town. . . .

My mother sent two dollars by return mail. That same day,
I spent it on a boat trip around the bay. It was almost two by
the time I walked to town, but I got to the dock in time. I was
last in line, but I got on. As the boat bounced along the choppy
waves, splashing spray in all of our faces, the captain pointed
to places of historical interest along the shore.

Are you here alone? I heard a voice beside me ask, and I
turned to meet his light blue eyes, and I said yes. My name is
Mario Diaz, he said—I am here from Barcelona. . . . I work for
Tommy Watson—know the name? No, I told him (as I wondered how a blond could come from Spain). Tommy Watson
is the president of IBM, he said—his son needed help with
Spanish in school, so they brought me here for the summer to
be his tutor— The Watsons have a home here on the bay—
Would you care to go out with me some day?

There'll be no stepping out with young men in the evening as
long as you are under my roof! Grandma said. I knew her

words were not meant for me; they came from long ago and far away, when she said them to another girl who looked like me. (I will never be as strict with my kids as my mother was with me, my mother always said.) Don't worry, Grandma, I told her—you needn't worry.

In the evening after supper, after we had turned down the madam's bed for the night (. . . fold the covers catty-corner like so—then fold them over again, and tuck in the side—pound the pillows—fluff them up—smooth the top case—creases must not wrinkle her face . . .), Grandma and I would sometimes go for walks together in the cool, sea-sweet air, past the beds of purple-and-yellow pansies, the gardener's pride, along the winding road that cut through the neighboring golf course. And she would tell me stories about her childhood in New York, and how her parents sent her to Germany to visit relatives the year she was thirteen, and how she met her husband at the dance, and how the barrel at the factory where he worked fell down and crushed his leg and made him lame, and how much she missed him since he'd died— Such-is-life-without-a-wife-and-worse-without-a-husband, she sighed.

Every weekday morning a young, black-suited minister from a church in town would come to the house to give the madam communion in her room. Sometimes he would bring her flowers, too, along with the bread and wine. Grandma said he was only nice to the madam because he hoped she would leave a pot of money to his church when she died. The minister spoke to me once, to my surprise. I was on my hands and knees, polishing the floor upstairs, and didn't hear him approach. He bent down and whispered close to my ear: You've got to come out to my house one day, he said; it must be awfully stuffy for you here— And then he winked.

The story of the madam's life, or so Grandma said, could be summed up in her name: Mary Louise Curtis Bok Zimbalist.

Her parents were the Curtises of the Curtis Publishing Company of Philadelphia. At the proper age she married Edward William Bok, and they had two sons. Years after Bok's death, she married again—the gifted violinist and composer Efrem Zimbalist, who was director of the Curtis Institute of Music, which she had founded and endowed. Mrs. Zimbalist was more than ten years older than he (he, mid-seventies and she, late-eighties), but they were very happy, Grandma said.

The first day I arrived I met the madam. Grandma brought me to her room, where she was sitting up in bed. She had white baby-hair and a bird's face. She held out her hand to me and I reached to take it. Did I touch it? I don't know. Her hand was a wisp that my rough hand went through. My dear, she whispered to me, it is so nice to meet you. . . . Your grandmother speaks of you often, with such pride. . . . I hope you will enjoy your stay in Maine. . . . It is good of you to help your grandmother in this way. . . .

Mr. Zimbalist is a strange little man, Grandma said one day as we were cleaning his room. Look at this jacket, how old and frayed. For years I've been telling him to get a new one, but he says, No, this one is comfortable, it's like a friend— Grandma shook her head. With all that money, he could buy a million jackets, she said.

Each day at four, Mrs. Braun, a widow from the estate next door, came over to play the piano to accompany Mr. Zimbalist's violin. The music that they played—classical pieces that I'd never heard before—would fill the house and greet me as I returned from my walks to town. Trying not to make a sound, I tiptoed up the servants' stairs and sat on the second-floor landing, listening to their music for as long as I could. Although they didn't know it, they had an audience of one; and it was hard not to applaud when they were done.

One Sunday morning Grandma said I'd been invited to go downstairs to hear a chamber orchestra perform. A group of students from the Curtis Institute were spending the summer in Maine, and they had requested an opportunity to entertain the madam. Grandma nudged me down the stairs, and Frieda pointed toward the door—I had never been downstairs in *their* part of the house before—and Mr. Zimbalist motioned for me to sit beside him on the sofa. I folded my hands in my lap and listened hard as the students played. They smiled at the madam and their heads swayed in time with the music.

That was the day that we had the salmon brunch.

The week before I left I walked slowly into town, stopping along the way to take pictures of my favorite places. I didn't have a camera, so I stood for a long time in each place, trying to burn the images on my mind. I still have a clear picture of the sheep grazing in the valley beyond the broken split-rail fence, and of the strange cows (front half black, back half white) that were specially bred on the farm down the road, and one of a headstone in the old cemetery in the woods I used to cut through. The headstone read: BABY SARAH JANE—BORN JUNE 1, 1825—DIED OF THE GRIPPE, DECEMBER 10, SAME YEAR—THE LORD GIVETH AND THE LORD TAKETH AWAY. And of course I took a picture of the dock with its lobster pots and salty old men. And I promised myself I'd come back again one day—with a camera.

Grandma pushed me through the music room door where Mr. Zimbalist stood facing the windows overlooking the bay. He was playing the violin and didn't hear me come in. Excuse me, sir, I said when I was just a few feet away. I've come to say good-bye. The little man—who was shorter than I—put his violin down, took my face in his hands, and kissed me on both cheeks.

And as I left the music room, I cried.

•   •   •

Part of her still marched to the beat of an inner drum. *You must be strong—you must go on,* walking tall and proud like her German grandmother, from home to office, to school and back again, doing her work, doing her best. But another part stum-

286

bled, crawled, and wept. *I can't go any farther; I'm tired, so tired; I want to let go—* In the darkness of this tunnel she saw only black: the fat, blind black girl getting off the bus with fresh blood staining the seat of her dress; the old, broken vagrant with a black hole where his right eye should have been; the black beggars on street corners rattling their tin cups to wake the sleepwalking passersby; the reeking, broken bag ladies raging to deaf ears; the crazy man with his black trousers rolled, exposing his filthy white skin, making deranged music on the pavement with drumsticks—clickety-click, clickety-click-click, click-clickety-click—and people walking past, ignoring him. This part of her felt one with them: *Yes, I know how it is; you've lost something—your vision? yourself? your grip? all hope?—and nobody listens or cares.*

She read the paper every day, the *New York Times* reports of the war in Rhodesia, and wept for the Africa she'd loved.

This part of her peered from her apartment window, imagining what it would be like to fall: like a water balloon, exploding with a POP at the bottom. Quick and sure. But who would have to clean up the wet mess? And who would take her white Persian cat and hold him, rocking, like an infant, the way she did? And what would her mother think?—"Oh, Bonnie, honey. Why? Why?"

The subway was a better idea. At Columbus Circle, where the IRT turns a corner before it comes to a stop at the platform. There, with the unseeing, uncaring crowd, she'd stand close to the edge. . . . If they could identify the mangled remains, her mother would be told it was an accident. Anyone would love her cat.

She wasn't well. She exuded sadness like a bad smell only a saint could tolerate, and there are few saints in New York. Fortunately, she knew one. "You need a break," her friend Maureen told her with deep concern in her eyes. "You need to get out of this city. New York in the summer is like the subbasement of hell. Let's go to the ocean on Saturday . . ."

In Penn Station, standing at the ticket counter, she clapped her hands like an idiot or a child, and people stared at her strangely. Maureen led her by the arm to the train.

During the two-hour trip they sipped coffee from Styrofoam

cups and spoke of pleasant things: Maureen, of what she planned to do when she finished law school; she, of the summer courses she was taking at Columbia—Shakespeare's comedies, journalism. And they read: Maureen, the latest *New Yorker;* she, *As You Like It:* In the forest of Arden, Duke Senior said, "Sweet are the uses of adversity, which, like the toad, ugly and venomous, wears yet a precious jewel in his head . . ."

At the beach they spread their beach towels on the hot, soft sand, and then she ran: fast and sleek as an African antelope, along the shallow edge of the water, past the Frisbee players, the sand castle builders, the teenage smoochers. Her body was pale, receptive to the sun, and strong; only her mind was sick and black.

"What would you do," she asked Maureen when she returned from her run, "if you had my life? If your child was missing and you couldn't forget her and there was nothing you could do to find her?"

"I really don't know," her friend replied. "Never having had a child, I don't know what I'd do or how I'd feel."

"Do you think you might get tired of it at some point and want to kill yourself because you saw no other way out? Death seems so peaceful to me—" (*Lucky Ruthie, lucky Ruthie.*) "No more memories, no more tears. I don't know why so many people are afraid of it. It has to be—I know it must be—better than this—"

Maureen looked at her with deep concern. "Have you read 'The Suicide' by Edna St. Vincent Millay?"

She shook her head.

"You must read it. It's about a woman who decides to take her life because she can't bear living anymore, and when she gets to heaven she's happy until she finds there's nothing there for her to do. So she goes to God and asks Him for a task similar to what the others are doing. But God tells her she can't have one because she never finished the job she had to do on earth. The last line goes something like this: 'Thou hadst thy task and laidst it by, He said.'

"You are a person of faith, Bonnie. You mustn't give up now. You must believe God has a job for you to do and you must stay alive and do it."

288

Do. Yes, of course, DO. Eat, sleep, breathe. Study, work. Pay taxes. Obey laws. Cross-at-the-green, not-in-between. Stare at the Puerto Rican mothers on the subway train babbling lovingly to their babies in Spanish and think: I am a mother, too. God, dear God, if you hear me at all, please tell me what you want me to do.

· · ·

She read in the *Times* of a group called Children's Rights, Inc., a national, nonprofit organization formed "to combat the crime of child-snatching." That day, while reading the newspaper and drinking her morning coffee, she learned she was not alone.

To fulfill a street-reporting assignment for her journalism course, she went to one of the Children's Rights meetings as a reporter. There, pretending to be an objective observer, a recorder, a conduit for information—hiding behind a dispassionate disguise—she met other victims, talked with them, and took notes. She noted their words, so much like her own: "I am going to school at night, taking courses to keep my mind occupied . . ."

"I mustn't fall apart, for the sake of my child . . ."

"I pray . . ."

"I hope I will locate my baby soon . . ."

"The authorities won't help me—they say, 'Sorry, lady, but you married the guy; you should'a known better' . . ."

"I can't afford more private detectives . . ."

"I don't know what I can do . . ."

She noted their faces and eyes: trying to be brave, blinking back tears.

She wrote her story, and when it was returned she saw that her professor had scribbled across the top: "Excellent—I wasn't aware—"

Then she knew what it was she had to do.

New York
April 1980

Dear Whitney,

In all the years since I've been back from Africa, I've wanted to write to you, but I haven't known your address. I've tried to find you, but without success. I even tried to forget you, but I could never do that.

It's been almost a decade since I last saw you, and in that time I've passed through several stages. My grief at losing you at first took the form of rage. I screamed at God, shook my fist in His face, and demanded an answer to my questions, *"Why—?"* I hated my country for not helping me to find you. I hated myself for being so helpless and powerless, for not knowing what I could do.

When the fire of my rage burned away, I became depressed. I swallowed my tears and got ulcers. I crawled alone in a dark place and prayed for death.

Now, it seems, I've reached a new plateau, and it is from this place that I write to you. In a sense, I have lived to write this story for you. For years I kept it locked inside, carrying it with me like a great weight, subconsciously waiting for the right time, when you'd be old enough to understand, when I'd be far

290

enough away from the past to write about it without bitterness, hatred, or self-pity.

Whitney, it may not be important for you to know *me,* but I believe it is important for you to know the truth about your earliest years, because truth makes us free. It is important, too, that you know something about my side of the family, and about me. I think you should know that I've never let you go.

For your sake especially I've tried to be strong. Professionally, I became a writer. Academically, I earned a degree. But writing to you, I found, required more than these credentials. It required a healthy frame of mind, a change of heart. God, whom I had shouted at for years, took care of this. He led me to a church on Palm Sunday last year, the first church I'd been to in almost fourteen years, where the minister preached on "the crown in the crisis." In every life, he said, there are crises; and in every crisis, there is a potential crown. . . . I had just learned I would be able to write to you even though I didn't have your address; I could see the crown.

Since then I have been writing this, alone in a small room. I've begun each day in prayer, begging God for the strength to remember all of the memories I've tried to forget, for the grace to forgive your father and to write about him without bitterness, for the right words with which to reach you.

Whitney, I confess, I have not written only to you, but to all the other Whitneys who go by other names, who have been taken from one parent by the other without reason. I used to think you and I were alone in this, but I recently learned there are thousands of others, children who are being deprived of their mothers' or fathers' love, and parents who don't know where their children are. I am writing also for those parents who don't know their children's addresses.

Now that my story is almost ended, I realize I've written it also for myself. Not for exoneration, but for exorcism. The unspeakable memories, like fierce dragons from which I'd tried for years to flee, have been faced, and in a sense, slain. All of the words that could never seem to leave my lips are out now on this paper. I no longer feel so heavy.

Over the years I've tried to keep in touch with our old

friends. I wrote to Margaret for a while, in care of Edwin at Barclays Bank. Edwin replied on behalf of Margaret, because she can't write in English, giving me her news and reports of their son, Gregory, and asking me whether I'd found "the piccanin madam" yet. Somehow, I couldn't answer his last letter.

I still write to Gigi. She is twenty now and says she hopes to come to America next year to visit me. Sue Pichanick and her daughter Jenny were here last summer for a holiday. I played tour guide and showed them the city. Mrs. Clarke wrote recently and said everyone there still remembers us. George phones occasionally to ask how I am. Once in a while we have dinner. I saw Mel last year in England. He is married now and has an infant son. Everyone asks about you.

My childhood friend Lindy and I were reunited a few weeks ago. I had Sunday dinner with her family, after which she and I went for a long walk and laughed about how little we'd changed in the twenty-two years since we last walked together to school.

My Gibbs roommate Kathy and her husband, Carl, will celebrate their fifteenth wedding anniversary next month. They have two children, are happily married and still in love.

My mother is well, still living in the house where I grew up. She is studying oil painting in preparation for her retirement. She is a gifted artist. We are close friends. The rest of our family is spread throughout the country. My brother is married and has two grown children; one sister is married and has two teenagers; and my other sister is married and has three children. Both of my sisters went back to school to earn their degrees at thirty. My father phoned me from somewhere in the Midwest a few years ago and offered to help me find you, but I've lost touch with him since.

This week Rhodesia became the new, independent country of Zimbabwe. The civil war that began the year I left is now over. There will be peace there, we all hope, at last.

Life goes on, and with it, hope. "Never give up hope," Goethe said and I keep repeating to myself, "because hope is half of life." I hope you are well and happy. I hope we shall meet again someday; I long to hear your story. In the meantime, I hope these words will take on a life of their own, that they as

292

my emissary will seek you and find you and reintroduce you to me.

Now, Whitney, I must go on with my life, as you must yours. Run. Pray. Think. Write. Dance. Read. Work. Sing. Strive. Stretch. Play. Grow. Love.